Golden Wings and Hairy Toes

Golden Wings and Hairy Toes

Encounters with New England's Most Imperiled Wildlife

Todd McLeish

UNIVERSITY PRESS OF NEW ENGLAND

HANOVER AND LONDON

Published by University Press of New England,
One Court Street, Lebanon, NH 03766
www.upne.com
© 2007 by Todd McLeish
Printed in the United States of America
5 4 3 2 1

Title page photograph by John Crane.

Library of Congress Cataloging-in-Publication Data

McLeish, Todd.
Golden wings and hairy toes : encounters with New England's most imperiled
wildlife / Todd McLeish. — 1st ed.
    p.   cm.
Includes bibliographical references.
ISBN-13: 978–1–58465–626–5 (cloth : alk. paper)
ISBN-10: 1–58465–626–3 (cloth : alk. paper)
1. Endangered species—New England. I. Title.
QL84.22.N47.M35 2007
578.680974—dc22   2007014835

 University Press of New England is a member of the Green
Press Initiative. The paper used in this book meets their
minimum requirement for recycled paper.

For Renay

Contents

Introduction

It was the spring of 1932 when the last heath hen on Earth took its final breath somewhere in the middle of Martha's Vineyard in what is now the Manuel F. Correllus State Forest. The 5,100-acre forest was created in 1908 to protect the rare bird from extinction, but by then its end was already predestined. A pheasant-sized relative of the endangered prairie chickens that are still found in small numbers on the Great Plains, the heath hen had ranged from Maine to North Carolina prior to the American Revolution, but by the 1870s its entire population was relegated to the now-famous island off Cape Cod where it eventually succumbed.

I was surprised on my first visit to Martha's Vineyard in the spring of 2006, well before the hordes of tourists descended there, that the center of the island where the heath hen once had lived still has considerable undeveloped areas. Like most of the islands in southern New England, Martha's Vineyard is a sand plain created when retreating glaciers deposited sediments once trapped in or dragged beneath the ice. The dry, sandy soils support an unusual concentration of rare species—especially moths—that thrive in the grasslands and heathlands that are dominated by pitch pine, scrub oak, blueberry, and huckleberry. Land clearing for agriculture was responsible for the destruction of heath hen habitat throughout most of its historic range, but the poor soils on Martha's Vineyard ensured that the land remained uncultivated and allowed the species to hang on long after it had died out elsewhere.

Matthew Pelikan, the island programs director for the Massachusetts chapter of The Nature Conservancy, gave me a tour of the island when I visited, noting the rolling topography, the twisted scrub oak trees that are constantly subjected to wind and salt, and the numerous depressions of fossilized stream beds called frost bottoms that are the coldest areas of the island. I was most interested, however, in the former Green Farm, where the last heath hen was observed on March 11, 1932. At one corner of the farm was the lek, the grassy area where the male birds converged on early spring mornings to perform an unusual courtship dance designed to attract females. The farm is still privately owned, but the area where the lek was located is visible through the trees of the state forest near a roadway pull-off marked with a stone monument honoring the extinct bird. Pelikan and I walked along a paved bike path paralleling the Green Farm hayfield and through the forest where the heath hen would have foraged and nested. Today, the forest has a thick understory of head-high scrub oak and scattered shrubs with a few taller oak trees leaving a mostly open canopy. A century ago, though, it may have looked very different, as the ecology of the island is based on frequent fires that turned forests to grasslands and then to shrublands in rapid succession. Fire suppression since World War I has altered the ecosystem and required extensive habitat management to protect the rare species that still remain.

Soon after the heath hen sanctuary was established, it appeared to be a resounding success. From fifty birds in 1907, the population rapidly increased to about two thousand in 1915. But a fire a year later burned a third of the island and killed 80 percent of the heath hens, and the species just couldn't recover. A harsh winter the following year brought an influx of goshawks—raptors that feed on chicken-sized birds—that suppressed the population further, and the remaining heath hens were victimized by a poultry disease that found its way to the island via domestic turkeys. By 1927, just thirteen heath hens were left, most of them males, and a year later just one survived. "It's a classic example of how a bunch of negative factors converged to reduce a population that was once extensive," said Pelikan. "The heath hen experienced catastrophic local impacts from the fire, but if it weren't also affected by disease, inbreeding, and hunting, they probably could have survived it."

The sole surviving heath hen was monitored closely by Bowdoin College professor Alfred Gross, who, on April 1, 1931, trapped and examined the bird before releasing it again. As he wrote in the ornithological journal *Bird Banding* later that year,

> the last heath hen is a splendid, well-groomed male. It is heavy, plump, and exceedingly strong and resistant. An examination of the bird revealed no trace of disease or external parasites, which were common among its last companions examined by the author in past years. There is no way of ascertaining the age of this bird, but since the last record of any young was in 1924, it is probable this individual is at least seven years old, and perhaps much older. . . . How many years the last heath hen will prolong the life of its race cannot be predicted, but it is truly remarkable that this lone

bird has been able to escape all of the vicissitudes of the elements and the constant danger of predators and disease. . . . Nevertheless, the last bird on Martha's Vineyard has fired our imagination and has served to focus public attention on the necessity of taking immediate positive steps for the conservation of our wild life. If this bird serves as a warning of what may happen to other game-birds, the thousands of dollars expended by the state and various organizations and individuals will not have been spent in vain.

A year later, the heath hen had become extinct, the first ornithological extinction observed in the wild down to the last individual.

The story of the heath hen is an important lesson for today. For, as the following fourteen chapters will attest, there is much that can be done to prevent future extinctions, but also immense challenges. And while extinction is indeed a natural process—as those advocating for progress at any cost emphasize time and again—the current rate of extinctions on Earth is anything but natural. Human actions have increased the extinction rate as many as one hundred to one thousand times greater than normal.

Without the benefit of a more complete understanding of the heath hen's life history, habitat needs, and the effects of human disturbance, biologists could do little to help the bird. It also didn't have the added benefit of being included on the federal endangered species list. Passed with bipartisan support in 1973, the Endangered Species Act is perhaps the most enlightened piece of environmental legislation ever enacted. For the first time, legislators acknowledged that wildlife has value in itself, regardless of the value it may have to people, and that it plays an important role in maintaining healthy ecosystems. Unfortunately, restoring the populations of endangered species is expensive and time consuming, and it affects the development activities in the communities where the species' live. Many people are unwilling to allow their lives to be affected by a creature for which they see little use. So maintaining funding for the Endangered Species Act has been a constant struggle, and adding new species to the list without court action has been a near impossibility in the last decade.

Nonetheless, the legislation has had numerous successes, not the least of which is the bald eagle, the symbol of the United States that was nearly extirpated from the Lower 48 before gaining federal protection. Today, its numbers have rebounded to never-before-seen highs in many places around the country. While the eagle is the most visible success story, it's certainly not the only one. Populations of the peregrine falcon, piping plover, humpback whale, puritan tiger beetle, and dozens more have also increased considerably. In the Northeast, populations of thirty-eight out of forty-one species on the federal list have increased or remained stable, and none have become extinct, according to a 2006 report by the Center for Biological Diversity. On the other hand, critics point to the fact that just one percent of endangered species have improved enough to be removed from the list. While this statistic is true, these critics ignore the fact that, based on the recovery plans prepared for species in the Northeast, the average length of time it is expected to take for a species' population to become healthy enough to be de-listed is forty-two years. And with the regular funding cuts forced by opponents of the act, some listed species may take even longer to recover.

Even with the protections and funding that come with inclusion on the federal endangered species list, ensuring that endangered wildlife doesn't become extinct is an overwhelming challenge. That's partly because, by definition, the creatures are extremely rare, so even finding them to collect the data that may ultimately save them is difficult. That is one of the frustrations that ornithologist Kent McFarland has articulated. The species he studies, Bicknell's thrush, is not on the endangered list yet, primarily because not enough is known about it to justify its inclusion. Yet it is so rare that it has taken him and numerous colleagues more than ten years to document the bird's status and begin to make a case that it belongs on the list.

Other biologists I spoke to struggle with the politics of wildlife protection. Government biologists often must speak carefully so as not to contradict the prevailing policies of each new administration, and in extreme cases they are silenced altogether, as was the case with NASA climatologists who sought to speak about global climate change in 2006. Because protecting habitat for wildlife has implications for regional economic development, recreation, and other activities, many politicians are unwilling to defend the need to protect species, and others intentionally stand in the way of protections, even when there is overwhelming scientific evidence that the animal is on a path to extinction. The soft support for such protections among the general public doesn't help the situation. While surveys have demonstrated for decades that Americans place a high value on wildlife protection, open space, and a healthy environment, these topics often are not among their priority issues when it comes time to elect public officials. It's even more difficult to drum up popular support when the species isn't one of the charismatic megafauna—the large or seemingly cuddly animals like seals, bears, eagles, or otters. The public is often willing to be inconvenienced to protect a cute fox or stately moose, but bats, mushrooms, insects, snakes, and the like are out of luck.

Couple these challenges with the seeming impossibility of fixing the major threats to wildlife populations, such as global warming, acid rain, and mercury poisoning, and it's understandable that many biologists have a pessimistic outlook, not only about the future of the species they study but about the health of the planet in general. One biologist, who preferred not to be identified, said of his work and that of others trying to protect especially rare species, "I think we're pissing in the wind. It's not that it's not worth doing, because it's important to strive to bring back populations that are in trouble. But I'm not terribly optimistic. For many of these species, the populations are so low that they're not likely to be sustainable without continual active intervention by conservationists who hate to see a species disappear."

Yet each rare species has an important story to tell about the causes of their population declines, the obstacles they face rebuilding a sustainable population, and the people who go to extraordinary lengths to give them a chance to thrive. Some of those stories are told in the following pages. Despite the sometimes overwhelming odds, the outlook for many of the species is quite hopeful. In some cases, the stories also include elements that are somewhat surprising, such as how lynx benefit from the clear-cutting of forests or how utility companies—often blamed for environmental degradation—have accidentally succeeded in creating excellent habitat for golden-winged warblers along their power-line corridors.

What was not a surprise, however, was the fun I had researching the stories of these imperiled creatures. There's nothing I enjoy more than sloshing around in the wilds with biologists as they do what they are trained to do: search, track, observe, follow, listen, study, collect, note, capture, photograph, count, and more. I'm not a biologist myself—though I often wish I were—so even on the days when the weather or the wildlife didn't cooperate, I can't imagine a place I'd rather have been. And even though the outlook for some of these species may not be promising, learning about them first hand was always exciting and, more often than not, a powerful and moving experience. I hope that by reading about them, you can share that emotional connection with this group of remarkable animals and plants, and help to postpone permanently the day that they, like the heath hen, disappear entirely.

Golden Wings and Hairy Toes

I

North Atlantic Right Whale

My father pretty much soured me on parades when I was a kid. He dragged my brother, sister, and me to every small-town parade in our area, from the ten-minute parades for nearly every holiday of the year to the blockbuster parade celebrating our town's three-hundredth anniversary. Along the way, we watched parades honoring veterans, youth groups, police, and anybody else being honored. We stood in rain, snow, and searing heat and always stayed until the very end when the last fire truck had passed by and the normal traffic resumed. As an adult, I think I've only been to one parade and only because my wife insisted we go. Admittedly, it was a pretty good one, but I feel like I saw a lifetime's worth of parades as a kid, and I'm no longer interested in them.

But this parade was different. There were only four "marchers" and they paraded back and forth in front of us for an hour. The parades of my youth paled in comparison to that spectacular sight.

It began unexpectedly as five biologists and I were returning from an all-day research cruise aboard the R/V *Shearwater* studying North Atlantic right whales in Cape Cod Bay. The cruise was designed mostly to visit eight "sampling stations" throughout the bay to assess the density of food available to feeding whales, but we also kept a sharp eye out for whales with the objective of identifying each individual whale and observing its behavior.

That day in mid-April 2005 was my second cruise with the biologists from the Provincetown Center for Coastal Studies, based at the tip of Cape Cod, and they claimed I had brought them good luck. A month earlier I joined them on what turned out to be a picture-perfect cruise with comfortable temperatures, bright sunshine, and calm seas, and we saw more whales that day than on any other cruise of the year. So when they heard that I was coming again, one of the biologists secretly confided to me that he had high hopes for the day.

I didn't, though. After such a great first cruise, I wasn't expecting much on my second visit, especially when the weekly reports of whale sightings and plankton abundance suggested the winter feeding season in Cape Cod Bay was fast coming to a close. But I wanted a second visit to make a comparison of how whale activity changes from month to month, so I made the three-hour drive to the Provincetown municipal dock early that morning anyway, expecting to simply go through the motions and maybe see some interesting birds migrating through. I figured that even if we saw nothing, that would be a telling indication of the plight of the rarest whale in the world.

But we didn't see nothing. In fact, less than half a mile out of the harbor, with flocks of common eider and white-winged scoters and red-breasted mergansers swimming and diving all around us, and with the cormorant-covered breakwater still within easy view, we saw our first whales. The call came out from the observers on the upper deck that a whale "blow" had been seen about half a mile distant, and that the whale's tail fluke was also visible as it made a deep dive. Those characteristics are important to notice, not only in sighting the whale in the first place, but in identifying it to species. Finback whales, one of the most common whales in the area year-round, don't flip their tail flukes in the air as they dive to deeper water, so because the tail was visible it became more likely that the whale we headed toward was a right whale. Many whale species also can be identified from a great distance by the pattern of the moisture emitted from their blowholes when they surface for air. Because of the position and angle of their blowholes, the blow of a right whale comes out in a V pattern when seen from in front or behind the animal, or as a bushy shape when seen from other angles. When finback whales surface, the blow is tall—up to 20 feet high—and elliptical. Finback whales also have a dorsal fin that's clearly visible when they are at the surface, and right whales do not.

The first whale we sighted that day brought on some confusion. I clearly saw a dorsal fin as we approached the whale, suggesting it was a finback, but one of the other observers was certain it flashed its tail flukes, indicating it was not a finback. It quickly became apparent that two different whales were cavorting nearby. When the finback resurfaced, the biologists took note of it and then scanned the water to find the other whale. The second whale resurfaced not far away, swimming side by side at the surface with a calf born earlier in the winter.

When the calf was first sighted, Moriah Bessinger, the biologist who coordinated the weekly research cruises for the Center for Coastal Studies, broke out of her usual professional mode and cried out excitedly in her best baby talk, "It's a baby!" Young whales like this calf haven't yet begun to flip their tails in the air as they begin a deep dive, and when it was apparent the whales were going deep, the entire team of biologists gave the calf vocal encouragement and cheered when a tiny bit of its tail became visible before the young whale disappeared on a six-minute deep dive.

While the whales were at the surface, Bessinger and the rest of the researchers did their best to take photos of the whales from all angles, watched through binoculars to check for distinguishing marks, and took notes of the length of each dive and the various behaviors they exhibited. They quickly identified the adult whale as #1245, also called Slalom, a whale seen several times in recent weeks during aerial surveys. Slalom was born in 1982—her mother's name is Wart—and she previously gave birth in 1996 and 2001. She has been sighted by biologists more than 160 times up and down the East Coast since she was born.

Later in the day, we sighted several more finback whales and another female right whale with a calf. This one was #1303, a.k.a. Slash, who has a large, distinctive white scar on the underside of her torn tail and additional scars on her tail stalk, likely from colliding with a boat propeller. Slash was first sighted as an adult in 1979, and her current calf is her fifth since 1984. According to Cyndi Browning, the biologist who conducted the biweekly aerial whale surveys of Cape Cod Bay for the center and who was the chief whale spotter on the cruise, no other known right whale has such a large scar on its tail. Browning first saw Slash on a research cruise in the Bay of Fundy two years earlier while she worked for New England Aquarium. Since she sees many more whales during her aerial surveys than do the biologists on the boat, Browning is the group's expert at identifying individual whales, though she admits that it's harder to do at sea than from the air.

As the nine-hour cruise came to a close and we headed back to Provincetown harbor, Browning called out again that a whale was directly ahead. Uncharacteristically, we all let out a sigh of disappointment when she made the announcement, since it had already been a long day and we were ready to call it quits and have some dinner. But duty called. And our collective disappointment didn't last long.

It was 6 P.M., the sun was setting amidst wisps of pinkish clouds, and the whale was extremely close to shore—just 50 yards from the beach at the extreme tip of Cape Cod where several people casually walked and picked up shells. The water was less than 30 feet deep, and for a 50-foot-long, 60-ton animal, there was no room to dive and little space to maneuver beneath the surface. As we soon found out, diving and maneuvering were not what this whale had in mind. It was Slalom again, the same whale we had sighted on our way out of the harbor at the beginning of the day. As the boat zigzagged to get a closer look, a second calf surfaced nearby. Twins are virtually unheard of among right whales, so we scanned the area looking for another mother, but none was to be seen.

And that's when the parade began.

Rather than feeding beneath the surface and only rising to the top of the water for a brief moment to breathe, Slalom performed a behavior called skim-feeding that got the entire boatload of biologists giddy with delight. It was a sight that some of the biologists had never seen before; the others had never observed it so closely or for such a long time. Opening her mouth wide and raising her head 5 or 6 feet out of the water, the adult whale skimmed the surface for plankton. With her head so high out of the water and the setting sun reflecting off her dark chocolate-colored face, the white, bumpy callosities that grow in distinctive patterns on the whale's head and lips were easy to see. The callosities—tiny, white, crab-like parasites called whale lice that congregate on warty patches of the whale's body and feed on its skin—are like fingerprints and are the primary means to identify individual whales. In her gaping mouth, row after row of baleen plates used to filter her tiny food stood out clear as day through my binoculars, the front plate slightly worn and frayed compared to those further back.

Ignoring the boat and its star-struck passengers, Slalom paraded like a proud parent in front of us just 30 yards from the bow, head held high while keeping the two calves within view. As the boat drifted silently and the whales passed by, the setting sun behind them filtered through the baleen plates in her open mouth. Shortly after passing the boat, the whales turned around and paraded back in our direction. But this time, a second mother whale arrived and joined the procession. It took a moment, but Browning finally identified this whale as #1703, a whale without any other name, born in 1987 to #1157 (Moon) and now with her second calf. Traveling straight toward us this time and with the heads of both adult whales still high in the air and with mouths wide open, they provided us with an unusual look down their throats, a view few but Jonah have seen. Back and forth they went along a narrow strip of water parallel to the shore, constantly shifting position—sometimes side by side, sometimes one in front of the other, sometimes crossing paths or approaching each other head on. They were like a synchronized swim team.

The biologists and I couldn't get enough. We were long past overdue back at the dock, but we took picture after picture of this amazing sight—though my camera battery died well before the procession began—with the Wood End lighthouse and the historic Provincetown tower as a backdrop. What amazed me most was the flexibility of the whales, for while their heads were held well out of the water, their tail flukes were often still visible, and sometimes their backs were, too, as they propelled themselves slowly through the water.

Stormy Mayo, the founder of the Provincetown Center for Coastal Studies and chief biologist on the weekly research cruises, perched himself way out on the bow pulpit to observe and photograph the whales. It was he who first noticed why the whales were acting in this unusual manner. As he glanced straight down into the water, massive swarms of what must have been billions and billions of krill and plankton at the surface were easily visible to the naked eye. Mayo took pictures of this unusual assemblage of food, grabbed a net to take samples, and stared in awe from the plankton to the whales and back again.

It was an impressive sight, but after an hour of observing the parade of skim-feeding whales, we had to leave. By 7 P.M., the parade was still going on, but the marchers had no one left to perform for.

The story has been told again and again that North Atlantic right whales got their name because they were the right whale to hunt. As whale biologist Bob Kenney of the University of Rhode Island said at a public lecture in March 2005, they're easy to hunt because "they float when they're dead, they live close to the shore, and they swim slowly so six guys in a rowboat can charge up on them and kill them with a spear. It's a good story, and I've told it many times myself, but it's probably not true." According to Kenney, the data manager for all right whale research in the North Atlantic, it's more likely that the name was coined because the literal translation of its Latin name, *Eubalaena glacialis,* means "true whale."

Nonetheless, they were indeed the right whale to hunt for several centuries, and as a result, there are only about 350 of them left, making them the rarest whale and one of the rarest mammals on the planet. The North Pacific right whale, which may have a population slightly larger than its North Atlantic cousin, and the southern right whale, which numbers several thousand and lives in the southern oceans, haven't fared much better.

Commercial whaling—as opposed to subsistence hunting—got its start in the Bay of Biscay along the Atlantic coast of France and Spain well before the eleventh century. The Basques, who lived in this region, were known throughout Europe for their fishing and maritime skills, and it was the North Atlantic right whale that they first hunted. The Bay of Biscay was probably a calving ground for the whales, and look-outs were set up in all the coastal towns. When a whale was sighted, the fishermen would row out to the whale, harpoon it, and tow it back to shore, where they would peel the blubber off, fry it up in big kettles, and capture the oil. There was little market at the time for whale meat, since there was no way to preserve it, but the oil could be collected in barrels and sold all over Europe for cooking and heating.

It didn't take long for the Basques to deplete their local waters of right whales, though, so they traveled as far north as Spitsbergen and Norway, in search of additional populations of the whales. Long before Columbus arrived in America in 1492—with many Basque sailors on board his ship—it's likely that the Basques were hunting right whales around the Canadian Maritimes. When John Cabot visited Newfoundland in 1497, he wrote in his logbooks that Basque fishing boats were seen on the Grand Banks off Newfoundland. The logbooks of Jacques Cartier, who explored the Gulf of St. Lawrence in 1537, indicated that he saw over a thousand Basque fishing boats there when he arrived. Basque settlements were established in the Strait of Belle Isle between Labrador and Newfoundland as early as 1530. Because the Basque fisherman kept such good records of the whale oil they shipped back to Europe, it is known that between 1530 and 1710—by which time the right whale population had been mostly depleted—they killed between twenty-five and forty thousand whales in that area. The Basques left, but New England whalers continued hunting right whales until about 1750, when the expense of outfitting a ship was too great for the small number of whales remaining to hunt. Yet even though commercial hunting of right whales ended at about that time, they were still hunted opportunistically for many years afterward by fishermen who happened to encounter one. The last North Atlantic right whale killed for its oil in American waters was taken off Long Island in 1913, and the last in European waters were captured off Scotland in the 1920s.

The first international treaty to regulate whaling was ratified by the whaling nations in 1935, and one element of this treaty banned the hunting of right whales. Article 4 of that document states in its entirety: "The taking or killing of right whales, which shall be deemed to include North-Cape whales, Greenland whales, southern right whales, Pacific right whales and southern pigmy right whales, is prohibited." But by then, there were probably no North Atlantic right whales left on the European side of the ocean, and probably just a paltry few on the American side. Even though the commercial hunt for right whales ended more than seventy years ago, the population hasn't recovered. That's because people are still killing whales, albeit unintentionally.

According to Kenney, only one-third of right whale deaths are by natural causes, and most of those are newborns. Most of the rest die as the result of a collision with a ship or from becoming entangled in fishing gear. Soon after the ban on hunting right whales took effect, increasing industrialization led to a dramatic increase in ship traffic. A report by the National Academies of Science noted that the world shipping fleet increased from 85 million tons of ship weight in 1948 to 550 million tons in 1998. The increase was most dramatic in the range of the right whale off the coast of the northeastern United States, which is now the most heavily traveled shipping region of the world. Since 1970, twenty-one right whales have been killed by ships, a huge number given the total whale population.

The use of commercial fishing gear has increased dramatically since right whale hunting ended, too, and that has had a frightening effect on the whales. Seven out of every ten right whales sighted show scarring typical of having been entangled. While it occurs most often in juveniles—the "teenage drivers," as Kenney calls them—many adults get entangled, too, sometimes more than once. When it happens, the gear may remain wrapped around the whale's body for years, affecting its ability to grow, feed, and reproduce. And the frequency of entanglements is getting worse. During the first thirty years of right whale mortality data collected (1970–2000), just three whales were killed by entanglements. Now it's more than one per year. In 2000, six whales became entangled in fishing gear, and five more became entangled the following year. In each of those years, one whale died and one was never seen again—and presumably has died—and the others survived but may still be entangled. In 2002, eight whales became entangled, the worst year ever. As of 2004, four of them were still wrapped up, and at least one of the others had died.

As a result of the high number of entanglements in 2002, the National Marine Fisheries Service proposed modifications to the gear that fishermen use offshore. Since whales must maneuver through thousands of vertical fishing lines connecting gear at the bottom with buoys at the surface, one proposal is to require installing "weak links" in the ropes so they come apart if a whale becomes entangled. Another proposal recommends phasing out the use of ropes that float to the surface from lobster pots and fishing nets.

"The only thing we know for sure that will work is to have no ropes in the water at all," Kenney said. "But that's not a politically realistic option in fisheries that have considerable political clout. Changes in the gear in the tuna fishery that had killed 300,000 dolphins a year were tremendously effective. Kills are now down to under 1,000 a year. But that's because the fishermen are there when [the dolphins are being caught]. No fisherman has ever actually seen a right whale get entangled. It's such a rare event, and it's hard to manage rare, accidental events."

That's where Stormy Mayo comes in. In addition to founding the Provincetown Center for Coastal Studies and directing its habitat research program, he is the director of its whale disentanglement program. He disentangled his first whale, a humpback, on Thanksgiving Day in 1984. Since then, the center has become the only government-authorized whale disentanglement program in the country, and Mayo himself is the only individual authorized to disentangle right whales. So in every effort undertaken along the East Coast to disentangle a right whale from fishing gear, Mayo is there. He explains,

Disentanglement is the only thing you can do for right whales that you know for certain is reducing mortality. But it's not the answer to the entanglement problem. And it's very dangerous. Right whales are nasty, difficult animals to disentangle. Humpbacks are larger, but they don't have the will of a right whale. Right whales are unbelievably powerful.

Entanglement mortality is probably as great as ship strike mortality, but you see more dead whales from ship strikes. Entangled whales probably go out to sea to die, whereas ship strikes are closer to shore and end up washing ashore on a beach somewhere. Both causes are impossibly high if the species is to survive.

Mayo grew up in Provincetown, and he's proud to say that his family has been in that community since 1660. After earning a graduate degree in fisheries—"fish are at least as fascinating as whales," he said—and working for the Environmental Protection Agency in Puerto Rico, he returned to Provincetown and eventually was hired as the first naturalist aboard the first commercial whale-watching boat on the East Coast. "After my time in Puerto Rico, I was trying to avoid doing any science," he stated without further explanation. It was aboard that whale-watching boat that he saw his first right whale. It was a turning point for him.

I was doing a lot of humpback photo ID work back then. Salt was the first whale we named, and he's still around. But then I shifted to right whales. It had been believed that right whales were only in Cape Cod Bay in April and May, but I kept hearing stories from friends and others of earlier sightings and winter records. We got our first research vessel, *Halos,* in 1985 and started accumulating data on right whales in the bay in winter. As a result of that work, the bay was designated critical right whale habitat.

So what's so special about Cape Cod Bay? No one really knows, other than that it's the only known winter feeding ground in the world for North Atlantic right whales. About thirty whales—10 percent of the total population—visit the bay each winter to feed. Where the rest of the population spends the winter and early spring no one knows for sure. Those whales that enter the bay can usually count on finding dense aggregations of copepods to sustain them for a few weeks.

Copepods are the insects of the sea. Some are carnivorous and feed on other copepods, while others are vegetarians and eat mostly phytoplankton. Those that the right whales feed on—species in the genus *Pseudo-*

calanus in the winter and *Calanus finmarchicus,* the dominant copepod in the entire North Atlantic, in the early spring—are about the size of a pinhead and weigh nearly a milligram. That's a pretty tiny creature to sustain a 50-ton whale. As Bob Kenney describes it, the difference in size between the copepod and the whale is a factor of about fifty billion, "sort of like if people fed on bacteria by swimming around their pool filtering out bacteria with their mouth open."

Kenney says that, because of this large size differential, right whales are very specialized predators.

> They can't just go out and strain these things from the water at average concentrations. They need to find places in the water where the copepods are packed close together. It costs them a lot of energy to take that huge baleen filter in their mouth and shove it through the water. Imagine yourself swimming through the water with a bushel basket in front of you pushing it ahead. That's a tremendous amount of work. The densest concentrations of *Calanus* anywhere in the North Atlantic have always been found by asking the whale where it is. They know how to find the patches, but we still don't.

The whales know that they usually can find the patches in Cape Cod Bay in winter and spring. Something about the bay makes for extremely dense aggregations of copepods. Maybe it's because it's quite shallow, or perhaps it's because there aren't strong tidal currents in the bay that might otherwise break apart or flush out dense patches of copepods. Or it may be some combination of factors—shallow water, the topography of the bay floor, and tidal currents—that physically concentrates the zooplankton. Regardless of the reason for the patchiness of the food, those patches occur in different places in the bay each winter, and it's Stormy Mayo's job to track them.

The first research cruise I went on with Mayo aboard the R/V *Shearwater* was in March 2005. The 40-foot boat was built by Jarvis Newman in the 1980s to serve as a tender for the *Stars and Stripes* yacht, which was competing in the America's Cup races in Australia. At the end of its life in big-time competitive yacht racing, *Shearwater* was sold and converted into a fishing boat, and then sold again in 1995 to the Center for Coastal Studies, which upgraded its engines and made several other renovations. On research cruises, it travels at 12 knots, the protocol speed for scientific investigations of this type.

While the weather was perfect that March day, the concentrations of copepods were quite thin. With water temperatures not much above freezing, everyone but the captain wore bright orange, bulky "survival suits." As the biologists prepared their gear for the day, I kept a keen look-out for seabirds as we pulled out of Provincetown harbor, and felt a mild satisfaction at getting a good look at a black guillemot and two red-necked grebes, birds that are hard to find at my usual birding haunts back home in Rhode Island.

About a mile and a half out, we stopped at the first of eight designated sampling stations scattered throughout the bay where a wide variety of tests are conducted to assess the quantity and density of the food re-sources available to the whales. First, a funnel-shaped net with a 12-inch opening was towed slowly behind the boat for five minutes to sample the copepod density at the surface of the water. Then, a similar net with a 24-inch opening was dropped straight down and pulled up by hand, a test the biologists call an "oblique," to determine copepod abundance in the vertical water column. The fine mesh in the nets is supposed to filter out food particles at the same rate that a whale's baleen plates would. In the first two samples, it was clear that any whale swimming in those areas would have gone hungry. In each case, the few copepods collected in the nets were placed in tiny jars and labeled with date and location. Later, at the center's lab, Bessinger would count the actual number of copepods in each sample, a tedious process that the biologist says is her least favorite part of the job. While the tow-net and oblique tests were being com-pleted, another biologist lowered a Secchi disk into the water to deter-mine water clarity, another method of assessing plankton abundance. The disk is patterned in stark black and white, and it's slowly lowered deeper and deeper into the water until it can no longer be seen by the unaided eye. The deeper it can be seen, the clearer the water—and the fewer copepods available for whales to feed on.

As we motored off to find the second sampling location, the observer on the top deck called out the location of some fishing buoys that ap-peared to be illegal gear. The researchers report all commercial fishing gear they see on their weekly cruises to the National Marine Fisheries Service for investigation. Though they never follow up to find out what becomes of any investigations that may occur, they say it's their duty to report the gear and help the government biologists protect the whales from becoming entangled.

As we continued, another report soon buzzed on the radio. The aerial survey team announced the sightings of two whales at coordinates 41.50.4 and 70.20.0, eight miles southwest of our then-current location and close to one of the sampling stations we would be visiting later in the day. One whale was doing six-minute dives, while the other was diving for ten minutes at a time, they reported, though they couldn't tell if the whales were actively feeding or not. The sighting raised the spirits of the biologists, although it seemed they were mostly excited that they probably would get to show me my first right whale. On several of the cruises earlier in the season, no whales were sighted at all.

The center conducts aerial surveys whenever the weather cooperates, which tends to average out to be about twice a week from January through April. Because the airborne biologists can cover more ground and see whales more easily from their small airplane, they always report seeing many more whales than the biologists on the cruises see. It had been a bad season for whale sightings so far, with a total of only eight whales sighted and never more than two on any one day. Mayo said the thin plankton samples are the reason. He thinks the whales arrive in the bay on schedule, but they soon realize that food is scarce and they leave within a day or two to seek a meal elsewhere.

At the second sampling station, the tow-net and oblique tests again returned disappointingly thin results. The group then conducted a pump station test, where they lower a hose overboard to fifteen different depths (from 1 to 31 meters) and pump water to the surface to filter out the copepods. It's a long process that seemed even longer as the weather conditions deteriorated and the boat was tossed back and forth. Conditions weren't bad enough, though, to abort the team's first planned use of an optical plankton counter, a high-tech device that uses a beam of light to count and determine the size of any plankton in the water column. As the device is dropped straight down into the bay or towed behind the boat, water flows through a central opening and passes by the light beam.

Dave Osterberg, a bearded engineer from Michigan Tech, was hired by the center specifically because he has experience with the optical plankton counter. He was a little nervous as his skills were put to the test for the first time, and he struggled a bit with how to connect the device to a laptop computer to provide real-time plankton data. He said the device gives the researchers an excellent picture of plankton densities every half second that it's in the water. "It gives a fine-scale distribution of plankton, unlike the tow-nets and the oblique which collect everything in one pile and can't tell you if one part of the water column had abundant copepods and another part of the column had nothing." While it took three people to lower and retrieve the bulky device, the first test was a success. It came back with similar results to the other sampling methods—copepod abundance was low.

The day continued in similar fashion at several more sampling stations, until we finally saw our first whale. It was about a mile distant, but its blow was clearly visible, and soon after we saw tail flukes. As we got closer, another whale was sighted, and then another, but none of them allowed us to get close enough for photos or identification. One would come to the surface, blow a couple times, and then dive deep before we could approach. Then a different whale would do the same thing in a different location. In all, Mayo believes there were four different whales within 1 square mile, but we'll never be certain nor know the identity of any of them.

While it was frustrating for Mayo and his team, for me it was truly memorable. I got my first clear look at the diagnostic V-shape of the blow, and it amazed me how long the moisture from the blow hung in the air. Like a lingering low fog, it was sometimes still visible four or five seconds after the initial surfacing blow. What also surprised me was how short each breath was at the surface. In my previous experience watching humpbacks, finbacks, gray whales, and several other species, they all seemed to blow at the surface and then swim beneath the surface for a minute before breathing again. These whales took four or five breaths within a minute's time before diving deeply for an extended period. They also exhibited what to me was another unusual behavior—a quick change of direction when diving. Usually when a whale initiates a deep dive, it raises its tail flukes into the air parallel to the water surface and dives straight down. These right whales seemed to be changing course with each dive, as their flukes always seemed to rise into the air and sink beneath the surface at what appeared to be an awkward angle. Bessinger suggested that perhaps they were changing direction with each dive, maybe to herd food together, maybe to avoid something (like us), or maybe just to retrace their steps. Whatever the reason, all the whales in this location were doing it.

"Bonanza!" yelled Mayo. As I was entranced with watching the whales, Mayo was sampling plankton. And they were much more abundant here than anywhere else we had sampled so far. As Bob Kenney said earlier, if you want to know where the patches of food are, follow the whales.

Despite the bonanza in that one sample, the winter of 2005 was a bad year for North Atlantic right whales, both in Cape Cod Bay and elsewhere. From November through March, five adult right whales were killed from ship collisions or fishing gear entanglement, an unprecedented rate of mortality for a long-lived mammal with a population of just 350 individuals. The dead whales included #1909, who bled to death after being struck by the U.S. Navy's amphibious assault ship USS *Iwo Jima* near the mouth of the Chesapeake Bay in November; an unidentified whale found 86 miles east of Nantucket in December; Bolo, who had given birth to a record six calves and was found dead 78 miles east of Nantucket in January; Lucky, who survived an earlier ship strike as a calf in 1991; and #2301, who died as a result of a severe entanglement and was found off Virginia in March. At least four of the dead whales were females of reproductive age, and two were known to be pregnant. With a breeding population of just eighty-four females, 5 percent of the species' breeding females died that winter. Another whale, identified only as #2425, had a large portion of its tail fluke nearly amputated in a collision with a recreational yacht off Cumberland Island, Georgia, and biologists don't expect it to survive.

Those that made it to their feeding grounds in Cape Cod Bay faced a difficult time finding food. Copepod densities were well below those found the previous year in nearly every weekly sample taken from January through early May when the last whales left the bay. While the availability of food didn't reach an all-time low that winter, it certainly added to the already difficult year the whales were having. Yet Stormy Mayo didn't appear to be particularly concerned. "This is a rare animal feeding on an ephemeral food source, so it's not surprising that its distribution varies dramatically from year to year," he said, although he believes that part of the variation in copepod abundance is caused by an influx of nutrients from human sources that find their way into the bay and negatively affect the ecosystem. "Every year is different, and we don't have enough historical data to tell whether this is an unusual year or not."

Moments before, Mayo had said it *was* an unusual year, but not for the lack of food. Instead it was unusual for a positive reason. Right whales had a baby boom earlier in the season. Biologists had counted twenty-seven right whale calves born on their breeding grounds during the year, the second-highest tally ever (thirty-one were born in 2001). As a result, Mayo said that Cape Cod Bay had an influx of mothers and calves greater than in past years. Six mother-calf pairs were sighted on a mid-April aerial survey, the most seen in the bay at one time in his twenty-one years of observations. Some of that could be attributed to the large number of calves born that year, but he said that even in years when similar numbers have been born, fewer visit the bay.

Mayo's optimism was short-lived on that April cruise. After reviewing his notes, he realized that one mother-calf pair sighted that day was feeding in the middle of the shipping lanes leading toward Boston Harbor. Most of the whale sightings in the bay are in the southeastern half, because that's where most of the dense patches of copepods form, but a patch of food had formed in the northwest and that's where those two whales were feeding just below the surface. He said that right whales are struck by ships more often than other whale species because they are slow-moving whales that are oblivious to their surroundings when they feed and socialize. He made a note to alert the Coast Guard and National Marine Fisheries Service to the unusual location of these whales, and he included his concerns in his weekly report to whale biologists throughout the region. Luckily, the whales safely left the area within a few days.

Where they went is anybody's guess. And that's one of the challenges of studying North Atlantic right whales. Little is known about where they go for much of the year, especially the adult males. Calving occurs off the coast of the southeastern United States, mostly between Savannah, Georgia, and Cape Canaveral, Florida, in early- to mid-winter, but very few males are ever sighted there. About 10 percent of the population—a mix of adult males, adult females, juveniles, and mother-calf pairs—feed in Cape Cod Bay in late winter and early spring, but no one knows where the rest go during that time. In late spring, many are seen in the Great South Channel in the Gulf of Maine. They then go north to Canada for the summer and fall, but the population splits: the mothers and calves go to the Bay of Fundy while the males go to the Roseway Basin off Nova Scotia. Again, not all of them go to those sites.

Given the advances in technology, you would think it would be easy to put a tracking device on a whale to learn where it goes from season to

season. Not so, mostly because they have such a boisterous courtship behavior that takes place at all times of the year. According to University
of Rhode Island's Kenney, courtship in right whales occurs in groups of
up to thirty or forty males and a lone female, who starts the action by vo-
calizing to attract the males to her. But when the males arrive, she rolls
upside down at the surface so none can mate with her.

> So the males all jostle to be the one next to her when she rolls right side
> up again to breathe. They're all banging into each other and they just beat
> the living daylights out of the tracking tags we put on them. Sperm whales
> will carry a tag for a year and still keep working. With right whales,
> though, we've had some thirty-day attachments, and then they rip them
> off during courtship. We've even tried putting little tags on the whales that
> stick below the skin and all that sticks out is an antenna. And the next day
> the antenna has a kink in it, and the day after that it's bent like a corkscrew,
> and the day after that it's gone.

But these challenges don't mean that everything about the whales is
still a mystery. In 1986, scientists from the University of Rhode Island,
Woods Hole Oceanographic Institute, New England Aquarium, and the
Provincetown Center for Coastal Studies got together to form the North
Atlantic Right Whale Consortium to study the whales and come up with
strategies for protecting them. One outgrowth of that effort is a catalog
of photographs of all the known right whales, maintained by the aquarium, which has helped to monitor individual animals and keep track of
births and deaths. The catalog contains over 37,000 records and 200,000
separate pictures of right whales; 474 different individuals have been identified. Twenty-five of those are known to be dead, and 118 have not been
seen in more than six years and are presumed dead.

The catalog isn't yet old enough to give an accurate picture of the average lifespan of a right whale, although a picture of an adult whale was
printed in a Florida newspaper in 1935, and that same whale was killed
by a ship in 1995. Bowhead whales, the closest relatives to right whales,
are still sometimes found with ivory harpoon points lodged in them that
Eskimos used in the late nineteenth century. A new technique being
used to age whales by analyzing the chemical makeup of their eye lens
suggests that a bowhead might have lived to be 230 years old. But other
than those hints, their lifespan is still uncertain.

There is more certainty about their reproductive cycle, but what is known is alarming. Despite the banner year for calves in 2005, a more typical year finds just twelve or thirteen calves born, and that's just not enough to sustain the species, especially with the high number of ship collisions and fishing gear entanglements. Scientists from Woods Hole suggest that at current rates of birth and death, the species will go extinct in two hundred years. Right whales don't give birth until they are about ten years old, and then they have just one calf every three to six years. What's more, the birthrate varies dramatically from year to year. In 1999, just four calves were born, followed by only one in 2000. But 2001 was a record year with thirty-one calves, after which the rate dropped again before rebounding to twenty-seven in 2005. "Bouncing from a record low one year to a record high the next is not good," said Kenney. "That kind of wild statistical variability is the exact thing you don't want in a rare population if it's going to survive."

So what's happening to keep right whale numbers low? Kenney thinks it's a combination of several factors. Habitat loss is clearly an important one. Writings from the colonial era suggest that Delaware Bay was once a calving ground for right whales, and Cape Cod Bay and other places may have been as well. But the whales may have been excluded from using those locations to give birth by human activities, and that likely has a significant impact on their ability to recover their population numbers. Kenney said that natural and man-made toxins in the water also may reduce reproductive rates, and the small population may result in inbreeding, which is known to cause low fertility rates, sterility, and a high rate of miscarriage. The "Allee effect" could be another contributing factor. When a small number of individuals are scattered across a large range, as Kenney says, "it's hard to find a date. Tiny whale, big ocean." The other limiting factor he points to is food. "They're not starving to death, but maybe the females aren't getting enough extra food to put on the necessary weight to support pregnancy, so they're having calves farther and farther apart."

Kenney has an idea about the bigger picture as well.

During the Basque times, the whale's feeding area probably extended from Cape Cod all the way to Greenland and Iceland, and all those whales probably migrated south. Like now, the whales that fed in Cape Cod had a calving ground in Georgia and Florida. Those that fed further north maybe calved in Delaware Bay, and the ones who fed off Greenland maybe had their babies around Cape Cod Bay. And whaling just cut the whole top population off. All that's left are those that feed off New England and calve off Georgia. All the northern whales disappeared and haven't come back.

If you're a mammal that lives in a big population range, the ones that live on the edge live in marginal habitat . . . where the habitat quality is usually lower. The whales we've got left are living in marginal habitat, so they go through boom and bust times—years when there's plenty of food and they have lots of babies and years when things aren't so hot and their reproductive rate is really low. They could probably get through that, except that on top of all that, we're still killing them.

But why haven't they gone back to Newfoundland and Greenland? Matrilineal-directed habitat fidelity, he said.

Junior learns where all the good feeding grounds are from mom, and after he weans he just keeps going back to those same places. Since there aren't any mothers taking their calves to Newfoundland and Labrador, they never learn [to go there]. In the last thirty years, there have been two or three right whale sightings in Labrador, a couple in Iceland, and a couple in the Gulf of St. Lawrence, so over generations of whales they will eventually find it. But can they do it quick enough to get through the tough times they're having now? That's the big question . . . What we need to do is to find ways to stop ship collisions and fishing gear entanglements, and then just let them be. They're good at having babies, so if we can stop killing them, then eventually, long beyond our lifetime, they'll probably re-colonize those other habitats and end up doing OK.

We can only hope.

2

Ringed Boghaunter

They witnessed the evolution and extinction of dinosaurs, and to the public they're among the most recognizable creatures on the planet, but most people know very little about dragonflies. Despite wearing dragonfly jewelry and dragonfly t-shirts, all that most dragonfly aficionados know is that they see them darting around in their gardens and parks in the warmer months, and that the insects are entertaining aerialists that come in a beautiful rainbow of colors.

Yet they're much more than that. Fossils of the ancestors of modern dragonflies date to 225 million years ago, and while ancient dragonflies had the same basic form and structure as those we see flying today, they were much larger. Wingspans often topped more than two-and-a-half feet! Like today's versions, they were generalized obligate carnivores, which means they ate whatever they could catch, primarily other insects.

Most people don't realize that adult dragonflies live on average just three or four weeks, although their entire lifespan lasts more than a year, and in some species, perhaps as long as five years. There are about five hundred species of dragonflies and damselflies—a close cousin—that make up the family Odonata in the United States. The smallest is less than an inch long and the largest more than four inches in length.

The characteristic that attracts the greatest attention, however, is their flying ability. Dragonflies are the only creatures that can fly backwards and forwards as well as straight up and down, and they can stop instantaneously in midair. Their remarkable flight skills are accomplished with four stiff wings that move independently yet in concert with each other. It's these great feats of flight that allow them to be such dangerous predators, easily capturing and devouring many other flying insects, including other dragonflies. They are such skilled aerialists that flight engineers have studied them in search of ways to improve military aircraft.

Dragonflies lay their eggs in the water, often in fish-free freshwater ponds of varying types and sizes, almost always ponds with emergent vegetation, as well as in lakes, streams, rivers, vernal pools, and all sorts of wetlands. It's this aquatic part of their life cycle that most people know so little about. When dragonfly eggs hatch, most larvae live for about a year in the water body in which they were born, feeding voraciously on other aquatic insects. According to Ginger Brown, one of New England's leading dragonfly experts, larval dragonflies look more like terrestrial insects than like aquatic insects, despite the fact that they live entirely in the water.

> I would describe them as short bodied—definitely not long and lean like the adults—but you can still see the insect-ness of them because they have six legs, eyes, and antennae that are visible just like other insects. They have three different body parts—a head, thorax, and abdomen—and wing pads that tell you that they're going to eventually fly around. They breathe through gills like fish, but they have internal rectal gills, so when they breathe they're actually pulling water in and squirting it back out again, which creates a jet propulsion-like movement. And they have a chitinous exoskeleton like all insects do, but it's definitely soft rather than the hard shell like on many terrestrial insects.

That's definitely an entomologist talking. Only an entomologist could describe a dragonfly larva with such eloquence and precision. It's obvious that I'm not a biologist, because every time I've tried to describe a dragonfly larva, all I can come up with is three words: ugly, brown, and squishy. And yet they intrigue me immensely, partly because I had never known about that part of their life cycle or seen one before I went looking for them. Mostly, though, they're intriguing because of their unique trigger mechanisms that tell them it's time to leave the water and fly.

That trigger is a combination of environmental and physiological elements: the water temperature in their natal pond, the amount of daylight, and various hormones and body rhythms. Some species are tuned in to some of these elements more than others, but for most, when the water temperature is right and the days get to be a certain length, something inside them indicates that it's time to emerge from the water. For the rare ringed boghaunter, for instance, that combination of triggers occurs primarily in April and makes it the earliest-flying dragonfly in New England. The trigger for other species is warmer water and longer days, so they don't emerge until later in the season, mostly in June or July. Regardless of when it happens, whenever their body tells them it's time, the larval dragonflies seek out a suitable support that's sticking from the water—often a stiff grass or sedge or other vegetation—and they climb up above the water line. Boghaunters only crawl an inch or two out of the water, while other species such as common baskettails might crawl 10 or 15 feet up a tree. In extreme cases, some of the river species like shadowdragons may walk 100 feet from the water to find a suitable support.

Then, when they're comfortably out of the water, the transformation begins. Much like a butterfly's metamorphosis from caterpillar to butterfly, the dragonfly experiences a similar metamorphosis from larva to dragonfly. But the butterfly goes through several other life stages and takes several days or weeks before its transformation is complete. Dragonflies do the whole thing in about ninety minutes. And it's fascinating to watch.

As Brown—who is occasionally called the dragon lady by friends—explained,

> it's mind-boggling to imagine the physiological changes that happen as it goes from being a fully functioning aquatic larva with all the components of an insect's body into a completely changed animal. The reorganization internally is something I really have a hard time understanding because you can't watch it happen. The animals apparently stop eating for a day or so before they seek out that emergence support. That reorganization inside results in an expansion once they're out of the water that creates a split down the back of the larva's exoskeleton. Then the adult dragonfly begins to back out of the shell. First comes the head and thorax. Then it has to reach forward with its legs to hold onto its support to pull out its abdomen.

After completing this process and pumping body fluids through its wings to stiffen them, it takes flight for the first time.

That's the process I was hoping to observe when Brown took me to a few of her favorite dragonfly ponds in search of ringed boghaunters (*Williamsonia lintneri*). This small, dark-brown member of the Emerald family has gray-blue eyes, a tan-colored face, and prominent pale yellow or orange rings around each abdominal segment. It ranges from southwestern Maine and southern New Hampshire down to eastern Connecticut, but most of its populations are found in eastern Massachusetts and Rhode Island. A distinct Great Lakes population was discovered in the late 1990s in Wisconsin and Michigan.

Our first stop was to the mother of all boghaunter sites, a one-and-a-half-acre pond in Richmond, Rhode Island, where three or four times more boghaunters are born in an average year than in any other place in the world. Because Richmond is home to ten of the state's twenty-nine populations of ringed boghaunters, we were joined by Suzanne Enser, a member of the town's Conservation Commission and its land trust, to learn more about how she can work to protect the species. To get there, we drove down a long, unpaved driveway and parked next to a rural home hidden in the woods. Cutting through the backyard, we trudged about a quarter mile through open woodland, across a small, rushing stream, and through a tiny cranberry bog where several of last year's bright red berries lay nestled against thick mats of sphagnum moss. At the top of a small rise, we glanced down into a large "bowl" surrounded by white pines and maples where the pond sat amidst a ring of leatherleaf, sweet pepperbush, and blueberry. Fighting our way through the bushes, we waded out into the pond. The surface of the fen-like pond was mostly covered with three-square sedge—new green shoots reaching 6 inches above the surface and last year's dead brown ones lying in the water—and just beneath the water surface were masses of submerged sphagnum. These two plants are indicative of ideal habitat for the inch-and-a-half-long dragonfly.

"There is rarely a direct association between an odonate and a particular plant species, but from my observation, *lintneri* is actually depositing eggs on sphagnum at the surface of the water," Brown said. "It may be that the eggs are actually adhering to the sphagnum, but I don't know this for sure."

After a dragonfly larva climbs up the emergent vegetation and meta-

morphoses into an adult dragonfly, it leaves behind its exoskeleton—
which is then called an exuvia—still clinging to the vegetation. That empty
shell is how Brown keeps track of boghaunter populations. Several times
a season, she visits many of the known boghaunter sites and inspects each
emergent sedge to collect and count exuvia. While she might not get
them all, she knows with a fair degree of certainty that her counts are a
good indication of the status of the population in each pond. At this site,
for instance, she and colleague Nina Briggs collected 222 exuvia in 1998,
more than 500 in 2000, 1,525 in 2001, and between 500 and 700 each year
from 2002 to 2005. No other site comes close to these numbers. In fact,
this site is almost certainly the source population for several other boghaunter sites nearby. Which is a concern to Brown because it's a site in
peril.

It was the third week of April 2005 when I visited, which is a few weeks
early for most songbirds to have migrated from their southern wintering
grounds, but the early arrivals—pine warblers, black-and-white warblers,
American robins, and Eastern towhees—let us know by their distinctive
songs that they had completed their long, nocturnal flights and were ready
for the breeding season. Unfortunately, their calls were often drowned
out by the constant rumbling and crunching of heavy machinery and the
incessant beeping of massive dump trucks backing up.

Immediately adjacent to the wetland is a gravel pit, which had recently
expanded its operation right up to the edge of the 50-foot regulatory
buffer required between its excavation site and the wetland. But the buffer
is hardly adequate to protect the aquatic environment. Like a desert sand-
storm, dust and debris was constantly in the air, and 50 feet of vegetation—
mostly white pines and maples, along with a variety of shrubs in the
understory—did little to keep it from settling in the water. Run-off from
the pit was also a problem. In many places, the sphagnum in the wetland
was covered in silt, so if the boghaunter truly does lay its eggs on the sphagnum, as Brown suspects, then much of the sphagnum at the surface was
being compromised. Equally important, once the insects complete their
transformation from larvae to adult dragonfly, they spend most of the remaining three weeks of their life in the adjacent forest. Yet the forest on
two sides of the wetland had been cut down, and residential development
encroaches on a third side.

"What are the ramifications of the upland habitat destruction? Does it matter to a boghaunter that there's a gravel pit and not forest?" Brown asked. "If you look at this population, it doesn't appear that it does. But it may be that there are other things going on that we don't know about. Maybe they're concentrated in smaller forests as adults, and because they're concentrated in a smaller area maybe they can find each other with greater frequency. Time will tell. But there's nothing good about what's going on out here."

It seems clear that the boghaunters know something is wrong, too. I visited this same site with Brown six years earlier, when the forest was much more extensive between the gravel pit and the wetland. Most of the exuvia we collected that day were found on emergent vegetation on the side of the wetland closest to the gravel pit. Back then, it appeared that the gravel operation's impact on the dragonflies was insignificant. But on my most recent visit, with silt covering much of the sphagnum at that end of the wetland, almost all of the exuvia were at the end opposite the gravel pit. That's also the only place we found frog and toad eggs, newly emerged tadpoles, and various other aquatic life.

As I strained to hear Brown's voice above the sound of the heavy equipment, she excitedly pointed out our first adult boghaunter of the day. "There's one, and it's on its maiden flight!" she called out. "Look at those wings shimmering. It's just emerged and it's heading right toward the forest. It sure knows where it's going." It was a teneral, she explained, which is the stage of life immediately after emergence, when the dragonfly's body is rather fragile and its wings are shiny and flimsy.

The gravel pit isn't the only threat to this particular wetland. In fact, some observers say the gravel operation isn't likely to survive much longer. Once all the gravel is removed, which likely will be soon, the operation will shut down. But now there is talk that the site is slated for major development, a combination of residential, commercial, industrial, and recreational. This kind of development is often disastrous to wetlands, as human development brings with it run-off of lawn chemicals, sewage concerns, invasive species, and hazardous wastes that find their way into nearby waterways. On one hand, if the development restores the buffer, the obvious signs of problems created by the gravel pit could be resolved and conditions could improve. On the other hand, large-scale development such as that being talked about around this site also brings with it significant withdrawal of water from the underground aquifer. And that, even more than the continued operation of the gravel pit, could cause disaster, because as water is withdrawn, the water level in nearby wetlands is lowered and the hydroperiod changes. Those species that require water in their wetland at certain times of the year or for a certain length of time—including salamanders, frogs, and dragonflies—may not have the water they require to complete their life cycle.

"We don't really know exactly what kind of hydroperiod these guys need," Brown said, "so I don't know how short that period could get before *lintneri* disappears. We know they are drought tolerant, but obviously at some point there's just going to be too little water for too little period of time."

While it's hard to predict the effect of development around the site, Brown's concerns are very real. No boghaunter site anywhere in Rhode Island is larger or more important than this one. It appears to be the primary source population for a number of other nearby sites. Adult boghaunters emerge from this wetland, fly into the forest, and make their way to other wetlands with the same habitat characteristics. Some of them then lay eggs at these other sites and start new populations. Most of the other sites have relatively small numbers of boghaunters, and in some years no boghaunters might emerge from the water. Without the annual influx of adults from the source population, many of these smaller populations would disappear. And with them, the best hope of saving the species.

Brown is also concerned because this key site is in private hands with four different owners. The property boundaries run right through the wetland, with the gravel pit operator owning half and three other landowners owning the rest. "I'm a firm believer in the fact that conservation of species is only going to be successful on protected lands," she said. "That assumes that at some point in Rhode Island there will be no undeveloped land left, and that these protected lands can hold their own and nothing degrades them. It also assumes that they're managed right. But only 50 percent of our boghaunter sites are on protected lands, and there are big populations unprotected. Those are the ones I'm skeptical about over the long term."

For now, though, Brown seems confident in knowing that this site is on the radar screens of the appropriate municipal and nonprofit conservation agencies. "We've communicated the importance of the site to everybody that needs to know about it. I'm looking at it in a very positive way and, because everybody knows about it, anticipating that they're going to make sure that something happens to improve the situation in the immediate vicinity here," she said.

Brown developed an interest in insects as a student at Kansas State University, where she got her fair share of ribbing while running around campus swinging her insect net. She carried that interest with her to a job as a naturalist at the Cape Cod Museum of Natural History, where she taught environmental science programs in local elementary schools, led field walks, and conducted marine science programs. That work left her one day a week to conduct research on dragonflies, first by teaching herself the necessary biology and later publishing *The Dragonflies and Damselflies of Cape Cod*. Arriving at the Rhode Island office of The Nature Conservancy in 1990, she continued her dragonfly work by reconfirming the state's three known ringed boghaunter sites and seeking out new populations.

One new population was found five miles up the road in the town of Exeter, where we visited a small fen on a quiet, forested road with scattered houses and numerous wetlands. This site is much more typical of the majority of known boghaunter sites in Rhode Island, according to Brown, but to me it looked rather similar to the site we had just left. The water surface area was about a third the size of the previous site, but it had the same sphagnum, sedge, and cranberries in the water, and a more extensive red maple and white pine forest all around it, with leatherleaf and blueberry bushes at the edges. Over the years, Brown and Briggs have collected an average of about thirty exuvia at the site annually, with a high of sixty-three in 2003. As we waded to our knees and began searching emergent vegetation for exuvia, Brown warned us that a huge snapping turtle resides beneath the waters somewhere. But we soon forgot about the turtle. Instead, our minds were focused on boghaunters—dozens of them—and they were all emerging from their larval shells at the same time.

I almost plucked the first one I saw off its stem, thinking it was an empty shell. Instead, its back had split and a live dragonfly head was just barely poking out, like the grisly alien emerging from a human in that 1970s B-movie that was too scary for me to sit through. The boghaunter's head appeared white and ghostly, adding to my uncertainty of whether it was alive or not. But the next one I found was much further out of its shell, squirming and straining to remove itself from the tiny confines of its earlier life-stage. Brown and Enser called out from other corners of the pond that they were seeing similar activity, and we carefully waded back and forth to see what each of us had found. We saw several tenerals making their first flights, and others that were entirely emerged from their shells but that hadn't yet completely pumped fluids through their bodies, waiting to firm up before taking flight.

A closer look at one emerging boghaunter reminded me of the dangers lurking around every corner in the natural world, even for a voracious insect predator like a dragonfly. The time it takes for dragonflies to emerge from their larval shell is the most vulnerable period in their life, and this boghaunter suffered the consequences. Halfway through its emergence, a wolf spider found it, immobilized it, and began feeding. Like the Cooper's hawk that regularly visits my yard to catch one of the many small songbirds that have been attracted to my birdfeeders, it's no surprise that dragonflies—and almost every other creature on Earth— face similar run-ins with those higher on the food chain. In the case of this boghaunter, however, it seemed unfair that this one was captured when its defenses were down and it couldn't fight back. Yet the success of so many predators is based on their ability to cull out the old, young, diseased, or otherwise vulnerable prey. I suspect that the tables are occasionally turned and wolf spiders sometimes fall prey to adult dragonflies.

Just when we thought we had found all of the exuvia and emerging boghaunters in the pond, we discovered another batch. In this last group was a dragonfly whose body was almost entirely out of its shell, but not quite. In order to complete the job, it needed to grasp the stem of the vegetation it had climbed onto for leverage, but it couldn't reach it. For long minutes at a time, it arched its body and tried to spin around and reach out with its legs to grasp the stem. And every time, the stem was just out of reach. Like a bound and gagged crime victim, it struggled mightily with its shackles until it was exhausted, then rested for another try. I asked Brown if we should try to help it, but she insisted that we let nature take its course. Besides, they are so fragile that any effort to grasp it likely would have crushed it. So we moved on. (Brown returned to the site the next day and found the empty exuvia of that dragonfly, so it probably made it out on its own.)

Brown felt slightly more confident about the future of the Exeter wetland than the previous one. "Even though it's right next to a road, the risks at this site are considerably less than at the other one," she said. "The upland is developable and a house could still get plunked in right next to the pond, bringing with it fertilizers and invasive species and trampling. But the level of threat is much less, and the owner is known by conservation organizations."

Before we left, I grabbed one last exuvia and put it into the orange prescription drug canister that Brown uses to collect the larval shells. I mentioned to her that this one was just barely above the water line, and she immediately rushed over to take a look. I'm thankful that she did, because in my haste I had grabbed a live larva that was still climbing out of the water and hadn't even begun its transformation. How did Brown know? I would have had a hard time forgiving myself if I was responsible for killing an individual of such a rare species.

Brown had one more site she wanted to show me before heading home for the day, and this one was as unexpected as could be. Driving north on interstates 95 and 295 from Exeter, we came to a clover-leaf exit in Johnston adjacent to an electrical substation and the intersection of miles of towering power transmission lines. This site couldn't be more disturbed or appear more unnatural, but it was here that in 2004 a single adult ringed boghaunter was found somewhat late in the season. Brown has been back to the site several times since then, unsuccessfully looking for exuvia or other adults.

It's a puzzling site. It has many of the same plant species as the more pristine sites—sedges, sphagnum, blueberry bushes, and small maple trees—but it also has exotic and invasive shrubs, muddy gravel roads around it, and almost certainly run-off from the nearby highway. The power lines had been there for decades, and the wetland probably had been there well before that. When Brown first visited the site, she expected it to have good dragonfly diversity, but she didn't expect to find a boghaunter. As we approached the site, the criss-crossing power lines crackled overhead, green frogs and bullfrogs leaped and croaked, and the songs of field sparrows and song sparrows occasionally could be heard above the din of the traffic.

"This may be one of those sink populations," Brown said. "But the scary thing about that is that means there should be a source population nearby that we haven't identified, which shouldn't be any more than a mile or so away. We don't know where that guy came from, but we presume there's some breeding going on here because the habitat looks fine.

Structurally it's right for it, even though it's taken a heck of a lot of run-off from the highway and it's been altered and there's only a limited amount of forest on one side."

It's places like this that give Brown hope. "Just when I think we've found them all, we find more. I don't think there are a lot more unknown sites out there, because we've put our antennae out for this species, but they keep dribbling in."

They keep dribbling in partly because Brown, her husband Charlie, and Briggs spend every available day in April and May looking for them. But they're not the only ones looking. Brown also enlisted a dedicated team of more than fifty volunteers (including me) to visit as many ponds, streams, and wetlands in Rhode Island as possible over the course of six years to census the state for dragonflies and damselflies. During that time, we found 136 different species scattered around the state, adding 23 new species to the state's official odonate list. We found several species that had never been found in New England before—southern species such as the southern sprite and blackwater bluet—as well as lots of new populations of rare species. One species thought to be rare, the New England bluet, was removed from the state's endangered list because seventy different populations of it were found. And we found an additional eleven populations of ringed boghaunter.

"You hear people say it all the time: If you don't know what's there before it's lost, you're never going to know what you've lost," Brown said. "And until you've been everywhere to look for it, you can't say it only occurs here. So that's why we did the dragonfly inventory. So we can draw conclusions about distribution and abundance, and so we know where the hotbeds of diversity are within this group of organisms. How does The Nature Conservancy know where to spend their money? This is a great way to inform them. Because if you protect a piece of land and water for a dragonfly, you're going to protect the fish that are in there, the frogs and toads as well, everything."

As an example, she said that her dragonfly survey project discovered high odonate diversity at a small watershed in the town of Foster that conservation groups in the region hadn't considered important. But when the census found beautiful forested streams and interesting ponds with rare species of dragonflies and damselflies, they took notice. And they already have begun spending money to protect land in the area.

"The other thing to know about this group of insects is their ecological significance," she added. "They're aquatic insects, and you might be able to tell something about the health of your aquatic systems by looking at this group of insects. That's pretty much where we're going with this project, to try and do this work so we can look at aquatic systems, individual sites, and watersheds, and see what our data can tell us about their ecological health."

So far, the Rhode Island data has told her a lot. For instance, she's found significant relationships between species diversity and forest cover. The more forest an area has, the more odonates are found there. Conversely, the more development and roads in an area, the fewer species live there. "Most people might not think there was a link between dragonflies and the forest," she explained. "People think of them as only aquatic insects linked to wetlands. You might expect the significant relationship to have been between dragonflies and wetland cover, but it wasn't. The data showed that the amount of forest adjacent to the wetlands is important."

With 14,000 dragonfly records from 1,100 sites in all thirty-nine communities in the state, Brown is now trying to get her data out to conservation groups in a useful form. "It's the only way to protect these animals," she said. "The results we found are directly applicable to conservation. We've come up with recommendations for how to manage sites, and brought in data from other areas that talk abut the impacts of recreation, forestry, and how big a place you need to protect the odonate fauna in that place. I want that data to get out there because I know that the conservation groups really want some kind of dataset to help them prioritize their conservation efforts."

The ringed boghaunter was first described in 1878 by Herman A. Hagen, a physician from East Prussia who devoted his life to the study of insects, especially dragonflies and damselflies. While living in his hometown of Koningsberg (now Kaliningrad, Russia), the Smithsonian Institution sent him hundreds of odonates collected by numerous American collectors and asked him to write a monograph of North American species. The resulting document, which he submitted in 1861 entirely in Latin, is considered the seminal publication on the subject, establishing his reputation in the New World as a leading expert in the field. He was soon offered a position at the Museum of Comparative Zoology in Cambridge, Massachusetts, a post he held until his death in 1863. Although he never be-

came fluent in English, he had significant influence on American entomologists and served as a mentor to many.

One of them was Edward B. Williamson, considered the most colorful and most famous dragonfly expert in the country, who also became a
noted iris cultivator later in life. It was he for whom the ringed boghaunter (*Williamsonia lintneri*) was named. Born just a year before Hagen
first described the species, Williamson discovered his first new dragonfly
species while still in college and named the next one for the woman who
would later become his wife. In all, he would describe ninety-two North
American species new to science and, though often in poor health, he regularly traveled throughout North and South America collecting specimens.

Williamson went to work in his father's bank in Bluffton, Indiana, in
1902, and he was serving as its president when it joined the long list of
failed banks following the stock market crash of 1929. Nonetheless, his
influence in the world of odonates was great. He was the first to correctly
describe how dragonflies mate, wrote extensively about their wing veins,
and studied the order's complex taxonomy. As Nick Donelly wrote in a
brief biography of Williamson in *Argia,* the newsletter of the Dragonfly
Society of the Americas, he

> was the master of the keen and thoughtful field observation, noting that
> in a single place, for example, there may be an abundant population of
> some species in one year, but that the same species might not be seen again
> for several years—if at all. He warned that the proper surveying of an
> Odonata fauna could not be realized unless one was careful to note that
> many species wandered widely from their place of emergence. "To say, for
> example, of some species of *Somatochlora* that it frequents woodland streams
> may tell about as much about it as the student would learn of the activi-
> ties of Charles Darwin, say, if his biographer told where Mr. Darwin spent
> his youth and gave the street address and house number of his later years.
> For the chances are that our *Somatochlora* from the date of its emergence
> till its final activity (mating) may never visit the woodland stream."

These observations clearly came into play during my search for ringed
boghaunters in Massachusetts. While they're clearly an aquatic insect, my
time with Jennifer Loose of the Massachusetts Natural Heritage Program
was spent mostly strolling through woodlands.

Loose grew up in Connecticut and in the Adirondack region of New
York, and credits her godmother, a botanist, with getting her interested

in a career in the outdoors. She earned an undergraduate degree in anthropology and biology at the University of Connecticut, working in the entomology lab and spending a semester in Costa Rica, where a visit to an insect collection piqued her interest in bugs. A master's degree in entomology at the University of Maine was followed by a job mapping habitat and developing conservation plans for dragonflies in Massachusetts. A week after my visit, she was headed out on a trekking vacation to Bhutan with her parents and brother, their second adventurous trip to the region.

I met Loose at her office in Northborough, where she enthusiastically told me about the state's endangered species law and the implications it has for protecting dragonflies. One of just four states to have enacted tough legislation protecting rare wildlife, Massachusetts' law works in conjunction with the state's wetlands protection act to protect not only the wetlands where dragonflies breed, but also the upland area for up to 250 meters around the wetland. According to Loose, no other state designates the upland area adjacent to a wetland as critical habitat for aquatic species.

"Ideal protection for dragonflies in Massachusetts is defined as the wetland itself, plus a 100-meter 'no-touch' area around the wetland, and then 150 meters around that where small-scale development is allowed as long as 50 to 70 percent of the original forest canopy is preserved," she explained. "So development is okay, but the development must protect the hydrology and the functionality of the site."

This strict legislation means that Loose, the state's only aquatic invertebrate biologist, has a lot of work to do, both in the field and in the office. With the help of a team of volunteers, she keeps a close eye on sites where populations of endangered species are known to live and searches for new sites. She also does a great deal of mapping work, and even found time to co-author a field guide to dragonflies in the state. Pulling out a massive two-volume *Natural Heritage Atlas,* she showed me page after page of detailed maps of wetlands where rare species have been found, each with the 100-meter no-touch zone and the 150-meter protected upland area delineated around it. Developers have to jump through plenty of hoops to justify encroaching on property delineated as critical to protecting the feeding and breeding areas of rare species.

Massachusetts has twenty-two sites where the ringed boghaunter has been found, all east of the Connecticut River, and four sites where the species was known to live historically but from which it is now considered extirpated. About one-quarter of the current sites were discovered in the last fifteen years, and the sites range from grassy fens and classic kettlehole bogs to Atlantic white cedar swamps and vernal pools. As in Rhode Island, all have sphagnum moss and emergent sedges or related vegetation. But most of the Massachusetts sites are much larger than those in Rhode Island, which makes Loose's monitoring strategies very different from those Brown employs in Rhode Island.

"I don't spend a lot of time counting exuvia like Ginger does, partly because the sites are so large and it's hard to do a good job," Loose explained. "I once spent hours at one site and found only one exuvia even though it was a site that we knew had boghaunters. And with thirty-one dragonfly species on the state [endangered] list, exuvia counting isn't an effective use of my time. It's really hard to count individuals here, so we don't know exactly which sites hold the largest populations. Instead we look at the risk to populations by landscape context rather than by population counts."

While monitoring strategies may differ, risks to the populations are very similar. In Massachusetts, most of the sites where boghaunters reside are inside the belt of Route 495 surrounding Boston, the most densely populated and developed place in all of New England. Boghaunters at all of those sites are at great risk of extirpation, primarily due to water-quality impacts and the drying up of the habitat from drinking-water wells. Loose said that many other odonates in the state are facing similarly dire circumstances, especially the pine barrens bluet and scarlet bluet. She's pessimistic about the survival of boghaunters in the sites closest to Boston, because it's almost certain that the wetlands will become further degraded.

Most of the state's healthy boghaunter sites are in areas that have been protected from development for quite some time. Unfortunately, they're also very far apart, so there's a good chance that populations could become genetically isolated if individual boghaunters aren't able to find and breed with other populations. That's why part of Loose's fieldwork is spent searching for potential boghaunter populations in between these healthy sites.

When I visited, she took me out to a site she had never been to before. The earliest records for ringed boghaunters in Massachusetts came from wetlands in the Upton State Forest, a 2,600-acre forest in the town of Upton not far from the Massachusetts Turnpike. Boghaunters were collected there in 1912 and 1916 and not again until 1988, although she believes there had been a continuous population during the interim. In 1991, the species was sought and not found at the site, but in 1994 one adult was sighted. Until my visit, no one had looked for it since.

After a couple of wrong turns, we found the first of two target wetlands across the street from a relatively new housing development. Professionally manicured lawns and an SUV in almost every driveway foreshadowed a dismal future for the health of the wetland, but we were hopeful that we would find a sign that boghaunters still lived there. The extensive wetland was mostly forested and separated from the road by 20 or 30 yards of shrubby growth, but we eventually found an open portion with sphagnum and sedges worth investigating. Wearing hip boots and carrying long-handled insect nets, we pushed our way through the undergrowth, past maples and birches, and slogged through the thick mats of sphagnum. Leatherleaf and sheep laurel ringed the wetland, and large juicy cranberries lay hidden among pitcher plants and sedges as Baltimore orioles, red-winged blackbirds, and song sparrows sang loudly. Loose called this a classic site, although there was much less standing water here than at the Rhode Island sites that I had visited. Trails through the sphagnum made by deer and muskrats left depressions of standing water where Loose said exuvia were likely to be found. We took slow, deliberate steps through the wetland, being careful to disturb the vegetation and aquatic life as little as possible. We often had to crouch low, nearly dipping our backsides in the water, to check each emergent stem thoroughly for exuvia. But it was quickly apparent that the few open-water areas had extensive algal growth, likely caused by roadway run-off and lawn fertilizers, and we saw no dragonflies of any sort even though activity had been reported further north.

"It's not looking too promising," Loose said after we drove up and down the road again searching for another appropriate location to survey. "Based on the water quality and the algal growth on the sphagnum, I would downgrade this site. It definitely looks like there has been some run-off pollution. Conditions were good to see *lintneri,* but this site is a 'no find.' I won't take it off the list entirely, but I'll certainly recommend downgrading the site."

A few miles further down the road was another wetland where boghaunters had also been found in 1994. But instead of pulling on our hip boots again, Loose directed us to walk down the nearby Swamp Trail, a meandering woodland path that hugs the wetland edge. She said this sun-dappled trail is the perfect place to find adult boghaunters flying around or perched on boulders, tree trunks, and leaf litter. Ten minutes of slow walking turned up nothing but nice conversation and a pretty view, until I nearly tripped so as not to step on what looked like a ringed boghaunter camouflaged perfectly among the scattered oak and maple leaves on the edge of the path. Loose quickly identified it as a female Hudsonian whiteface, a similar-looking dragonfly but with a white face and more extensive pale yellow markings on its thorax and abdomen. Loose noted that boghaunters fly in a much more lazy fashion than the whiteface. She slapped down her net over the specimen and held it by its folded wings to point out the differences, then opened her hand to watch it fly away unharmed.

Dragonflies are remarkably sturdy insects. Unlike butterflies, which when caught in nets and handled are often irreparably harmed, dragonflies can be caught and handled again and again and still behave normally after being released. Holding a dragonfly in the hand is a breathtaking experience. With their folded wings held together over their back, they're virtually immobilized, allowing for close-up examination of their massive eyes, unusual anatomy, and beautiful colorations. If you let them, they'll grasp your hand with their rough legs and hold on tight, and sometimes even try to bite you, although all but the largest species have jaws so tiny that they are unable to break through our tough skin.

The hard part is catching them. It's not unexpected, even for expert dragonfly catchers, to swing and miss a dozen times before catching a target specimen. Their remarkable eyesight and flight skills enable them to taunt would-be collectors by dancing within reach, only to side-step being captured with a quick flick of the wings.

As Loose and I continued walking the Swamp Trail, we saw several more Hudsonian whitefaces, including a mating pair clamped together like a wheel, with the appendages at the end of the male's abdomen grasping the female behind the head and the female's abdomen curled forward to bring her sexual organs in contact with those of the male. After turning around and retracing our steps, I pointed out another whiteface, which Loose excitedly captured. Another mistaken identification on my part became the first record of ringed boghaunter at the site in eleven years! Removing the squirming individual from the net, Loose opened her mouth wide and breathed warm carbon dioxide on the boghaunter to calm it down. It was the first adult boghaunter I had seen close up, so Loose pointed out its key characteristics: its blue-gray face, chocolate-brown body, and pale orange rings around its abdomen. She said she could tell it was a female because its abdomen was fatter than the male's, but without a comparison specimen it was hard for me to see that its abdomen was fat. So she handed me the boghaunter and I nervously held it as she swung her net at several of the passing whitefaces, hoping to catch a male to show me the difference. After swinging and missing a dozen times, and seeing my expressions of concern for the specimen still in my hands, we let it go. But it didn't appear to want to go anywhere. It sat on my hand for a full minute—increasing my concern that I had injured it—until Loose gave it a nudge and it took off unharmed, eventually landing in the leaf litter and disappearing into the background.

Returning to the trail head, we briefly walked into the wetland—which Loose called a wetland in transition, as maple trees were encroaching in abundance—but it was too deep for our hip boots and much too large to make an exuvia search worthwhile. So we stood around in the thigh-deep water, listening to singing blackbirds, catbirds, and warbling vireos, and called it a day. A day that, at least at this one site, just might raise the level of optimism for the future of the ringed boghaunter.

3

Bicknell's Thrush

Just as I arrived at the lodge at the base of Mount Mansfield near Stowe, Vermont, a violent thunderstorm swept through the area, tossing tree limbs around like beach balls and causing scattered power outages for miles. At the top of the mountain, a team of six biologists and assistants ran for cover to the ski patrol hut and huddled in fear as several bolts of lightning struck dangerously close. After an hour of drenching rain and powerful winds, the storm drifted off eastward, allowing me to start the drive up the winding, dirt toll road to the summit.

Mount Mansfield is the highest peak in Vermont, at 4,393 feet, and the most frequently visited mountain in the state. From the east, its ridgeline is said to resemble the profile of a human face, so prominent features on the mountain have come to be known as the Adam's apple, chin, nose (the highest point), and forehead, although to me it's quite a stretch to make the connection. It's a popular site for hikers in summer as an extensive trail system criss-crosses the mountain, and it's even more popular in winter as the site of one of the New England's most famous ski resorts.

The drive up the 4.5-mile toll road traverses a thick deciduous forest of maples, ash, some of the largest birch trees I have ever seen, and a thick understory. Climbing higher, the road repeatedly crosses overgrown ski trails and the chairlift corridor that would have been crowded on a snowy winter day. In June, it was pleasantly peaceful with only a single, singing red-eyed vireo and a soft breeze breaking the silence. Passing the Mountain Chapel, a stone structure halfway up the road, frequent signs directed skiers to trails of varying difficulty levels, and occasional breaks in the foliage revealed spectacular views of the northern Green Mountains and distant villages in the valleys. Nearing the top, balsam fir becomes the dominant tree, with numerous dead and dying specimens on exposed ridges protecting adjacent newer growth.

When I reached the end of the toll road, the visitor center was closed, the parking lot was empty, and a thick fog reduced visibility to less than 100 yards. Just then, three cars pulled in behind me and out piled the team of bird researchers still talking about the thunderstorm that had chased them below the tree line. The leader of the group, Kent McFarland, reminded me of Curt Schilling, the Red Sox pitcher who two years earlier led the team to its first World Series in eighty-six years, but his attitude reminded me of a laid-back ornithology professor I knew. Moments after we met, he took a call on his cell phone and told the caller, "this is quintessential Bicknell's thrush weather. It's a misty mountaintop. It's perfect."

Bicknell's thrush (*Catharus bicknelli*) is a highly secretive bird, closely related to the American robin but smaller and slimmer, with an olive-brown back, contrasting chestnut tail, whitish underparts, and a spotted throat and chest. Breeding exclusively in the high elevations in the Northeast, from the Catskills to Cape Breton and the Gaspé Peninsula, it prefers dense, stunted balsam fir forests above 2,800 feet, characterized by a cool, wet, and windy climate, where it can find an abundance of caterpillars to feed upon. It was one of only two bird species that breed in New England that I had never seen before.

Since, as McFarland said, "you hardly ever see the darn thing," its most distinctive characteristic is its melodious song. "I always think about the evening time when they're starting to call," he said. "And then they start singing, and that's when you get that metallic, multi-sounding, flute-type song. And then they spin off a flight song and go flying off around the mountainside. You don't even need to say it's a neat brown bird; that song is enough to conjure up all kinds of interesting thoughts, especially in this forest type because it's sort of ethereal." The song has been described by some biologists as "chook-chook, wee-o, wee-o, wee-o-ti-ter-ee," although there is considerable variation in the song. The bird also has been known to mute its song, making it sound considerably farther away than it really is.

On top of Mount Mansfield, McFarland and his team of research assistants, graduate students, and volunteers had been setting up a series of mist nets along several hiking trails when the storm swept through, so they returned to finish the job before the birds became active again at dusk. The group split in half, and I headed off with McFarland, Juan Klavins, a biologist from Argentina who joined the Bicknell's thrush project several years before and moved to Vermont full time after falling in love with a fellow researcher, and Brendan Collins, a middle-school teacher who was spending his sixth summer vacation volunteering on the project. The narrow trails traverse varied terrain, most of it slick and challenging walking, but the researchers moved at a quick and determined pace, debating where to set the next net as they trekked. As Klavins trimmed vegetation that might become entangled in the nets, the rest of us strung 6- and 12-meter nets along the paths, supported them with 10-foot poles borrowed from the ski patrol hut, and tied the poles to adjacent trees with old pieces of string. Once a net was set, it was difficult to maneuver past it because the wind was blowing and the trails are so narrow that the fine mesh easily became entangled on our eyeglasses, buttons, binoculars, and watches. The aim of the nets was to ensnare Bicknell's thrushes as the birds crossed from the vegetation on one side of the trail to the other.

The site is part of Mount Mansfield State Park, although some is owned by the University of Vermont, and the trails—Amherst Trail, Cliff Trail, Long Trail, and Lake View Trail—are maintained by the Green Mountain Club. The habitat there is mostly stunted balsam fir, much of it no taller than the researchers, with small numbers of red spruce, mountain ash, mountain holly, and paper birch scattered amongst them. The vegetation is impenetrable, so even if we wanted to walk off the trail, it would be impossible to do so. It's also impossible to see more than a few feet into the trees, so while we could hear some birds singing—mostly white-throated sparrows, winter wrens, and blackpoll warblers—it was challenging to actually see any of them. Yet with the trees so short and located on a mountainside, the view above and to the mountains beyond would have been gorgeous if only the weather had cooperated.

It took us an hour to set up the rest of the nets. Just as the wind picked up and the fog rolled in thicker, I heard my first Bicknell's thrush song. It sounded to me very much like a veery, a common thrush found at lower elevations across the northern tier of the United States, whose flute-like song spirals downward. The Bicknell's song, however, had an extra note or two at the beginning and end. The bird wasn't far away, but as I listened to its beautiful voice, it wasn't anywhere to be seen.

At 7:30 P.M., the team scattered to check the nets for the first time to see what was caught. When we all reconvened fifteen minutes later, most of us were empty-handed. Just one white-throated sparrow and one yellow-rumped warbler had been caught, both very common birds. On the next "net run" at 8:30, three yellow-rumps and two blackpolls were collected. Although they weren't the target species, we took an extensive variety of measurements anyway—beak, foot and wing length, weight, fat composition, age, feather wear, and an assessment of the quantity of ectoparasites found on them. The birds were then banded with two colored rings on one leg and one colored ring and an aluminum ring on the other. The banding station was the back of McFarland's SUV parked in the empty lot. It had an unusual trailer hitch with a raised flat platform about a foot in diameter that was used as a table. Whoever collected the bird was responsible for processing it, quickly calling out the measurements and codes to a designated data recorder. I was impressed by the speed at which they assessed the birds. A quick blow on the belly of a female revealed a brood patch—a large area free of feathers that helps the bird keep its eggs warm—and a similar breath of air on the genitals was used to assess the cloacal protuberance, which determines the bird's sex, age, and reproductive condition.

As McFarland and I left to check the nets again, a snowshoe hare with a stem of grass in its mouth hopped along the trail toward us, unconcerned with our sudden appearance. Just before we were within arm's reach, it casually hopped into the bushes. It was nearing dusk and the fog had rolled in thicker by then, yet blackpolls, white-throated sparrows, and winter wrens were still singing regularly. Occasionally, we heard the call note of a Bicknell's thrush, but I still hadn't seen one and I was beginning to feel frustrated at my inability to see a creature that appeared to be so close. McFarland said that they typically perch on the top of a dead fir tree, but the thickness of the vegetation and the foggy conditions made it impossible to see them. As the wind died down and the darkness set in, the soupy fog gave us an eerie feeling, something the research assistants kept calling a "Blair Witch night."

Walking down the Cliff Trail to the lone net sited there, we heard two Bicknell's thrushes singing very close to the net, then uttering their call note, and finally making a growling sound that I hadn't heard before but that McFarland described as meaning "they're really pissed off." He excitedly played a recording of a Bicknell's song that he had made in that exact place earlier that morning, hoping to get the birds to defend their territory and lure them into the net. He set the recorder on the opposite side of the net from where the birds were singing, and we crouched just out of sight, but the birds ignored the recording and continued calling from their original location. So McFarland tried another strategy: He pulled out his microphone to record their notes for immediate playback, but just as he got his equipment ready to record, the birds went quiet.

Although McFarland said that the last net run before darkness envelops the mountain is usually the best time for catching Bicknell's thrushes—the birds are crepuscular, so they're most active at last light—we returned to the parking lot empty-handed once again, as did everyone else. The look on McFarland's face reflected the frustration in his voice. "Looks like we just wasted five hours of work," he said as we packed up our gear and left.

Bicknell's thrush took a long and circuitous route to becoming recognized as a species unto itself. It was in 1881 that amateur ornithologist Eugene Bicknell heard an unfamiliar bird song in the Catskill Mountains of New York. As was typical of naturalists in those days, he shot the bird to examine it more closely and decided it must be a gray-cheeked thrush, an uncommon but widely distributed species. He later sent the specimen to the American Museum of Natural History, where the museum's curator of birds, Robert Ridgway, determined that it was a subspecies of gray-cheeked thrush and named it *Catharus bicknelli,* Bicknell's thrush. Although it was a remarkable discovery so close to New York City where many well-known ornithologists lived, the bird was ignored for fifty years until another budding ornithologist, George Wallace, chose it for his research subject in the 1930s. Comparing specimens of the gray-cheeked thrush with the bird collected by Bicknell, Wallace noted that the Bicknell's thrush was considerably smaller and had a brighter yellow color at the base of its lower mandible. Nonetheless, he agreed with Ridgway and categorized it as a subspecies of gray-cheeked.

It was another sixty years before the taxonomic status of the bird was revisited once again, this time by Henri Ouellet of the Canadian Museum of Nature, who published his findings in 1993. He claimed that the breeding and wintering ranges of gray-cheeked and Bicknell's thrushes did not overlap, that the songs of the two birds were considerably different, and that Bicknell's did not respond to the song of the gray-cheeked. He also demonstrated that the two birds differed slightly in the color of their upperparts, tail feathers, and throat. Another researcher, Gilles Seutin of Parks Canada, examined the mitochondrial DNA of the two birds and found significant differences, concluding that they probably separated from a common ancestor about a million years ago. This information was enough to convince the Committee on Classification and Nomenclature of the American Ornithologists' Union, the group that has the last word on taxonomic decisions for birds, to elevate Bicknell's thrush from subspecies to full species status in 1995.

The story of the bird's taxonomy doesn't necessarily end there, though. The committee makes updates to the official bird list regularly, and they have been known to change their minds when new information is presented. The most recent change to the list occurred in 2006, when two populations of the blue grouse, a species found primarily in the mountains of the western United States and Canada, were split into separate species called the dusky grouse and the sooty grouse. There also have been numerous occasions when birds that have been split off from other species later have been lumped back together again, or vice versa. The Baltimore and Bullock's orioles, for instance, are eastern and western counterparts that were lumped together into one species, the northern oriole, back in the 1970s and then split again twenty years later. So there is no assurance that the Bicknell's thrush won't be lumped back with the gray-cheeked thrush sometime in the future. In fact, some biologists and taxonomists recommend that such a change should happen soon. Others, though, have a very different opinion on the subject.

After Gilles Seutin used DNA evidence to convince the ornithological authorities that Bicknell's thrush and gray-cheeked thrush were separate species, he and Canadian colleague Yves Aubry did the analysis again using a new set of DNA samples. Once again, they found that there was a significant distinction between the species. Another team of biologists then compared Bicknell's and gray-cheeked thrushes with the other three related thrushes found in the Northeast—veery, hermit thrush, and Swainson's thrush. "They found that the species broke down into two groups," explained Aubry. "Gray-cheeked, Bicknell's, and veery were in one group, and hermit and Swainson's were in a separate group. The distinction between gray-cheeked, Bicknell's, and veery was the same. Veery is as closely related to Bicknell's as Bicknell's is to gray-cheeked. They create a triangle."

That evidence pleased McFarland considerably, since he is somewhat bothered by those who think that Bicknell's shouldn't have been separated from gray-cheeked in the first place. "The bottom line is that if you're going to lump Bicknell's with gray-cheeked, then you've got to lump them with veery," he said, almost certain that no one would suggest combining the three species into one, especially since the habitat preferences and plumage characteristics of veeries are so different from the other two birds. "I'm not a geneticist and I'm not a taxonomist, but it raises my hackles that some people don't think Bicknell's is a 'good' species."

Regardless of its taxonomic status, Bicknell's thrush is facing a number of challenges that threaten its long-term future. Due in part to its new status as a full species and the relatively little research that has been conducted on it, the bird is not included on the federal endangered species list. However, it is listed by the U.S. Fish and Wildlife Service, Birdlife International, the Committee on the Status of Endangered Wildlife in Canada, the World Conservation Union, and Partners in Flight as a species of high conservation concern, but this designation doesn't provide it with any legal protections. As is true of so many other species, chief among the threats facing Bicknell's thrush is climate change. As the planet warms, habitat tends to move northward or higher in elevation, but since Bicknell's already nests at the treeline on the top of mountains, its habitat cannot migrate upward any further. According to McFarland, the bird's population always has been relatively small because it is a habitat specialist, preferring a very narrow type of habitat that has never been in large supply. McFarland has created a computer model that tracks Bicknell's thrush habitat as average temperature increases, and the results are alarming. "It doesn't take much—just 2 degrees Celsius—to remove 50 percent of the Bicknell's habitat," he said. "The 50 percent that is lost is the low end of the habitat where Bicknell's aren't so dense, but [with an increase of] 6 degrees, there's none left anywhere in the United States. It goes really fast. Just 1.5 degrees and it's gone from the Catskills. . . . If climate-change scenarios are right, this bird won't be around in a hundred years."

While climate change may be the most significant threat to the species in the long term, its short-term prospects look somewhat bleak as well due to a series of smaller threats that, when combined, significantly jeopardize the bird's health. Acid rain, a subject that has seen little public attention in recent years, is one issue that likely won't threaten the species on its own but may be an important contributing factor to its demise. When highly acidic rain falls—mostly as a result of pollution from power plants—it leaches the calcium out of the rocks and soil, reducing the quantity of calcium available to birds. "Birds have to get calcium from somewhere for the formation of their eggs," noted McFarland, "and we know they can't store it. There was a study done at Cornell that shows a high correlation between acid rain and populations of wood thrushes that are in trouble." Acid rain may also be a factor in the decline and degradation of balsam fir and red spruce forests.

Added to this are threats from loss of habitat on the Bicknell's wintering grounds in the Caribbean (just 8 percent of its original winter habitat remains and half of that is in jeopardy), ski resort development on its breeding grounds, blood parasites that compromise its immune system, and one quite surprising threat: mercury.

The presence of mercury in lakes and streams has been well documented for two decades, which is why numerous health organizations advise the public to restrict their intake of freshwater fish in many places in the Northeast. The mercury comes primarily from the emissions of coal-burning power plants in the Midwest, which drifts eastward and settles on water bodies, where it is converted to toxic methyl mercury by anaerobic bacteria. The mercury enters the food chain through tiny creatures on the lake bottom, and its concentration becomes magnified as larger organisms feed on smaller ones. Common loons, which feed entirely on freshwater fish during the breeding season, have been found to have highly elevated levels of mercury in their bloodstream, reducing their reproductive rates and making them lethargic. But no one expected mercury to be found in songbirds, especially not those living at the tops of mountains.

McFarland and colleagues from the Vermont Institute of Natural Science and the Biodiversity Research Institute decided to test for it anyway. Biologist David Evers found unusually high levels of mercury in the blood and feathers of all 178 woodland birds he tested in New York State in 2005. He believes that the mercury is absorbed by soil and fallen leaves, which are fed upon by worms and insects and which are in turn consumed by songbirds. Of all the species that Evers tested, wood thrushes had the most mercury in their blood: 0.1 parts per million, which is below the federal standard for fish for human consumption but still probably high enough to affect the birds' ability to reproduce. It may be one reason why wood thrush numbers have dropped by nearly 50 percent in the last forty years. It is unknown what its effect is on the Bicknell's thrush.

"It's not like the high levels found in loons feeding on fish," McFarland explained. "It's chronic low-level mercury . . . We don't even know what would be considered high levels for a songbird. At this chronic level, we don't know if [it's causing] some insidious behavioral effects, or if it's just another thing to knock their viability down just slightly. One thing we do know is that they actually obtain three times as much mercury [on their wintering grounds] in the Caribbean. Here, they're getting it from power plants mostly. In the Caribbean, we don't know. It could be cement factories, or maybe it's from a nickel smelter in the Dominican Republic."

What McFarland does know is that there are a great many human activities negatively impacting the Bicknell's thrush, and that there's little he can do to protect them. "It's not just one thing, it's a lot of these insidious things that could turn out to be really hideous for them," he said. "And the problem is that it's a lot of things we can't do anything about. Coal-fired power plants, for example. If mercury turns out to be a big problem, I don't know if we can do anything about it. Climate change? What the devil are we going to do about that? There are some big issues behind this bird that are not solvable."

After completing our unsuccessful night of trapping Bicknell's thrushes on top of Mount Mansfield, the team of biologists and volunteers retired to the ski patrol hut in complete darkness. The smell of sweaty, moldy clothes permeated the tiny space, but I had no right to complain since I was only staying there for one night; the researchers spent two months in those conditions. The makeshift kitchen table was actually a workbench scattered with odd tools, ski parts, and a stack of rescue sleds, but we ignored them as we had a quick sandwich, listened to the end of a Red Sox game, and shared stories of misidentified birds and mispronounced species names.

After just four hours of sleep, we awoke at 3:30 to partly clear skies with a crescent moon darting in and out of the clouds. Little was said as everyone prepared for another long day in the field, and then we headed silently to the mountaintop. It was breezy and chilly in the visitor center parking lot, where white-throated sparrows and winter wrens sang loudly. The researchers who arrived ahead of me went to open the nets and reported hearing several Bicknell's thrushes singing, so my expectations for the morning grew. By 4:30, the clouds had moved in again, although a nice sunrise was visible in one corner of the sky. On our first run to check the nets, only one wren and one sparrow were collected, and worse, no Bicknell's were even heard singing.

My partner on my first net run was Rose Graves, a recent college graduate from Barnet, Vermont, who had spent the previous summer monitoring loons for New Hampshire Audubon Society and later conducted a survey of animal tracks crossing a section of Route 2 in the northern part of the state to determine the need for culverts and other animal passageways. She said the hardest part of the Bicknell's thrush project for her was the split shifts—working seven hours early in the morning, then a five hour break, and then working six more hours until late at night. She yearned to catch up on her sleep. Although Graves was the only woman living and working with five men on the research team, she said it wasn't a problem for her. "It might have been different if I were a girly girl," she said with a smile, "but I'm not."

At 5:30, I joined McFarland for the next net run, where we collected two entangled blackpoll warblers and one Bicknell's thrush feather, apparently from a bird that bounced off the net and escaped. Returning to the banding station, we found the group working on the first Bicknell's thrush of the season. While a bird in the hand doesn't count as my first wild sighting of the bird, it was still exciting to get my first glance at a live Bicknell's. Up close, the contrast between the olive-brown back and rusty tail is more obvious than is indicated in the field guides I had brought with me, and the spotting on the breast is less distinct. The bird was also considerably smaller than I expected, appearing closer in size to a large sparrow than to a small thrush. McFarland said it was a rather typical second-year bird, and it had never been captured before, as evidenced by the lack of any bands around its legs. That, however, was rectified rather quickly as the bird was processed. In addition to the usual measurements done for all the other birds captured, the researchers also pricked a vein on the underside of the wing of each Bicknell's thrush to collect a blood sample for mercury and DNA analysis.

By 6:15, the researchers were constantly coming and going, checking the nets and processing an increasing number of birds. One returned with a male black-throated blue warbler and a Swainson's thrush—another Bicknell's look-alike—while another retrieved two blackpolls. McFarland said that the black-throated blue looked "a little droopy" after it was banded, so the biologist fed it a tiny amount of orange juice in the crease of his palm and held the bird against his exposed stomach to warm him before release.

At 6:30, McFarland ran from the trails to the parking lot to process a female Bicknell's thrush he found in a net on the Lake View Trail. A quick puff of breath on the belly revealed a huge brood patch, so McFarland was certain that the bird was sitting on eggs; he wanted to get her back to her nest before the eggs could get cold. The bird had no fat reserves whatsoever and weighed 33.5 grams, the largest Bicknell's McFarland had seen in a long time, suggesting that she may still have had additional eggs to lay. While McFarland quickly took measurements, two helpers plucked feathers for analysis and called out measurements so quickly that I lost track of what was being measured. After struggling for a minute to collect a blood sample, they gave up and rushed back to the area where she was captured to release the bird. But in a surprise move, McFarland handed the bird to me.

Taking her in my right hand with her back in my palm and her head between my index and middle fingers, I could feel how warm the bird was and even feel her heart racing—just like mine. I stared at her large, dark eye momentarily and saw my own reflection, then, as much as I wanted to hold the bird longer, I set her feet on my open left hand to release her. But she didn't move. So I stroked her back to straighten her ruffled feathers, and still she just stood there. A very long five seconds later, McFarland blew gently on her and she took off in a straight line down the path, flying low and fast to avoid the net, until she was no longer visible. McFarland and I immediately followed her to make sure she didn't get caught in the nets further down the path, which she didn't, and then I finally let out the breath I seemingly had been holding from the time the bird was first placed in my hand. It was a special moment.

The activity at the banding station continued unabated, but I decided to walk off by myself for a few minutes to focus on the singing birds, the majestic mountains, and the unique habitat in that unusual place. I headed a short distance down Long Trail, enjoying the singing sparrows, black-polls, and wrens, and occasionally hearing a distant Bicknell's thrush call. But in the thick fog and dense vegetation, I couldn't see any of these birds. Finally, I spotted a sparrow on top of the tallest balsam fir and took it as a sign that it was time to return to the banding station. On the dirt road leading to the parking lot, I stood quietly for a long moment, feeling an emotional sense of awe about the place and the experience I was having. A slight movement in the trees just ten feet from where I stood caught my attention, and then all of a sudden came a loud series of Bicknell's thrush call notes seemingly yelling at me. I moved just an inch or two, craning my neck in vain to see the bird. Unexpectedly, it flew across the road at chest height just a few steps in front of me and continued deep into the woods in a location so dense with vegetation that I would have swore that it would have been impossible for the bird to even spread its wings. And then it began singing its incredible warbling song. Standing there all alone with that beautiful bird singing nearby was just as powerful an experience as holding the nesting female in my hand minutes before, feeling its heart beating, and watching it fly away. Again I let out a deep breath and continued to the banding station.

Two more Bicknell's thrushes were captured at 9:15, which was when the sun came out, the black flies emerged, and numerous other birds—robins, purple finches, chipping sparrows, juncos, and yellow-rumped warblers—became active around the parking lot. At 10:00, the toll road opened to the public and a crowd of tourists arrived soon after, taking pictures, exploring the area, and trying to catch a glimpse of the nearby mountains through the clouds. The last Bicknell's we captured was another large one, and it already had a band on its leg from when it was first caught in 2000, making it just two years shy of the oldest Bicknell's thrush on record. While the bird's wings were the longest of those caught that day, McFarland was especially impressed with its unusually large cloacal protuberance. "This is not a Christian bird we've got here," he said with a grin.

He's right. Male Bicknell's thrushes outnumber females by a ratio of two to one, and recent evidence has shown that both males and females mate with a variety of partners. In fact, the eggs in every nest tested are of mixed paternity, so several males are usually found feeding young at each nest. While polygamy is not unusual among songbirds, seldom does more than one male bring food to a nest.

"We knew something weird was going on, so we started using radio tags to look at how birds were moving through the ski area here," Mc-Farland explained.

And we found that the males were moving all over the place, crossing over the top of each other's territories, so it didn't take too long to figure out that something crazy was going on. Jim Goetz (a graduate student) put a blind up at a nest and he noticed that all different individuals were coming to the nest. It turns out that the males have many females and the females have many males. It looks like the females have small territories— 3 to 4 hectares—that they guard against other females, but the males have territories that are twice the size and they overlap a lot. So you can have seven or eight males overlap on the same piece of real estate.

We think the males try to mate-guard the females as well as they can, but the habitat is so thick and so nasty that the female loses them all the time. I've been tracking two or three males at the same time, and then the female moves but the male doesn't notice. And then all of a sudden he starts singing like mad because he loses her and he freaks out because he knows another male is going to get her . . . It looks like a female has the ability to assess how much prey is available in her territory each year, and based on that, she determines how many males she's going to copulate with, because that's how many helpers she needs to bring enough food in . . . There's a direct correlation between how much prey she has on her territory and how many males she has.

When Bicknell's thrushes complete their breeding cycle and have raised their young to a healthy age, they migrate south over the course of several weeks to a number of islands in the Caribbean. Most of the population winters in the Dominican Republic, but smaller numbers are found in the mountains of eastern Cuba, the national parks on the southern peninsula of Haiti, in the Blue Mountains of Jamaica, and, rarely, in Puerto Rico. Unlike on their breeding grounds, where 90 percent of the habitat consists of balsam fir trees, wintering birds will be found in almost any moist, broadleaf forest from sea level to 9,000 feet. "The structure of the wintering habitat is very similar to the breeding habitat," Mc-Farland said. "It's thick, impossible to walk through, really wet, and it often has clouds and mist coming over it. It has a lot of similarities even though one is subtropical and one is semi-boreal."

That's not to say that even on their breeding grounds the birds all use the exact same habitat. The further north they go, the mountains get lower and lower, so birds that nest in Canada find themselves breeding much closer to sea level than those in the United States. And while they still prefer dense stands of balsam fir, forestry practices in Canada make it more of a challenge for the birds to find appropriate habitat.

"In Quebec, forestry is the primary threat to Bicknell's thrush," said Yves Aubry, a biologist with the Canadian Wildlife Service. "Because of paranoia about the potential for a spruce budworm infestation, foresters reduce the density of balsam fir through pre-commercial thinning. After they log the balsam fir stands, the trees regenerate themselves, and when they are about 2 meters tall—about twelve to twenty years after harvesting—right when they become good habitat for Bicknell's thrush, they remove about 90 percent of the stand and open up the habitat," making it less susceptible to a spruce budworm infestation but also less useful to Bicknell's thrushes.

Aubry said that the other major threat facing Bicknell's thrushes in Canada—and one that is just beginning to become an issue in the United States—is wind power development. "The windmill industry in Quebec is expanding in every direction and it is totally chaotic now," Aubry said. "And many of the areas where they are expanding are the same places where Bicknell's nest. Once the habitat is cut for windmills, it will never recover because the area around the windmill is kept clear or it is converted to roads and power line corridors to plug the windmill into the electricity network. That habitat will forever stay clear of trees."

The good news, according to Aubry, is that in Canada the Bicknell's thrush appears to thrive in a small area of balsam fir habitat that may be interspersed with other habitat. "Bicknell's don't need a large plot of habitat," he said. "They will use small patches of good habitat, as long as the habitat is dense and the climate is cool and humid and there are a lot of invertebrates to feed on. As long as there is a patchwork of balsam fir in the landscape, there is a good chance of keeping Bicknell's thrush around."

Vermont's Kent McFarland said he became interested in birds through a series of accidents. Growing up in rural Pennsylvania where hunting and fishing were the most popular activities, he studied environmental science at Allegheny College and went into the Peace Corps in Paraguay to work with small farmers. "I got there and I had this good friend who was way into birding, and so I started looking at birds with her," he said. "Then I got to my little village and there were lots of birds everywhere, so I decided I needed some binoculars. I hopped on a bus to the capital and got this cheap pair of binoculars and a field guide in Spanish, and I totally got addicted to bird watching." When he returned home, he went to graduate school to study the birds of Belize, then met Chris Rimmer of the Vermont Institute of Natural Science, who was looking for some help studying Bicknell's thrush. McFarland has been studying the rare bird ever since.

The institute is a small nonprofit organization based in Woodstock with six conservation biologists on staff, and it survives entirely on grants for such work as a butterfly atlas of Vermont, studies of grassland birds, salamander research, and the Bicknell's thrush project. It also has a staff of educators conducting environmental outreach programs in local schools, and a bird rehabilitation center where permanently injured eagles, hawks, and owls live out their lives while educating visitors.

The fieldwork that McFarland and his Vermont Institute research team were doing on Mount Mansfield—and similar work on Stratton Mountain and East Mountain, both in Vermont—is intended to gain a better understanding of the long-term demographics of the Bicknell's thrush in Vermont and establish whether the species is decreasing in population. "This mark and recapture work is giving us really good information about how long the birds are living and correlating that to weather events. Pretty soon we'll be able to find out which part of the annual season is the nasty part—whether their survivorship is worse in winter, migration, or summer," McFarland said. The research is also seeking to understand the complexities of what he calls "natal dispersal" or where the young birds go when they return north on their first spring migration. Do they all return to the same mountaintops where they were hatched, or might birds hatched on Mount Mansfield end up in the Adirondacks or the White Mountains or Cape Breton? If the birds return to the same mountains, it might indicate that they maintain close-knit populations on their wintering grounds and do not interact with Bicknell's hatched elsewhere. And that might suggest that there are distinct populations of Bicknell's that eventually could diverge genetically from each other (if they last that long).

What little genetic research has been done on the birds so far suggests that there may be two distinct populations of Bicknell's thrush in the United States, with birds hatched in the Catskills and the southern Green Mountains interbreeding with each other but not with those in the northern Green Mountains, White Mountains, and Adirondacks. Canadian nesters were not included in the genetic analysis, but the great distance between the U.S. birds and those that breed in Cape Breton, New Brunswick, and the Gaspé Peninsula might suggest that the Canadian birds may be another distinct population.

All combined, McFarland believes the total population of Bicknell's thrushes is between twenty-five and forty thousand. The computer model he and his colleagues created of Bicknell's thrush habitat suggests that there might be as many as fifty thousand of the birds, but he said "it's a pretty weak number" since not every bit of available habitat gets used. More likely, he said, there are closer to half that many left.

To get a better handle on Bicknell's population numbers across the entire landscape, the Vermont Institute of Natural Science launched Mountain Birdwatch in 2000. From the Catskills to Mount Katahdin in Maine, trained volunteers conduct dawn surveys of Bicknell's thrushes and other mountain birds along more than two hundred remote routes on June mornings. At each of five stations along the 1-kilometer transects, the volunteers watch and listen for five minutes and count the number of individual birds they identify.

"We started the project primarily because the main tool for monitoring bird populations in North America is the Breeding Bird Survey, but it's a road-based count, so there's a big blind spot in monitoring in remote locations," explained Dan Lambert, a Vermont Institute biologist and coordinator of the project. "The idea is to fill in the gap in our understanding of population trends by placing survey routes in the high-elevation forests."

Although just five years of data are not enough to make accurate estimates of Bicknell's thrush population trends, a great deal has been learned from the Mountain Birdwatch data so far. In 2005, for instance, Bicknell's thrushes were found on 66 percent of the survey routes and more individuals were counted than in any year since the surveys began, the first increase following four years of decreasing abundance. The count data also have been used to create the first detailed distribution map of the species. By integrating latitude, elevation, and forest type, the map shows nearly 340,000 acres of red spruce and balsam fir forest in mountainous regions of Vermont, New Hampshire, Maine, and New York. The map was found to be 92 percent accurate at predicting the presence or absence of the thrush at a given site. "We also learned that New Hampshire contains about 40 percent of U.S. Bicknell's thrush habitat, so it's an especially important state in terms of managing the population," Lambert said. "Fortunately, close to 95 percent of that habitat is conserved in the White Mountain National Forest and elsewhere." Yet despite the protected habitat in New Hampshire, Lambert estimates that the Bicknell's thrush population there declined at 7 percent per year between 1993 and 2003, based on data collected in the national forest. Mountain Birdwatch data soon will help to determine whether that trend continues throughout its range.

Data from Mountain Birdwatch, coupled with McFarland's studies, has also uncovered some unexpected results, such as the relationship between red squirrels, balsam fir cones, and Bicknell's thrush nests. "Predation rates on open-cup nesting birds like Bicknell's are elevated in years following a major cone crop," Lambert said. "So there is a big cone crop of balsam firs every other year, and the red squirrel populations track the availability of this cone mast. When red squirrel numbers are elevated, predation rates on Bicknell's thrush nests are also elevated and breeding success is reduced."

Ultimately, the researchers hope to amass enough data from Mountain Birdwatch and other studies of Bicknell's thrush to develop a conservation plan that will maintain the population at a steady and healthy number, despite the limited breeding and wintering habitat available. If their numbers drop precipitously, as many fear is likely, then inclusion on the federal endangered species list will be a necessity to provide the funding to restore them again. By then, however, it may be too late.

"When I'm in my eighties, I think Bicknell's will be a very uncommon bird," McFarland predicted. "I don't think you'll be walking around and hearing them singing like we have in the last few days here, unless serious things change both on the wintering grounds and in the more insidious things on the breeding ground."

After a moment's reflection, he said: "That's pretty dismal, isn't it? I really think that, but it doesn't mean I also don't have hope. It's like Sisyphus rolling the rock up the hill. One day he might just get it up to that pinnacle and be like, 'Yeah!'"

4

Northern Red-Bellied Cooter

At an environmental science museum called the Ecotarium in Worcester, Massachusetts, nestled among dioramas of African animals, exhibits on energy and astronomy, and a children's play area, is a dark corner devoted mostly to turtles. Seemingly out of proportion to the hordes of kids gathered around it excitedly, a giant tortoise looked around blankly in its pen, oblivious to the commotion. A sign on a massive terrarium nearby invited visitors to search for seven species of native turtles amidst a recirculating freshwater pond and upland habitat. Several rare Blanding's turtles and a musk turtle were clearly evident in the water, and a brief glance around turned up an Eastern box turtle hiding under a log. As I searched for the others, I spied the bizarre-looking head of a spiny softshell turtle peeking out from beneath the sand at the bottom of the pond, its shell and appendages entirely covered. I never found the other three species—wood, spotted, and painted turtles—and I'm convinced they weren't actually there.

A smaller tank in the corner looked a bit like it was in transition, more like the one I had at home growing up. It was big by residential aquarium standards, about 4 feet long and 2 feet high, but it didn't have the fancy trappings of more typical museum exhibits: no real or artificial plants, no gravel bottom, and nothing to make the setting appear natural. Instead, it was simply illuminated with a fluorescent lamp, filled with 6 inches of water (continuously filtered of contaminants), and one artificial rock attached to the wall with suction cups provided the tank's inhabitants with a place to rest. Covering nearly a third of the surface of the water were eight large leaves of romaine lettuce. And swirling around and beneath the lettuce were seven young northern red-bellied cooters. Looking similar to the red-eared sliders sold by the millions in pet stores when I was a boy, the cooters tore off pieces of lettuce, floated at the surface, and occasionally dove to the bottom, seemingly less concerned with escaping than any of the turtles I ever tried to raise.

The northern red-bellied cooter (*Pseudemys rubriventris*) is the only terrestrial turtle in New England on the federal endangered species list. Found only in a small number of freshwater ponds and lakes in Plymouth County, Massachusetts, the adult turtles easily can be mistaken by casual observers for the abundant eastern painted turtle—both have a mostly brownish shell and body with a few yellow streaks on the face. But as juveniles, the cooters are quite distinctive: Their shells are mostly bright lime green, and when they are turned over, their plastron glows a beautiful coral red. In addition, their skin is a complex mix of dark green and bright yellow swirls that reminds me of a steep section of a topographical map.

The turtles at the Ecotarium, and at several other environmental museums and science centers around Massachusetts, are part of a "head-start" program designed to protect the young turtles from predators during their first year. They're just the size of a quarter when they hatch in early summer, making them vulnerable to hungry herons, fish, bullfrogs, and raccoons. By providing the turtles with an all-they-can-eat diet and the right conditions through their first winter, the science centers allow the turtles to grow as big as a three- or four-year-old turtle in just nine months. They are then released back into local ponds, much less susceptible to predation and healthy enough to sustain and increase the population. Since 1981 when the head-start program began, the cooter population in Massachusetts has more than tripled.

Mike Hamilton, a young and enthusiastic wildlife keeper at the Ecotarium who looks forward to a career studying snakes, keeps a close eye on the growing cooters and is proud of the success he has had at raising them. "The water is maintained at optimum growth temperatures of about 75 to 80 degrees (Fahrenheit) to speed up their metabolism so they will eat more and more," he said. "The more they eat the faster they grow. We want them to get as big as they can as fast as they can." In the fall, he feeds the group of seven young turtles a full head of lettuce every day, but by the time the turtles are ready to be returned to the wild, they'll be consuming four or five heads of lettuce daily. "Other head-start locations feed them other kinds of greens, too, and even worms and other food, which sounds like a healthier diet, but when the turtles are turned back over to Mass Wildlife in the spring, our turtles are always the biggest and the healthiest."

While they're at the Ecotarium, the turtles are handled just once a week when they are weighed and measured. This batch of cooters came from four different nests and hatched between June 17 and July 13. They arrived at the museum on September 20 weighing between 8 and 9 grams with shell lengths of 24 to 27 millimeters. By the first week of November— just seven weeks later—their shell length had doubled and their weight had quadrupled. One turtle went from 8.3 grams to 43.8 grams, more than a five-fold increase!

Four months later when I visited the museum again, the water level in the tank was up a few extra inches to accommodate the growing turtles, who then weighed between 155 and 322 grams. Their shells no longer had even a hint of lime green, and only the smallest of the turtles had any noticeable pink on its plastron, but the yellow swirls on their heads and necks stood out dramatically on their darkening heads. Lettuce still littered the surface of the tank, which was a bit murkier than during my previous visit, due largely to the increasing amount of waste generated by the growing turtles.

On a Monday afternoon the following June, I met up with Peter Mirick, a biologist with the Massachusetts Division of Fisheries and Wildlife and editor of *Massachusetts Wildlife* magazine, to release the turtles into Pocksha Pond and Great Quitticas Lake in Middleboro, Massachusetts. All the science centers participating in the head-start program had turned in their cooters the previous Friday, and Mirick had checked their health and notched each turtle's shell so they could be identified if they were caught again in the future. He had released about a hundred turtles in Great Quitticas a few hours before I arrived, and now he was ready to release the other fifty in Pocksha. The two ponds are the largest natural bodies of freshwater in the state—Quabbin Reservoir is larger, but it's not natural—so it's a huge area of excellent habitat, but no cooters were found there before the first release of turtles from the program. The ponds looked too large to me for the more common pond turtles, with not enough floating vegetation and places to climb out and sun themselves, but Mirick said there are plenty of hidden coves for resting and nesting, and the few emerging shoots of vegetation visible were just a hint of the abundant aquatic vegetation still to come.

Mirick said that the head-start program was a key reason why the northern red-bellied cooter population in Massachusetts is on the upswing. Back in 1980, the population was down to about 350 mostly geriatric turtles, almost all in one pond, and they were reproducing very slowly. Soon after they were declared endangered, the 200-acre Massasoit National Wildlife Refuge was established to protect them, the first refuge in the nation created exclusively to protect a turtle. Today, there are approximately 700 to 800 breeding age turtles in two dozen ponds, and the overall population is believed to be growing at a significant rate.

"We know this program is working because several head-started turtles have been seen laying eggs," he said. "So we know it's successful at reproduction, and we know the turtles are behaving naturally. The population is definitely on the rebound. They are the crown jewel of biodiversity in Plymouth County."

In the back of Mirick's state-owned pickup truck were several gold plastic bins, two of which held an inch or two of water and dozens of turtles climbing over each other and clamoring to get out. The size and color of the turtles varied tremendously: Some of the largest ones had shells that were nearly black like full-grown adults and with yellowish plastrons, while others had paler shells with red markings, pinkish plastrons, and a lingering hint of green skin. Mirick said that for some unknown reason—maybe due to their diet, constant water temperature, or their extreme growth rate—the plastrons of captive turtles turn yellow. But they return to their natural coral pink once they are returned to the wild.

We carried the two bins to the edge of the release site, and one by one we dropped the cooters into the water by some small boulders. They all sank like a rock for a brief moment before kicking out their legs, extending their neck, and beginning to swim. The first few immediately dashed off into deep water and disappeared, while others lingered near the bottom a couple feet from shore, floated at the surface nearby, or hid amid the rocks directly below the release site. The clear water and sandy soil made it easy to keep an eye on them until they swam about 20 yards from shore. The entire process of releasing the cooters took less than five minutes.

As Mirick drove off, ten tiny turtle heads were visible at the surface of the pond up to 30 yards out, enjoying their first minutes of complete freedom in the biggest body of water they had ever seen. As I sat at the water's edge, one cooter that initially had swum away reversed direction and swam back toward me, only to change its mind again and head back to deep water. Five minutes after the release, four turtles were still clearly visible hiding beside some rocks at the bottom within an arm's reach of the release point, and then the smallest of them surfaced briefly for air before disappearing for good. Fifteen minutes later, eleven turtle heads were still visible at the surface, but they were spreading out farther and farther. Catbirds and song sparrows flew back and forth in the shrubbery at the edge of the pond as I watched the turtles, and several dragonflies and a host of unknown flying insects hovered at the surface of the water. By then, just two turtles were still within reach below the surface, one very large one that hid beneath a rock two feet from shore immediately after being released, and a smaller one that repeatedly surfaced every five minutes to breath and then dove back to the rocks below to hide.

The cooters were clearly shy, and any movement I made seemed to make them swim farther away. The big one nearby looked at one point like it was ready to surface for air, but when I slowly reached for my camera to take its picture, it changed its mind and withdrew back to the rocks below, still clearly visible. Finally, twenty-eight minutes after the release and just moments after a northern water snake swam by, the large cooter finally surfaced to breathe. It was the first time it had ever done so in a wild body of water, and it looked uncertain, not only about my presence, but also in its effort to judge how far up it had to swim to reach the surface. After apparently misjudging the distance and trying to take a breath while still under water, it shook its head as if it had sneezed and then rapidly surfaced. It remained there watching me for about twenty seconds, then quickly turned around and raced into deeper water. As I prepared to leave, having seen what I thought was my last cooter from the head-start program, one of them swam rapidly toward me at the release site, surfaced in the sunlight, and then disappeared again before I could take

its picture. As I got in my car to leave thirty-five minutes after the release, just one turtle was still visible off in the distance, its blackish head
and pale shell reflecting the sunlight as a great blue heron glided toward
the opposite shore.

How northern red-bellied cooters got to Plymouth County is a mystery.
They are a disjunct population of a species whose next closest population
is in southern New Jersey. While originally thought to be a genetically
distinct subspecies, DNA analysis has determined that they are identical
to the race found in New Jersey. While they eventually may evolve into
a distinct subspecies due to their isolation, for now they are simply the
northernmost population of a southern species.

"We'll never know how they got here," said Mirick, who also studies
the state's four populations of the rare black rat snake. "I suspect that Native Americans carried them here. In indigenous cultures, (live) turtles
are a good thing to pack. They're easy to carry and the food doesn't spoil.
They may have been traded among Native American groups. It's also
possible, though, that there was a natural expansion of their range during a warm period in history." A population on Staten Island, New York,
disappeared seventy-five to a hundred years ago.

Cooters are found in coastal plain ponds with sandy, low-nutrient
soils. According to Mirick, there is little protein available in this habitat,
which may be why the cooters became vegetarians, unlike most of the
rest of the turtles in New England that feed on worms, bugs, and other
invertebrates. Instead, cooters feed on aquatic vegetation such as milfoil,
although they occasionally eat crayfish or invertebrates when they are
young. Although similar to the abundant eastern painted turtle, cooters
are much less approachable than their common cousin and prefer to live
in more remote ponds further from human presence. Mature cooters are
also considerably larger than painted turtles—they can grow up to 12
inches long and weigh as much as 10 pounds—and their shells are noticeably more domed as well.

Northern red-bellied cooters aren't the only turtles found in New
England to be included on the federal endangered species list. All four
species of sea turtles that regularly occur off southern New England—
the leatherback, loggerhead, green, and Kemp's Ridley—are on the list.
And while the cooters are the only terrestrial turtles on the list, they're

not the only rare terrestrial turtle in the region either. In fact, of the eleven terrestrial turtle species found in New England, nine are included on at least one state's list of rare species. Just the painted turtle and common snapping turtle are abundant enough to be left off the lists. Of those that are listed, Lake Champlain is the only location in the region where the map turtle and eastern spiny softshell are found—the northeasternmost point in the ranges of the two species—and while they are relatively common and secure elsewhere, the map turtle is considered a species of concern in Vermont and the softshell is listed as threatened in the state. The musk turtle is on the Vermont list as well, although it is found in all six New England states and considered locally common in most of them. The spotted turtle, a denizen of small, shallow ponds, and the wood turtle, which prefers slow-moving streams, were once both common species throughout much of New England and are now considered rare most everywhere they are found. Similarly, the eastern box turtle, the region's most tortoise-like turtle and the one least likely to be found in water, has declined rapidly in the Northeast and is included on the endangered species lists of all five New England states where it is found.

The bog turtle is the smallest terrestrial turtle found in the region, with adults growing to just 4 inches in length; next to the northern red-bellied cooter, it's also the rarest. Found in sphagnum bogs or wet meadows in scattered colonies in extreme western Massachusetts and western Connecticut and south to North Carolina, bog turtles have suffered from intensive development pressure and the draining of their wetlands. In addition, their small size makes them an easy target for predators seeking a meal and a popular species for collectors, although the international sale and trade of bog turtles was banned in 1973.

An endangered species in Canada, the Blanding's turtle is another species whose populations are scattered widely. In New England, they are found exclusively in eastern Massachusetts, coastal New Hampshire, and extreme southern Maine, where they prefer shallow waters with abundant aquatic vegetation. A distinctive-looking species with a bright yellow chin and a domed shell speckled with numerous yellow flecks, the Blanding's range centers around the Great Lakes states and extends to Nebraska, but it is considered rare or threatened everywhere it is found.

The diamondback terrapin is one of the only turtles in the world that lives almost exclusively in the brackish water of tidal marshes, estuaries, and lagoons. Found from coastal Cape Cod to the Gulf States, it was once abundant but was hunted to near-extinction when turtle soup was popular. Its population has rebounded, and in Connecticut there is even a regulated capture season, but in Rhode Island, where it is found in just one location in upper Narragansett Bay, and in Massachusetts, it is included on the state endangered lists.

Peter Mirick is more worried about these species than he is about the protected cooter. "They live in the habitats most coveted by developers; do not nest in discrete, easily observable areas; and are scattered over the landscape, rather than concentrated in specific water bodies like redbellies," he wrote in an email after my visit. "So as their populations continue to collapse, there will be no easy solution for rapidly boosting their numbers or restoring them to former haunts, which by then will be housing developments, roads, and malls. For these species, only large, protected areas—wildlife management areas, state forests and parks, etc.—containing entire populations will be able to maintain them as viable units of our biodiversity, and even then, given the horrendous record of turtles disappearing from public lands (pet collection), I don't have much hope short of intensive management, including captive breeding."

One thing that favors the northern red-bellied cooter is that it is a long-lived species. Those that survive their first year can expect to live forty to fifty-five years, but that also means that it takes them a long time to mature. Females don't lay their first clutch of eggs until they are about ten to fourteen years old, so while the head-start program has been in place for about fifteen years, the first hatchlings from the program have been breeding for less than five.

The key to breeding is habitat. In late June or early July, female cooters emerge from their ponds to find a suitable site to lay their eggs. Nests are typically found within 100 yards of their pond, but some have wandered as far as a quarter mile in search of a preferred site. What they're looking for is sandy, unvegetated soils where they can easily dig down 5 to 7 inches. Unfortunately, increasing development around preferred ponds has reduced suitable nesting habitat and altered land use in the areas, resulting in long-term changes to the environment.

"Loss of habitat is the number one cause of its endangerment," said Tom French, assistant director of the Massachusetts Division of Fisheries and Wildlife. "It's not only the amount of habitat, but the quality of habitat that is a concern. One major problem is there is so much fire suppression. Around these ponds, we probably once had disturbed clear areas where there were places for the turtles to lay their eggs. But now, some of the ponds are surrounded by dense, closed canopy and huckleberry, so there's nowhere for the turtles to nest. They also need open areas where they can bask in the sun to warm up their bodies."

French believes that the northern climate is also a key concern for the species' success. "This is a southern turtle at the northern edge of its range. Our summers are barely long enough to carry out its necessary metabolic processes. This is a species that is asleep for most of its life, but they have a hard time with limited warm weather to find enough food to give them a healthy enough body to last through their next sleep cycle. This is one of those species that would do wonderful as a result of global warming."

The other chief threat to the cooters continues to be predation on hatchlings. While the turtles in the head-start program bypass that threat, fewer than one-quarter of the approximately seven hundred hatchlings per year are collected and enrolled in the program. The remainder are released into the wild, where 99 percent are eaten by predators. "Bass get the most attention for eating the turtles," French said, "but what we've found is that bass snatch them immediately when the hatchlings hit the pond and then they spit them out. Bullfrogs are the real horrendous eaters of baby turtles." French said that one biologist collected eight bullfrogs near a red-bellied cooter nesting beach and examined the contents of their stomachs. Six of the frogs had each eaten a cooter hatchling and one frog had eaten two!

Once the turtles reach a certain size, they face very few threats. While the number-one killer of most other turtle species in New England is cars striking them on roads—a significant factor, since it is mostly breeding females that are killed because they are the only ones that wander from their ponds—there has never been a documented road-killed cooter in the region. The other potential threat is poor water quality from the use of pesticides at cranberry bog operations adjacent to some cooter ponds. While French acknowledges that there hasn't been any attempt to assess the impact of water quality on the turtles, he noted that "turtles are generally robust and resilient to those kinds of insults."

The greatest challenge to ensuring the long-term health of the cooter population in Plymouth County is habitat protection and management. The priority is to acquire additional habitat for the turtles, but limited appropriate land is available. That's why head-start turtles are being released at Pocksha Pond and Great Quitticas Lake, where there are no records of historic occupancy. It's the only area left with abundant habitat. With little additional land available to protect, biologists are focusing on improving habitat at existing cooter ponds. Trees have been cut down around some ponds to provide sunny places for them to nest, and logs and other supports have been placed directly into the ponds for the turtles to bask on. In most cases, these modifications have met with immediate success.

In addition to habitat conservation, the key to the increasing population of northern red-bellied cooters in Plymouth County appears to be the continued success of the head-start program, and the program's success depends on finding cooter nests and collecting hatchlings before predators do. That's where John Crane comes in. He's a biologist and environmental consultant who makes most of his living flying around the country assessing cell phone towers for cellular telephone companies looking to upgrade their service. But Crane also has been a reptile and amphibian fanatic since childhood and spends a great deal of effort creating habitat for the creatures around his home on the edge of Great South Pond in Plymouth. The shallow, sandy pond has been part of the water supply for the area since the 1850s, and with no public access, it has become an excellent place for cooters to call home.

Beyond a small dock leading from his yard is a partially submerged platform that Crane has placed in the water for the turtles to use as a basking site. Since few other floating structures are available for that purpose, most days he sees between two and twenty turtles sunning themselves there. Cooters must bask in the sun as often as possible throughout the summer months because that accumulated warmth helps keep them healthy through the winter. Crane's basking platform is perfect for that purpose.

When I visited Crane's home, dozens of damselflies were dancing around the edge of the pond, some clinging to the tall vegetation that was growing in about a foot of water, which included the rare New England boneset and Plymouth gentian. Nearly every step I took around his yard, I came close to stepping on tiny Fowler's toads that had hatched recently from the pond and were moving to the uplands around Crane's house. Some as small as my pinky fingernail, the toads have a whiter belly than the more abundant American toad and are found in and around coastal plain ponds from southern New England to the Gulf Coast.

Crane has a contract with the U.S. Fish and Wildlife Service and the Massachusetts Natural Heritage Program to monitor the nests of northern red-bellied cooters and collect hatchlings for the head-start program. From May through October each year, he visits a series of ponds several times a week to look for cooter nests, protect the nests from predators, and watch for emerging young. He invited me to join him on one of his monitoring runs in July 2006, a year when abundant rain in May and June delayed the nesting season by several weeks. From late May to early July, he drives around the dikes of cranberry bogs adjacent to his designated ponds and looks for the trails of turtle tracks emerging from the ponds. "When a track starts to meander, I know that's the area where the nest is," he explained. "I also look for turtles 'taxiing' in the ponds as they line up and wait to emerge to nest. That's when I know the next day will be a good day for finding nests."

Cooter nests typically contain from eight to seventeen eggs, and more often than not they dig their nests close together, with three or four nests within a few feet of each other. Once Crane finds a nest, he places a wire mesh cage over the top of the site and digs it into the soil a few inches so predators like raccoons, skunks, and foxes can't get to the eggs. The cage also prohibits the hatchlings from escaping once they emerge from the ground. Sometimes the turtles nest in what Crane considers an inappropriate location—on a path where the cranberry bog workers might inadvertently drive over it, in a shaded area where the nest won't get enough sun, or next to maple trees whose roots tend to invade the nests—so he digs the eggs out and moves them to a better site. When I visited, all of the nests already had been found, but they need regular monitoring to ensure that animals haven't tried to dig under the cages or vegetation hasn't grown over them. During dry periods, Crane even pours water on each nest to mimic two rainy days a week so the eggs don't dry out.

As we drove around the bogs from nest site to nest site, Crane excitedly pointed out adult cooters on logs in the distance or tiny turtle heads peeking out of the water. He explained that the ditches and canals between the cranberry bogs were used as "grow-out" areas for juvenile turtles, places where the water is warmer and the competition from adult cooters is reduced. He doesn't think that the juveniles in these canals are head-start turtles, but rather young cooters that are making it on their own.

Red-bellied cooters take between seventy and eighty days to hatch, so by late August Crane shifts into hatchling collection mode. Every day through early October, he visits each of the nests—he monitored sixty-five nests in 2006—and removes any young cooters that have hatched and emerged from the sand. He takes two or three turtles from each nest for the head-start program and releases the rest into the nearest pond. "Sometimes they stay in the nest chamber after hatching, and they occasionally die in there or get infested with insects, so sometimes I'll pour water on the nest to induce them to climb out," he said. "When I do, they immediately pop to the surface."

Before leaving the first pond where most of the nests were located, Crane glanced into a canal between the pond and a cranberry bog and saw what he thought was a small snapping turtle peeking its head above the surface. Without hesitation, he ran into the canal to catch it to show me. It turned out to be a musk turtle instead, a species I hadn't seen since my turtle collecting days as a ten-year-old. It was clearly unhappy with us, opening its mouth wide in a threat display, but thankfully it didn't release the nasty odor that gives it its colloquial name "stinkpot."

Our last stop of the day was at Massasoit National Wildlife Refuge, a site that is closed to the public and that Crane claims has the densest population of red-bellied cooters anywhere in the state. Yet with 90 percent of those turtles being male, a nest discovered in 2006 was the first one on record for the site, although none of the eggs survived to hatch. We drove through two locked gates and down a long narrow dirt path through a forest of pitch pine and black oak with a thick understory of sweet pepperbush and huckleberry. An abundance of robins and eastern towhees flitted through the branches as we approached the pond and walked down a steep incline to a tiny sandy beach where the nest and its protective cage were located. Nothing seemed to be threatening it, other than a wandering glider, a large, bright orange dragonfly that occasionally perched on the mesh. Several cooter heads and shells were clearly visible as they rested at the surface of the deep pond, but we retreated to Crane's pickup and continued down the path another 100 yards to a peninsula that extends partway into the pond. The 20-foot-wide sandy peninsula had been partially cleared of trees and shrubs recently to create additional turtle nesting habitat, and a sign posted there warned of a $150,000 fine for taking or harassing the cooters.

During his regular nest monitoring, Crane often tries to catch adult turtles to weigh and measure. On the day of my visit, he invited me to join him as he snorkeled in a large pond to try to catch a few cooters. I hadn't been swimming in a freshwater pond since middle school, and it had been nearly a decade since I had snorkeled, but there was no way I was going to pass up the chance to swim with an endangered species. Sitting on a tree trunk at the edge of the water, we pulled on our swim fins and dive masks and waded into the still water. Several turtles were visible basking at the surface, so we slowly made our way in their direction, hoping to sneak up on them before they dove to the bottom to escape from us. The water was clear and the bottom was covered in soft vegetation, but my old foggy mask made it difficult to see anything clearly.

Crane said the trick to capturing turtles while snorkeling is to sneak up to within 10 or 20 feet of a basking turtle, and then to follow it when it dives and trap it against the bottom of the pond. He made it sound like it was going to be a breeze, but my optimism faded quickly. As we approached the first group of turtles, all but one dove well before we got close enough to swim after them, and the last one turned out to be just a bit of vegetation sticking above the surface and not a turtle at all. So we tread water and slowly moved around the pond looking for a cooter to pop up to breathe. Crane quickly became frustrated at our inability to find any of the numerous turtles he was sure was there, but on a 90-degree day, I was content to dive to the cool lower layers of the pond and relax at the surface. While scanning for turtles, I excitedly noticed a comet darner—the largest dragonfly in North America—flying back and forth across the pond in search of insect prey. Despite spending several summers actively seeking dragonflies throughout Rhode Island and knowing that comet darners were resident in the state, I had never seen the massive insect with the green head and long red abdomen before that moment. I quickly pulled the snorkel out of my mouth to try to get Crane's attention and point it out, but all I managed to do was choke on a mouthful of water.

At that point, Crane suggested that we swim around the peninsula and try to find some turtles on the opposite side of the pond. By the time we navigated our way over a submerged tree trunk and around some large boulders to the other side, we had been swimming and treading water for twenty minutes and I was exhausted. That side of the pond was deeper, perhaps 30 feet in some places, making our tactic of trapping turtles on the bottom even more of a challenge. But one turtle head was visible at the surface, so we did our best turtle imitation and slowly moved toward it. We got surprisingly close before it dove, but Crane and I judged that it was still too far away to attempt to swim after it. Instead, we tread water in place and hoped it would soon surface for a breath of fresh air. Alternately scanning above the water and putting our faces in the water to scan below us, we hoped that when it came up for air, we would see the cooter before it saw us.

After about five minutes of searching, I heard a loud splash behind me and saw Crane take three strong swimming strokes and dive beneath the surface. About twenty seconds later—long enough for me to worry whether I was going to have to rescue him—he popped to the surface with a large turtle held high above his head. Handing the dinner-plate-sized turtle to me, he described how the turtle briefly popped his head above the surface and then dove to the bottom, where Crane trapped him just as he said he would. Treading water with just my legs while holding the 4-pound turtle in the air was exhausting, but my adrenalin kept me going for a few minutes longer. Its shell was nearly black with rough concentric circles on its scutes, unlike the smooth shells of the painted turtles I had caught so many of as a child. Its head was mostly black, with a few narrow yellow lines that are so much more noticeable in younger cooters, and its plastron was a gorgeous coral red, the one feature that doesn't change through the years. As it alternated between withdrawing into its shell and digging its toenails into my hands in an effort to escape, Crane pointed out the vague remains of the notches on the edge of its shell that were made a decade earlier to identify it when that turtle was part of the head-start program.

By then I was winded, so I handed the turtle back to Crane, put my mask and snorkel back on, and signaled him to release it. The cooter immediately dove nearly straight down, and I took a deep breath to follow it. Despite my larger muscles and fancy snorkel gear and flippers, I struggled to keep up with it as it pumped its tiny legs back and forth and dashed to the bottom. The first 20 feet of my pursuit was through stunningly clear water, but a second later the turtle disappeared into a murkier area where I had stirred up mud and vegetation while treading water moments earlier. I kept kicking my feet as fast as I could as I sped through the detritus, and I got another quick glimpse of the turtle on the other side as it continued to make a beeline to safety. Nearing the vegetation on the floor of the pond, the cooter turned slightly to the right and around a massive boulder I hadn't even noticed, then disappeared briefly into the weedy vegetation. Knowing I had only a few seconds left before I needed to surface for air, I continued swimming deeper in the direction the turtle was traveling until it reappeared from behind the vegetation briefly and then disappeared for a final time. I was much deeper than I realized as I fought my way to the surface, gasped for a fresh breath of air, and made my way to shallow water. The whole dive lasted less than fifteen seconds, but my excitement made it seem much longer.

The northern red-bellied cooter has been a protected species since 1980, when it was added to the federal endangered species list. Adding a species of plant or animal to the federal list is an enormous challenge, but placing a species on a state list of rare wildlife isn't particularly difficult at all. Assuming the species warrants listing, all it takes in most states is the recommendation of a couple of state wildlife biologists and the approval of a top-level environmental official. The reason for the relative ease of the process is that inclusion on a state list does not necessarily provide species with any particular protections, require additional spending, or have implications for development or other regulatory matters. With few exceptions, Massachusetts being one of them, state endangered lists are prepared mostly for informational purposes.

The federal endangered species list is a totally different story. The legislation that created it includes punitive measures for those that violate it, requires spending considerable tax dollars to protect listed species, and restricts development and other activities that may harm wildlife on the list. It's the strongest endangered wildlife protection law in the world—something Americans should be proud of—but there is tremendous political opposition to expanding the list, regardless of how imperiled a species may be. So the process of adding new species to it is complex and onerous.

Historically, the process most often has been initiated by the U.S. Fish and Wildlife Service or, in the case of marine species, the National Marine Fisheries Service. But for political reasons and due to a backlog of proposed additions, most species in recent years have been petitioned for inclusion by environmental organizations or nongovernmental biologists. When a formal request is made, the Fish and Wildlife Service is required to decide within ninety days whether "substantial information" is available to indicate that listing may be warranted. If that finding is positive, a formal status review is conducted and a decision is made within a year on whether the listing is warranted. But a positive finding during the status review doesn't necessarily mean the species will be added to the endangered list. In many cases, species that are determined to warrant inclusion on the list are deferred for any number of reasons, often because other higher-priority species take precedence in the process. Those species chosen for listing and not deferred are then published as a proposed rule in the *Federal Register,* which initiates a sixty-day public comment period and, in most cases, a series of public hearings. It's during this period when the process is most politicized as advocates promoting and opposing the listing rally their forces to provide as much comment and support for their side as they can. While the decision to add a species is supposed to be based entirely on science, seldom is that the only factor considered. If the proposed listing survives the hearing process without being withdrawn for lack of evidence supporting it or extended due to disagreements within the scientific community, a final rule is published in the *Federal Register* and the listing becomes effective thirty days later.

That's the process that retired Worcester State College Professor Terry Graham initiated in the late 1970s to get the northern red-bellied cooter added to the federal list. Graham is the one who did most of the early research on the species and was its primary advocate throughout the listing process. The complexity of that process, and the considerable opposition that many proposed species receive, is due to the protective measures that listed species receive. By law, species included on the federal endangered species list receive extensive protective measures, including protection from the adverse effects of government-sponsored activities; restrictions on taking, transporting, or selling the species; development and implementation of a recovery plan; and land acquisition for habitat protection.

Thanks to these protections, the outlook for northern red-bellied cooters is very positive. Because their wetlands are largely protected and they don't wander far from their aquatic habitat, biologists are generally optimistic about their future. It doesn't hurt that the head-start program has generated considerable local interest in the species, and many residents in the areas surrounding their ponds have expressed interest in creating nesting habitat on their properties. And as the head-start program has demonstrated, it is easy to locate and monitor cooter nests and the species is easily reared in captivity.

"But the head-start program is not the silver bullet," noted Tom French. "That program is not going to restore the species to a self-sustaining population if we don't secure more habitat as well. Head-start is basically farming the turtles. But because of that program, the probability of hatchlings surviving is enormous; it's guaranteeing that most of those turtles will survive to adulthood. If we turned out 200 hatchlings into the wild, we would probably get one that survived to adulthood, but if we turned out 200 head-start turtles, we'd get 175 that survive.

"Because of that program, we've gotten to a point where we can guarantee that this population will never become extinct," he added. "They will probably require perpetual oversight, though not necessarily head-starting forever. I do think they will require long-term monitoring, because, while they can be farmed, that doesn't mean they can survive in a healthy, wild setting. But they won't require the kind of intense oversight that roseate terns or other species will need."

One other factor is in the cooter's favor, according to state biologist Peter Mirick. "There is almost no interest in this species for the pet trade," he wrote in an email. "Because they grow so large, require big aquariums, and produce large amounts of waste, very few hobbyists here or overseas want one of these animals. The opposite is true of our land turtles, all of which are in high demand and command high prices. As a result, the incentive to collect and sell [these other species] illegally is very high. I have already received a report this year (2006) of a poaching group taking eighty spotted turtles in the Foxborough area and selling them to a Florida dealer, who is likely to get a minimum of $200 to $300 apiece for them. With very few exceptions, it is probably time to end all trade in turtles from anywhere, or at least require stringent proof that any animals offered for sale are the product of captive breeding, not taken from the wild."

Oddly enough, while global warming is predicted to have devastating ecological effects around the globe, it might be the one factor that ensures the future health of the northern red-bellied cooter in Plymouth County.

5

Sandplain Gerardia

The Rhode Island Historical Cemetery Database, completed in 2005, identifies 2,833 historic cemeteries in the state with a total of more than 430,000 grave markers. The earliest, from 1647, marks the resting place of John Coggeshall, Sr., president of the colony of Rhode Island. The database lists 93 historic cemeteries in one small, rural community in Washington County where, in September 2004, I was drawn to a particular cemetery that at first appeared quite similar to many others I had passed by through the years, although it had an odd mix of old graves and new. Some headstones date to the 1820s, and many have simple, lichen-covered stone markers identifying the burial places, but not the names, of even earlier Americans. Others display the more modern adornments of recent deaths: plastic flowers, American flags, and homemade crosses.

In the midst of this well-manicured, 2-acre graveyard was an unusual overgrown patch of grasses, blooming asters, and broadleaf weeds. The 15-by-30-foot roped-off section held Rhode Island's last wild sandplain gerardia (*Agalinis acuta*), one of the rarest plants in the United States. Known from less than a dozen sites in the country—many of them historic cemeteries—this site in southern Rhode Island held just one solitary plant. It was a single, branched stem, barely visible among the similarly colored grasses, no more than 12 inches tall, with tiny narrow leaves and the beginnings of thirty-one seed pods emerging from where delicate, pink, bell-shaped flowers recently had dropped to the ground.

Despite being surrounded by the graves marking the end of dozens of human lives, this one plant was perhaps the saddest sight in the cemetery.

One hundred miles away, the Congregational Church cemetery in Waquoit, Massachusetts, wasn't nearly as sad. Although one corner of the cemetery looked unkempt—so much so that family members of the deceased might rightfully complain—it was a joyous site to botanists. Not only do a few specimens of the rare lady tresses orchid and bushy rock rose grow there, but a thousand sandplain gerardia plants were counted there the day before I visited in 2005. And there were two hundred times that many in the Waquoit Bay National Estuarine Research Reserve right next door. Yet despite the species' apparent abundance there, it's still a plant in great peril.

A member of the foxglove and snapdragon family, sandplain gerardia was never abundant. Just forty-nine historical sites were ever known in a narrow band of coastal plain extending from Cape Cod to Maryland. Today, it is found in just one site each in Rhode Island, Connecticut, and Maryland, and a handful on Cape Cod and Long Island. Some of these were only recently discovered. Massachusetts once had as many as twenty-four populations, all of which have disappeared, although two sites in historic cemeteries were rediscovered in 1980 by botanists Bruce Sorrie and Caren Caljouw. A report in 1923 claimed that Montauk, Long Island, had "untold millions" of sandplain gerardia plants, and eighty years ago a local naturalist described how the Montauk grasslands turned pink every year in August and September. But it didn't take long for the species' seventeen populations to be extirpated from that state. Or so it was thought. Today, Long Island is the plant's stronghold with six populations occurring in Nassau and Suffolk counties, including locations on a golf course, a railroad right-of-way, a roadside, and a community college campus, the latter of which was formerly the site of an airfield. The lone population in Maryland was discovered at what is now Soldiers Delight Natural Environmental Area in Baltimore County in 1950, although the plant's identity was unknown until 1984. This population is large and healthy, and it remains the only site where active management has not been deemed necessary, though the site has been protected from disturbance for several decades.

Most of the historic populations throughout the plant's range disappeared between the 1890s and 1940s, well before the development boom that has imperiled so many other species in recent decades. Farmland abandonment and fire suppression, which results in healthy grasslands becoming shrublands and forests, may be one explanation.

Long before the plant's listing as a federally endangered species in 1988, Chris Raithel and Rick Enser, wildlife biologists for the Rhode Island Department of Environmental Management, along with a team of interns and biologists from The Nature Conservancy, spent several years searching for the species in more than 150 historic cemeteries throughout Rhode Island and eastern Connecticut. Rhode Island once supported as many as six populations, but all had disappeared by 1941 mostly due to changes in habitat caused by succession. Similarly, it had been a century since Connecticut's last two sandplain gerardia populations, in Farmington and Voluntown, had been extirpated. Using soil maps and other clues, the Rhode Island team first visited cemeteries in spring in search of plants such as birds-foot violet that prefer similar conditions. They followed up in August and September during the plant's blooming season. After years of effort, they finally hit pay-dirt. As Raithel wrote later in *Rhode Island Naturalist,* "Eventually, fate intervened. As I was driving to work one day, I saw an historical cemetery that I had passed many times before but had never visited. I pulled in and had barely left the car when I saw the object of my long search, *Agalinis acuta*—in full flower. That moment remains one of my more memorable field experiences."

Strangely, in one of those small-world coincidences typical in Rhode Island, a cluster of the plants was found at the foot of a gravestone marked with the name Hoxie, which is the same name found on a gravestone in Massachusetts that identifies the location of one of that state's sandplain gerardia populations.

After Raithel's success finding the plant in Rhode Island, he urged Connecticut biologists to search a few cemeteries that he thought showed promise, and it was found in that state a short time later as well.

"Nearly all the current sites in the Northeast are old cemeteries," said Rick Enser, a retired state wildlife biologist in Rhode Island who worked with Raithel in managing the species. "Thousands of years ago, after glaciation, most of the landscape was open, scarified land with fairly little soil cover and not much organic matter. It was alpine-like with scattered grasses and lichens and other plants. That was probably the heyday of *Agalinis.* Nowadays, with the landscape being very different, they're relegated to places that are mimics of those historic habitats."

The Ice Age glaciers began retreating from southern New England between 19,500 and 17,000 years ago, and ice had left Rhode Island completely by 16,000 years ago. The landscape looked very similar to the way the arctic slope of Alaska looks today—mostly grasses and wildflowers. The earliest radiocarbon-dated vegetation from the state was a dwarf willow, a species now common on the tundra, from 13,000 years ago. As the climate warmed, trees emerged, starting with spruce and fir about 11,000 to 12,000 years ago, followed by birch, oak, and chestnut, the dominant species in the area when Europeans eventually colonized the area.

Historic cemeteries typically were located on high, well-drained points of land with good sun exposure that weren't useful for agriculture, often because they had acidic, infertile soil. These conditions helped support healthy populations of sandplain gerardia, because plants that might compete with it couldn't survive there. The plant's wild, natural habitat was dry, sandy, prairie-like areas with sparse vegetation on the coastal plain. It also prefers locations that are disturbed occasionally, whether by livestock grazing, sporadic fires, or other means. As grazing has declined and fire suppression increased, woody vegetation has taken over many coastal grassland habitats. Most of the appropriate habitat that has not become overgrown has been destroyed by development. But historic cemeteries have survived. Enser and other biologists believe that the regular but infrequent mowing at these cemeteries could be another form of disturbance that helps trigger the plant's success. They say the plant can't be managed like a lawn and be mowed frequently, yet for some reason it seems to thrive when it is mowed once or twice a year, as long as it isn't mowed after mid-summer when the plant is preparing to bloom and set seed.

When grass and flowers and other plants are mowed, some receive an indirect benefit as competing vegetation is reduced in size or vigor, which allows the "weaker" plant access to more light and nutrients. Mowing also may change a plant's hormonal activity and, therefore, its growing behavior. In the case of broadleaf plants, a hormone called auxin is produced in the apical meristem near the top of the plant's dominant stem. Like a Christmas tree or a human fingernail, new growth just behind the tip pushes the tip higher and higher. But when the apical meristem at the top of that dominant stem is cut, the source of the auxin hormone disappears. A free-for-all results within the rest of the plant as it generates auxillary buds that begin to grow into new branches and stems. Without the auxin in the meristem, no single stem has dominance and so the plant becomes bushy all over. That's why many gardeners "pinch" their mums or other ornamental plants—to create a hormonal balance and make them bushier. After mowing or "pinching," the secondary growing points are no longer inhibited by the hormones produced by the dominant stem, resulting in additional growth. While it's probably untrue to say that some plants *like* being mowed, many have found competitive niches in which periodic mowing is somewhat beneficial. It appears this may be true for sandplain gerardia.

Like the Rhode Island team of biologists, Bruce Sorrie also spent years searching historic cemeteries for sandplain gerardia. A botanist with the Massachusetts Division of Fish and Wildlife in the late 1970s and 1980s, he has been described by colleagues as a "phenomenal finder of rare plant records." He started out as an ornithologist working at the Manomet Bird Observatory, but he had a keen interest in plants as well and was hired by the Massachusetts Division of Fisheries and Wildlife in 1979.

"He hit the ground running," said Paul Somers, who took over for Sorrie as the state botanist when Sorrie moved to North Carolina in 1991. "One of the first things he did was visit herbaria around the region and find historical plant records and create a list of rare plants for the state. His next task was to go out looking and trying to relocate these species based on the clues he found on the herbarium specimen labels, talking with local naturalists, and from what he learned about the habitat needs of the species."

When I visited the Waqouit cemetery with Brendan Annett, stewardship coordinator at the neighboring Waquoit Bay National Estuarine Research Reserve, Hurricane Ophelia had just been downgraded to a tropical storm and was sitting off the coast of Delaware on its way to Cape Cod. A scattering of pre-storm rain showers was already dampening the region. The cemetery appeared to have been filled to capacity decades ago, as most of the gravestones dated from the 1800s and early 1900s. Several were broken or propped up with two-by-fours. The 20- by 30-yard section where sandplain gerardia bloomed hadn't been mowed in three months, so small shrubs had begun growing, weeds were abundant, and the grass was thin and scraggly. As we walked around the site, Annett pointed out the tiny pink flowers that were hardly noticeable at first glance. I never would have guessed that only the day before he had counted a thousand blooming plants there.

Surprisingly, I felt the same way at the research reserve next door. Annett said that more than two hundred thousand plants had been counted in one small section of the reserve the previous year, and though they hadn't been counted yet in 2005, he figured there were at least half that many when I visited. But I glanced around when I first arrived and only saw what looked like an abandoned lawn. Which is exactly what it is. As in the cemetery, there were few healthy turf grasses. Instead, the reserve was a mass of weeds, invasive plants, knee-high patches of little bluestem grass, early stages of shrubs, bare patches of ground, and moss. An osprey nesting platform sat on a pole at one edge of the property, and two eastern phoebes darted about after the abundant grasshoppers and other insects still active in the rain. I didn't see even one pink flower, let alone a hundred thousand.

The reserve was established in 1988 at the site of a former summer estate that was damaged by the massive hurricane of 1938 and later abandoned. When the state took the property by eminent domain, the estate's 23 acres were linked with an additional 3,000 acres of barrier beaches, uplands, and other lands, and became one of only twenty-five estuarine research reserves in the country. Its mission is to protect the site's natural resources, but also to make it available for environmental research. The estate's former gatehouse is now a dormitory for visiting researchers, the carriage house is a laboratory and classroom facility, and the boathouse is used for workshops. Much of the research at the site focuses on the impacts on water quality in Waquoit Bay caused by changes in land use in the surrounding communities, but other studies address atmospheric sources of nitrogen, changes in marine vegetation, anadromous fish, and nutrient use by shellfish.

During our short conversation in the visitor's center, Annett warned me that the numbers of sandplain gerardia were down a bit and the individual plants were smaller than in previous years, probably due to the very dry summer. He then led me to the area where I had glanced around earlier and saw no flowers. But they were there. Tens of thousands of them. It took a moment to refocus my eyes to ignore the big picture and zoom in instead on the smaller scale. Throughout the entire visible land-scape, five or six tiny blooming pink flowers perched on stems standing less than 6 inches from the ground, each bloom no larger than my pinky fingernail. Careful to avoid the delicate plants, I crouched on hands and knees to get a better view of the beautiful, pale pink, tubular flowers. Mist beaded on the petals, and dozens of buds on each plant seemed ready to burst.

State botanist Paul Somers explained that the research reserve site was cultivated from the original cemetery population in the late 1980s and used as a test site for management methods. After experimenting with periodic burning and scarifying of the soil, it was determined that a simple mowing regime—once in June and again in December after the seeds have dropped—was all that was necessary to maintain the popula-tion. And it's working. Numbers increased rapidly from 1,159 in 1995 to more than 50,000 in 2000 and to a record high of 227,600 in 2004. The neighboring cemetery population also has increased—from 73 in 1981 to about 4,000 in both 1998 and 2004, although major fluctuations have seen the population drop to as low as 42 in 1992 and 89 in 2002. Assuming that the mowing regime isn't altered, the remaining challenges to the long-term health of the population are competition with the nonstop on-slaught of invasive species and potential weather impacts. A major win-ter storm in 1991 may have been the reason for the population crash the following year, as salt spray and howling winds turned many stems com-pletely black.

"We assume this species was much more common on the Cape Cod landscape many years ago when much of the area was grazed," explained Somers, who unexpectedly discovered that several of his ancestors were buried in the Waquoit cemetery when he began monitoring the plant's population there. "It has only been the mowing of the cemeteries that has perpetuated the habitat. Most of the area has become reforested now. We don't know why it hasn't persisted as a roadside weed or along power lines, though the mowing regime may explain it."

When most biological reference materials mention sandplain gerardia, its Latin name is followed by the name Pennell. The former curator of botany at the Academy of Natural Sciences in Philadelphia and director of the New York Botanical Garden, Francis Whittier Pennell (1886–1952) was an international expert on the family *Scrophulariaceae,* which includes sandplain gerardia, in the early 1900s. He traveled widely throughout the Americas, collecting, discovering, and naming plants. He described hundreds of species new to science—437 in the *Scrophulariaceae* family alone—and authored numerous botanical books, scientific reports, and travelogues.

A Quaker, he graduated from the University of Pennsylvania and, in the summer of 1911, arrived at the Marine Biological Laboratory at Woods Hole Oceanographic Institute on Buzzards Bay in Massachusetts to collect and study marine plants. He didn't stay long. A year later, he was collecting terrestrial plants throughout the Southeast, including the first specimens of Virginia dayflower and axilflower, and soon undertook trips to the central states, the Rocky Mountains, and the desert Southwest, as well as multiple trips to Colombia, Peru, Chile, and Mexico, and still later to the Himalayan Mountains.

While Pennell discovered numerous new species and was the unchallenged authority on the genus, he was not the first to find sandplain gerardia. That distinction lies with Merritt Lyndon Fernald (1873–1950), another botanical expert with hundreds of plant discoveries to his name, who collected the first sandplain gerardia specimen on the dry, sandy downs of Edgartown on Martha's Vineyard on September 12, 1901. And yet even that discovery is slightly muddied, because while Fernald collected what is known as the type specimen—the specimen from which the plant was described originally for science, which now resides in the herbarium collection of the Missouri Botanical Garden—it wasn't identified as a new species until Pennell described it in the *Bulletin of the Torrey Botanical Club* in 1915. The original label on the type specimen lists it as *Agalinis skinneriana,* a similar species found from southern Ontario to northern Louisiana and Oklahoma. On the same type specimen is a handwritten note in pencil from 1914 identifying it as *Agalinis decemloba,* another look-alike species found from eastern Pennsylvania to Mississippi and Florida. It also can be confused with *Agalinis setacea* of the mid-Atlantic states and *Agalinis tenuifolia,* which ranges widely from Maine to Manitoba and south to Florida and Texas. Soon after the specimen was misidentified for the second time, Pennell got it right.

There is a great deal that still isn't known about sandplain gerardia, though. For instance, no one is quite sure what insect serves as its primary pollinator. Some biologists think it may be a bumblebee, another suggests it's a flower fly in the family Syrphidae, and still another claims it may self-pollinate. It is certain that individual flowers bloom for just one day, with fresh blossoms opening in early morning and dropping off by mid-afternoon, but it has been difficult to determine its anthesis, or time of full bloom. How the plant disperses its seeds is not well understood either. Perhaps small mammals such as rabbits and mice ingest and distribute the seeds—there is considerable evidence that the plants are grazed upon by herbivorous animals—but maybe the tiny seeds are carried by the wind or simply germinate where they fall. Like other members of the figwort family, the plant is probably a hemiparasite, attaching its roots to the root systems of other plants to gain additional nutrients while giving nothing in return. Many hemiparasites are restricted to attaching to just one or two host plants, but it is unknown what host plant sandplain gerardia parasitizes, although it is believed it may be some kind of grass.

Despite the biologists' best efforts, the plant's population at the Rhode Island cemetery site—once numbering as many as one hundred individuals—declined to twelve plants in 2001. In an effort to stave off extirpation from the state, they searched for a site to establish a new population.

The headquarters of the New England Wild Flower Society sits amidst a 45-acre botanical garden in Framingham, Massachusetts, called the Garden in the Woods. This beautiful setting features winding paths, hundreds of well-cared-for plants, a museum shop, and frequent plant sales. Not far from the main building is a small, unobtrusive cinderblock out-building that holds the society's archives and photographic slide collection. Sitting in the midst of this fire-proof structure is a waist-high, white freezer chest, just like the kind many families have in their basements to store the Thanksgiving turkey, a couple pounds of hamburger, an extra loaf of bread, and some frozen dinners. But inside this freezer is a most unique and valuable collection: seeds from three hundred of the region's rarest plants.

This "seed bank" holds the genetic fingerprints of species on the edge of extinction and may be the last hope for the survival of plants such as sandplain gerardia. Bill Brumback is the gatekeeper of the seed collection. He's the conservation director of the New England Wild Flower Society, and he has been charged with collecting a large percentage of the genetic variability inherent in each population of rare plants in the region. He and his volunteers do this by collecting and storing seeds so that if it becomes necessary to reintroduce that species into the wild, he could create a population with as much genetic variation as the original wild populations have.

"We've got different criteria for determining what species we collect from," he said. "We look at the rarity of the plant (how many populations there are), the threats to those populations, whether or not the populations are reproducing, and whether you can get permission to collect from those sites. When you combine those factors, you come up with a priority list." Brumback noted that he also looks at plants that may not be especially rare but that may have disjunct populations—populations separated from the main populations by 100 miles or more and that therefore might differ genetically from the populations that are closer together and have a more convenient flow of genes among individual plants.

When members of Brumback's team arrive to collect seeds from a population of rare plants, they first count the number of individual plants at the site and collect seed from as many individuals as possible. No more than 10 percent of the seeds from any one plant are collected, and no more than 10 percent of the seeds from the entire population are collected. The rest are left to fend for themselves and sustain the plant in the wild.

Once they've collected the seed, they clean it, count it by hand (or, in the case of extremely small seeds, by weight), package it into open packets, and put it into a drying cabinet for a month. At 25 percent relative humidity, the seeds soon go dormant and any moisture in them evaporates. Moisture is the enemy at a seed bank, because if seeds contain moisture when they are placed in the freezer, the seeds will soon crack, and cracked seeds don't germinate. After the seeds have been dried, they're placed in heat-sealed foil envelopes and placed in the freezer at −20 degrees Centigrade, which is a safe temperature for seed storage. Native New England plants are used to freezing winter temperatures, and they can last for many years in a frozen state. The New England Wild Flower Society established this seed bank—the largest in New England—in 1984 in cooperation with the Center for Plant Conservation, a collaborative of thirty institutions working to protect the country's rarest plant species. In the 1990s, the society developed an expanded program focusing on regionally rare species.

Sandplain gerardia poses interesting challenges to the seed bankers,

partly because the orange-colored seeds are so tiny—Brumback estimates that one teaspoon could hold more than ten thousand seeds. But
the bigger problem is that their germination rate is extremely low. While
each plant may produce up to twenty-four hundred seeds, just 1 percent
of them are likely to germinate. Seedling mortality is also high, so even
fewer will grow healthy and large enough to bloom and create more
seeds. Since the plant is an annual, next year's plants are almost entirely
dependent on the seed output and germination of this year's plants. In
addition, since sandplain gerardia is a hemiparasite and needs a host plant
with which to grow, the seeds must germinate in harmony with its host.
In test plots, Brumback has had success growing *Agalinis* with little bluestem grass as a host, and has raised the germination rate to 2 percent. But
that rate is still way too low to make him comfortable about the plant's
future.

Sandplain gerardia seeds have been in the New England Wild Flower
Society seed bank since 1988; seeds from the Rhode Island population
were added in the mid-1990s. After careful consideration, the Rhode Island biologists decided that the Eppley Wildlife Sanctuary, a 1,030-acre
preserve owned by the Audubon Society of Rhode Island and closed to
the public, had appropriate habitat in which to introduce an experimental population. So they made a withdrawal from the seed bank.

"Audubon is more singularly focused on managing properties exclusively for wildlife," explained Larry Taft, executive director of Audubon,
"so our property is easier to manage for a rare species than almost any
other place that must be managed for a variety of uses."

In the fall of 2002, Taft and Chris Raithel began their reintroduction
experiment. "To extract as much information as possible, even if the introduction failed, we established an experimental design at the Eppley
site whereby each of two 9 × 9 meter areas was subdivided into three
zones—left, middle and right," Riathel wrote of the project in *Rhode Island Naturalist*.

Each of these 3 × 9 meter zones was further separated into 1 × 1 meter
plots. We used two sources of seeds in this experiment. We collected
about eight percent of the fresh mature seed capsules from the existing
population during the fall of 2002. We broke apart the capsules and
counted the tiny seeds, separating them into lots of about 100 seeds within
glassine envelopes. We received the other seeds from the New England

Wild Flower Society. These seeds, originally from Rhode Island, had been seed-banked for just such an occasion during the fall of 1995. By using both sources of seeds in the same experiment, we could compare germination rates in the field while controlling for other effects (such as weather and predators) that also influence seed germination. Before introducing the seeds during November 2002, we prepared the introduction area by mowing down the existing grassy vegetation and scarifying the plots with garden rakes. We then introduced 100 fresh seeds to each of several randomly selected plots in the left-hand zones and placed 100 1995 seeds in each of several plots in the right-hand zones. We left the middle zones as non-treatment control areas to prevent confusion that might arise if some seeds "wandered" from their initial placement site. *Agalinis acuta* seeds need a cold period to spur germination, so while they lay dormant on the ground during the snowy winter of 2002–2003, we wondered, as we shoveled our walks and tried to stay warm, about the result of our effort.

He needn't have worried. A year later, Raithel was rewarded with thirty-three new plants—all but four from the fresh seeds. "There was some concern about how long the seed at the seed bank actually lasts," said Rick Enser, a quiet, ponytailed biologist who described the Eppley project as a stop-gap to protect the current population's genetic material. "We've had germination from both seed sources, though the fresh seed did much better." A follow-up planting of additional seeds in 2003 produced very little, but by 2004 there were thirty-five healthy plants at the new site.

In Connecticut, Nancy Murray was following a similar path. When sandplain gerardia was first discovered in a historic cemetery in Windham County in 1990, there were only four plants. The Department of Environmental Protection biologist described the site as a typical historic cemetery on town-owned land containing about a hundred gravesites surrounded by a stone wall, with housing developments encroaching nearby and a wetland on one side. Municipal officials have been cooperative in adjusting the mowing schedule at the site, and Murray is working on several other efforts to increase the population.

"We've taken seeds from our population, grown them at the New England Wild Flower Society to get them started, and then put them back into our site," she said. "That strategy hasn't been especially successful, though. So we've tried scarifying the soil and distributing seeds at the site ourselves, and that's been more effective."

While part of the federal recovery plan for the species is to establish new populations, as is being done in Rhode Island and Massachusetts, that's not in the cards for Connecticut. "It's always been a very restricted species in the state, and we don't have any good habitat left," Murray said. "And we would need to find a place that can be managed in perpetuity. We don't have a place like that."

Murray's efforts at the Connecticut historic cemetery—as in Rhode Island, the location of which is being kept secret so the plants aren't disturbed or removed by collectors—are paying off. From four plants in 1990, the population grew to 160 by 2004. "I'm optimistic we can maintain what we have through good management, but the long-term survival of the species is unclear to me," she said.

It's not just sandplain gerardia that is making its strongest stand in historic cemeteries. Grass is, too. Some of the earliest lawns in America were planted in colonial-era cemeteries, and most of these sites receive little maintenance, and have, in effect, been treated with benign neglect for decades or longer. And yet grass still grows there. If I did nothing but mow the lawn at my house twice a year and ignored every other standard maintenance practice—such as fertilizer and lime and raking the leaves and dethatching—that lawn wouldn't last long. The grubs would get it and the weeds would take over and the leaves would accumulate and it would quickly die out. And yet, for some reason, healthy grass tends to persist in many historic cemeteries.

That's where Richard Skogley comes in. He was a turf scientist at the University of Rhode Island for forty years who spent the latter half of the twentieth century going on wandering tours looking for healthy grass plants in historic cemeteries. I played high school soccer with his son in the 1970s, and later, when I went to work for the university, stories of Skogley's adventures were legendary. The professor visited centuries-old cemeteries in early American settlement communities such as Newport, Rhode Island, and Plymouth, Massachusetts, and ancient villages in the Canadian Maritimes, seeking out thriving grass plants. Sometimes he would find European or Mediterranean grasses that likely were planted by early colonists. He would go to cemeteries in hostile environments— coastal cemeteries exposed to frequent salt spray, northern cemeteries where the growing season seems to come and go in an instant—and he would wander during extreme drought when most grasses were dead or dormant. If he found a healthy patch of turf in these inhospitable conditions, he knew it was a survivor with something special in its DNA. That's what he was looking for.

When Skogley found a healthy patch of turf in an old cemetery, he'd take a plug of it, wrap it in wet newspaper, and take it back to his lab. Once there, he would nurture it, grow it in his greenhouse or back field, and after ten generations or so, if it was still thriving, he might make it the next grass seed available at the local hardware store. Or maybe he'd combine it with other grasses that he had selected and nurtured for their special characteristics: a plant with especially good color, or one with a preferred texture, perhaps one that was insect resistant or grew particularly dense. In the old days, before gene splicing and DNA fingerprinting, Dick Skogley was a master at finding and creating hardy grasses. His Jamestown chewings fescue and Kingstown velvet bentgrass, still popular lawn varieties today, originated from plants he found at historic cemeteries in Rhode Island.

But while grass flourishes in many places besides cemeteries, sandplain gerardia does not.

The formal recovery plan prepared for *Agalinis acuta* by the U.S. Fish and Wildlife Service delineates the steps that biologists hope will lead to the population gaining in numbers and the species being removed from the federal endangered species list. The goal the report established for considering the species fully recovered includes a total of "twenty stable, wild populations located throughout the species' historic range to ensure against any unpredictable events that could lead to reproductive failure and subsequent population decline." It defines a stable population as one that maintains a five-year "geometric average" population size of at least one hundred individual plants. The recovery goal also requires that at least fifteen of the populations be located on protected sites where maintenance of the species is the "predominating management objective."

Given the current population numbers, it's not likely that the recovery goal is within reach any time soon. That's partly due to the fact that the plant is an annual, so the adult plants die out each winter and new plants must start from seed the following spring. Typical of annual plants, population numbers fluctuate widely from year to year. In the late 1980s, for instance, the Maryland population went from 30 individuals to 1,000 to 150 in three years. More typical is one Massachusetts site that ranged from 220 to 50 to 130 to 18 to 94 over a string of five years. The trend at many of the sites in recent years, as at the Rhode Island site, has been a downward spiral.

That's not true, however, at one of the Long Island sites. In 1991, the sandplain gerardia population at the Sayville grasslands was at an all-time low of three plants, but it recovered to the point where it supported a couple hundred plants for several years in the 1990s. In 2002, the population shot up to sixty-five hundred plants, and the cool wet weather in 2003 produced more than eighty thousand plants! Marilyn Jordan of the local office of The Nature Conservancy enthusiastically described it as a "sea of pink."

Maintaining that sea of pink is an ongoing battle. While the recovery plan lists the most significant threat to the species as "the direct loss or degradation of its habitat," it also notes that most populations are on private property, so protection efforts necessarily must focus on ensuring landowner cooperation and active support. Most landowners are less than enthusiastic about making an effort to protect a rare plant. But even without their help, a great many management steps are being taken to try to better understand the species, including tests of cultivation techniques, pollination and herbivory studies, hand sowing of seeds for population augmentation, determination of potential parasitic hosts, and assessment of the effects of habitat disturbance. In Massachusetts, the state Natural Heritage Program is using occasional prescribed burns as well. Yet despite all these monitoring and management efforts, sandplain gerardia numbers at most locations are still declining.

"I think the species will survive, unless there's something out there that we haven't predicted, some unforeseen circumstance like a pest we haven't identified or a catastrophe that takes them all out at once, which is unlikely," said Rick Enser, the retired Rhode Island state biologist. "But whether it becomes possible to [remove it from the endangered species list] or not, I don't see that happening anytime in the near future."

With just one wild plant at the Rhode Island site in 2004, it would be easy to be pessimistic about its chances of survival. But Enser isn't. "That population varies from year to year. We've seen ups and downs before, but obviously this year is the lowest number ever," he said. "It's an annual, so it's dependent on the amount of seed production in a given year.

But an individual plant produces in the realm of a thousand seeds, and if they fall in the right place, you can get a comeback."

Enser's optimism seems to be working. A year after the lone plant at the Rhode Island cemetery withered and died, its seeds sprouted into fifty-nine plants that bloomed and dropped seeds, resurrecting the population for at least one more generation.

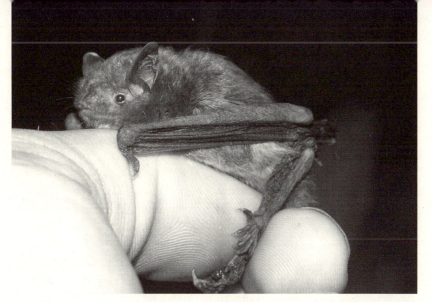

6

Indiana Bat

Beginning bird watchers often complain about the difficulty in identifying sparrows. Their common coloration, similar face patterns, and abundance at backyard bird feeders can easily turn enthusiastic nature lovers into frustrated hobbyists. Instead of studying and practicing until they're adept at distinguishing the various species, many beginners quickly ignore or give up on sparrows and simply lump them together into a category often referred to as "little brown things." That's certainly what I did. Warblers—that colorful group of neotropical migrants with the buzzy voices—can cause the same response, despite their more varied plumage. The problem with warblers is they just won't sit still long enough to let you get a good look at them. And even when they do, they're perched so high up in the trees that a new ailment has been coined to describe the pain they cause—warbler neck. Shorebirds are another problem all together, particularly when they're not in their breeding plumage, which seems to be most of the year.

But these frustrated birders should count their blessings that they're not trying to identify bats. There are over nine hundred species of bats in the world, mostly in the tropics, and they comprise about one-fifth of all mammal species on Earth. Just forty-five species are found in the United States, which, when compared to the seven hundred-plus species of regularly occurring birds in the United States, might suggest that identifying them should be easy. It's not. Since almost all are only active at night, getting a good look at them is difficult and binoculars are virtually useless. While it's sometimes easy to see thousands of them leaving their daytime roosts at dusk, distinguishing the diagnostic physical differences among most species of bats in flight is impossible. Even in the hand, they can challenge all but the most dedicated bat fanatic.

Take, for instance, the distinction between the little brown bat (*Myotis lucifugus*), the typical species found in many home attics and one of the most abundant and widespread species in the northern United States, and the Indiana bat (*Myotis sodalis*), an endangered species that is often found foraging in the company of little brown bats. Both weigh about a third of an ounce and have a 10-inch wingspan and brownish fur. While they sometimes can be distinguished in the hand by the slightly lighter brown fur on the underside of the little brown bat or by the color of their noses, there's enough variability in these features to make identification by those characteristics alone unreliable. No, the features you have to look at to identify these two species confidently are a small lobe of cartilage along the edge of the tail and the hair on their toes! The hair on the toes of Indiana bats is slightly shorter—it doesn't extend beyond their toenails—than the hair on the toes of little brown bats. Yet even seeing the hairs requires the ridiculous challenge of backlighting the bat's toes. Who would have guessed?

Regardless of their identification challenges, Indiana bats are in trouble. Although they range from Vermont to Wisconsin and south to the southern Appalachians and northern Arkansas, their population has been plummeting. When they were first declared endangered in 1967—making them the first officially designated endangered species in the nation—there were believed to be about 800,000 Indiana bats in the country, but by 2000 just 325,000 were left. Like most bats in temperate regions, Indiana bats hibernate by the thousands in dense clusters in caves and mines, which bat biologists call hibernacula, sometimes as many as three hundred bats per square foot. Protecting these caves from disturbance is one key to protecting the bats.

When bats hibernate, they enter a state of torpor in which their metabolism rate drops dramatically, allowing them to live for more than six months on their fat reserves alone. But they require a very specific microclimate within their caves. In the case of Indiana bats, it is critical that the temperature in their hibernation cave remains constant at between 37 and 43 degrees Fahrenheit. Any warmer than that and their metabolism doesn't slow down enough to maintain their fat reserves through the winter and they starve to death before spring arrives. Similarly, if a disturbance in the cave awakens the bats or forces them to move, their metabolism speeds up and, again, they starve to death. Unfortunately, human visitation to hibernacula in winter—and worse yet, intentional vandalism—has wiped out many bat populations and threatened the Indiana bat with extinction. In the last thirty years, efforts have been made to install gates on many hibernation caves to keep people out. Sadly, many poorly designed gates restricted exit and entry by the bats, too. Others altered air movement inside the caves and caused cave temperatures to rise, ultimately resulting in as much or more harm to bat populations than might have occurred without the gates.

Vermont has twenty-four known caves and mines where bats hibernate, but only three are known to harbor Indiana bats—one each in Dorset, Manchester, and Brandon—and all three have very small numbers of them. The Indiana bat population in Dorset cave, on Mount Aeolus, was at its peak in the 1930s and then declined rapidly in the 1940s, so that by the early 1950s they were gone. "It had been fifty years since we documented an Indiana bat in Dorset cave," explained bat biologist Scott Darling, "but spelunkers located a new part of the cave a few years ago. What often happens is that bat biologists will only go into the section of the cave that's easiest to get to, while cavers will generally go to places that bat biologists will not. So when they came back and reported finding a new room that was 100 feet long and 30 feet high with bats in it, we were forced to go down into it."

Dorset cave is the winter home to twenty thousand bats, including small numbers of Indiana bats, as well as the state-threatened small-footed bat and the more common little brown, big brown, northern long-eared, and Eastern pipistrelle bats. Using a cadre of volunteers, staff, and bat experts to lug 5,000 pounds of iron up a steep, rocky trail to the cave entrance, The Nature Conservancy installed a specially designed gate at the site in 2004 to restrict access during the hibernation season.

The only place in New England where Indiana bats are found to breed reliably is in the Lake Champlain Valley of northwest Vermont. It's there that I first met Darling, a wildlife biologist with the Vermont Department of Fish and Wildlife. A native of Connecticut, he has worked as a state biologist in Vermont since graduating college, first monitoring the wild turkey population and then black bears. When a maternity colony of Indiana bats was discovered in the state in 2000, he volunteered to take the lead role in protecting the population.

I joined Darling and a team of other biologists and bat enthusiasts on a June afternoon for two nights of bat trapping at Shelburne Farms in Shelburne, Vermont, a beautiful 3,800-acre estate overlooking Lake Champlain. Built in 1886 for William Seward and Lila Vanderbilt Webb, the estate was designed as a working farm to demonstrate turn-of-the-century, cutting-edge agricultural practices and included a breeding facility for hackney horses and a spectacular family residence. But it was more than just a working farm. The property was designed by renowned landscape architect Frederick Law Olmstead, who supervised the planting of one hundred thousand trees a year and the sculpting of 20 miles of roads and carriage trails. Borrowing from the English landscape tradition of the early eighteenth century, Olmstead created wide-open meadows scattered with occasional shade trees, thick woodlots, and numerous ponds and wetlands, all designed to create an atmosphere to relax the mind and spirit. In the summer and fall, as well as during holiday periods, the Webbs entertained the political and social elite of the nation.

After years of decline during the middle part of the century, family descendants established an environmental education center at the farm, and later donated the entire property to a nonprofit group founded to manage and maintain it. Today, Shelburne Farms remains a working farm, with a dairy herd of 125 Brown Swiss cows, a cheese-making facility, and a garden that grows organic produce.

In addition to creating a spectacular setting for learning and relaxing, Olmstead's tree plantings and carriage trails created excellent habitat for forest-dwelling bats. Indiana bats raise their young in mixed hardwood forests scattered with large dead and dying trees that have sections of bark that separate from the trunk, providing protected crevices for the bats to roost under. "They literally come right out of their roost trees one after another [at dusk] and go down these forest roads at a tremendous clip, foraging a little on the way, but for the most part just traveling to where they're going to feed," said Darling. Like most bats, they eat just about whatever insects they can find, mostly flies, beetles, and moths.

The goal of the bat-trapping effort at Shelburne Farms was to determine if any Indiana bats were found there. "This is a site that we think has potential habitat for Indiana bats," Darling explained. "It's at the right elevation, it has the tree species composition that seems to work in our favor, it has saw-timber size trees, and it has the travel corridors [through the forest] they might use and where we'd be able to catch them if they were here. The idea is to trap beyond their known range to see if we can delineate the boundaries of their range. We're trying to see just how far north they've come. We know they're found just south of here. And we've trapped just a little north of here and haven't been successful. It takes a lot of negatives to be convinced of the exact range."

So after a quick round of introductions in the parking lot, the eight of us climbed into three vehicles and drove the many roads and pathways through the farm to assess where best to put up the traps. Bat traps are like oversized volleyball nets: poles on either end holding a fine, mesh net that's nearly invisible to the naked eye. Unlike a volleyball net, though, this net can extend from the ground to the top of the 10-foot poles, and up to three poles can be stacked on top of each other so bats flying up to 30 feet above the ground can be captured. Since Indiana bats travel forest corridors to and from their feeding grounds, the plan was to set up several traps in potentially high-traffic areas. The ideal trapping site was at a spot along the path that was just barely wide enough to stretch the net taut between the forest edges—about 20 yards wide—and which had a canopy of trees overhanging it so bats couldn't fly over the top of the net. After an hour of site selection and two hours of setting up the traps, we grabbed some dinner and returned to the farm as dusk was approaching. Three of the seven traps we set up were double height (20 feet high), while the rest were singles. Susi vonOettingen, a U.S. Fish and Wildlife Service endangered species biologist who oversees protection of rare plants, mussels, and bats in New England, enthusiastically tried to convince the rest of the team to set up a triple-high trap, but an appropriate location was never found.

In addition to vonOettingen, Darling, and I, the bat-trapping team included a University of Vermont graduate student, a Fish and Wildlife Service enforcement officer, an enthusiastic volunteer, and a Vermont Forest Service biologist and his stepfather. It was an eclectic group, few of whom were required to be there but all of whom were excited about the potential for working closely with bats. Everyone except me had been inoculated against rabies because they had worked with bats before—a bat-handling requirement for which I was sadly unprepared. After dividing into teams, we went to our designated traps to await the right time to open the nets. Nets opened too early might capture birds that are still active, diverting our attention during the crucial first moments of dusk when bats leave their daytime roosts and begin foraging for food. An announcement from Darling over the radio at about 9 P.M. set everyone in motion opening the nets, and then the waiting began.

We didn't wait long. The game plan was to check each net every fifteen minutes so that any bats caught wouldn't be stressed for an extended period of time. My team—me, Darling, vonOettingen, and volunteer Barry Genzlinger—had three traps to monitor, each set up about 50 yards apart. The first time we stumbled through the total darkness to check the traps, we got one. As we approached the net, the bat sat quietly entangled, seemingly resolved to its fate. But when Darling began the sometimes challenging task of untangling it, the tiny bat came to life, squawking and fluttering. I didn't realize that bats made any sound other than their silent-to-humans echolocation, but this one (and others later) made a high-pitched noise like the sound made by pushing the rewind button on a cassette tape player when the tape is already in play mode. It was uncomfortable to hear—almost like the bat was crying—and I was pleased when Darling finally removed it from the net and it calmed down.

Wearing a miner's headlamp and one leather glove, Darling had set up the tailgate of his truck as a laboratory, with notebooks, measuring instruments, tools, and other gear used to collect the necessary data quickly before releasing the bat. This one was a northern long-eared bat (*Myotis septentrionalis*), identified in part by the long, spike-like piece of cartilage called a tragus sticking up in its ear. Darling put it briefly in a plastic bag to weigh it with a hand-held scale—it weighed a whopping 8.5 grams, which probably means it was pregnant—then measured various body parts and delicately placed a band on it. Unlike birds, which are banded with tiny aluminum or colored plastic rings around their legs, bats are banded on the "forearm" of their wing. Extreme care must be taken to ensure that the metal band doesn't puncture the wing membrane, which eventually could lead to difficulty flying and foraging.

Despite years of working with dozens of biologists on their wildlife research, this was the first bat I had ever seen up close. I suppose that's partly an endorsement that my house is well-built and bats have never found their way into the attic (that I know of). Just in case the rest of the evening was a bust, I took a few moments to focus on this incredible creature. With Darling holding it in his gloved hand, I stroked the bat's wing and found it felt as I expected, like a doctor's rubber glove. What I didn't expect was how incredibly thin the bones were that the wing membrane stretched between. A bat's wing is essentially the biological equivalent to a human hand, and the membrane stretches between the bones of its "fingers" sort of like the webbing of a duck's foot. Yet the bones of this bat's wing were no thicker than a pin and amazed me with their flexibility and durability. I stroked the furry back of this bat, feeling its warm body and beating heart and occasionally feeling a pulsing like a shiver that Darling said happens when the bat echolocates. We couldn't hear the sound it was making, but with my hand on its back I sure could feel it.

Many people, maybe even the majority, are afraid of bats. It's mostly old-wives' tales and misinformation, of course, about bats getting tangled in their hair or sucking blood (though some do). I've made it a point of telling these frightened individuals of the benefits of bats and that there's nothing they should be concerned about. I'll still do that, but in the interest of full disclosure, I must admit that their teeth are pretty scary. This tiny northern long-eared bat squirmed and chattered in Darling's hand, all the while constantly flashing a mouth full of sharp teeth and trying to bite its handler. Its mouth is so small and weak that its teeth can't really do much damage, but I imagine that anyone who was already afraid of bats would be even more afraid if they saw their teeth. And there's no way I would ever be able to dissuade them.

The traps were empty the second time we checked them, but fifteen minutes later we had our second capture, a big brown bat (*Eptesicus fuscus*). Living up to its name, this bat weighed more than twice as much as the previous one and its wingspan was three times as long. And the teeth on this species can cause serious harm. VonOettingen refuses to handle big browns, preferring to leave that job to the experts, and Darling insists on wearing his leather gloves even though he sometimes leaves them off when handling the smaller species.

A second big brown bat was in the trap the next time we checked, and then graduate student Kristen Watrous called on the radio to report that she was on her way with five little brown bats that needed processing.

Bats don't just live in the forest at Shelburne Farms. Thousands of them also live in the inn, barns, and other outbuildings scattered throughout the estate. The traps that Watrous was monitoring were near the coach barn. Most of the bats living in buildings are little browns, the species that most humans are somewhat familiar with because the females typically roost in buildings in the summer, especially in hot attics where nursery colonies can number in the hundreds or thousands. Virtually identical in size and coloration to Indiana bats, little brown bats swarm out of their roosts each evening and forage along set hunting patterns around houses and forests.

The bats living in the Shelburne Farms Inn and other buildings became an increasing concern to the site's manager in 2000. So he called in one of the region's leading bat-house builders, Barry Genzlinger, to build a custom-designed bat house to encourage the bats to relocate from the farm buildings to what is now the largest bat house in Vermont. Genzlinger, who calls himself the bat guy ("the name Batman was already taken," he said with a smirk), owns the Chiroptera Cabin Co., a sidelight activity that allows the software designer to indulge his passion for bats.

"About ten years ago I noticed a bat emerging from the rafters in my house, and I got curious about them," he explained. "So I did a little studying and built a bat house, but no bats moved in. After some additional research, I moved the house to a pole, and that was my first successful bat house." Since then, he's become obsessed with bat-house designing and has become a national expert on the subject. Genzlinger has designed thirteen different kinds of bat houses and conducted studies in collaboration with the nonprofit group Bat Conservation International of bat preferences for house size, shape, and color. He reports that most bats prefer a ¾-inch gap to squeeze themselves into the house. He also said that he was the first to discover that Indiana bats seem to prefer an odd rocket-shaped house on a pole, perhaps because it mimics their preference for roosting on tree trunks.

In addition to building bat houses, the somewhat nerdy-looking bat guy has recruited his wife and daughter to his "bat team" as well. Together, they travel in their equally nerdy-looking minivan covered in bat illustrations and slogans, visiting schools and community groups throughout the Northeast and educating anyone who will listen about the bats of the world.

The bat house that Genzlinger constructed at Shelburne Farms can house more than twenty-five hundred bats. And while not all of the little brown bats roosting in the inn and other buildings have relocated to the bat guy's bat condominium, visitors to the inn are now far less likely to be spooked by a bat emerging from the building to feed.

"Lazarro Spallanzani, an Italian scientist in the late 1700s, provided the first insights on how bats operated in the dark," wrote York University bat biologist M. Brock Fenton in *BATS Magazine*. "He put a bat and an owl in a semi-dark room and found that both could orient well in low light. The bat also flew effortlessly in complete darkness, but the owl bumped into objects in its flight path. When he placed a sack over the bat's head it, too, became disoriented. Spallanzani concluded that bats used a 'sixth sense' to orient."

Since then, biologists have learned that bats "see" in the dark not with their eyes but by emitting high-frequency pulses from their mouth or nose. When the sound waves hit an object in its path, an echo reflects back to the bat, which can determine what the object is, how far away it is, and whether it is moving. A bat can even tell the size, shape, and texture of the object using echolocation.

When we released the second big brown bat after processing it, Genzlinger pulled out a small, hand-held device he called a bat detector. The device converts a bat's echolocation into a clicking sound audible to human ears so we would know when a bat was around us even if the darkness prevented us from seeing it. As the big brown flew away, the bat detector clicked loudly to indicate that the bat was still nearby and echolocating every few seconds. It didn't take us long to determine that the bat was perched on the trunk of a tree just 20 feet above our processing station. By periodically turning on the bat detector or sweeping the tree with a flashlight, we knew that big brown bat remained nearby for close to half an hour before moving on.

"The frequency and the rate they emit the pulses is often associated with the habitat they are in," explained Darling. "A northern long-eared bat, for example, is in a much-cluttered forest and therefore needs to know a lot more about what's going on around it compared to bats that feed in more open areas like the hoary bat. Most of the forest bats don't really pick up on anything [with their echolocation] unless it's within 2 to 6 meters away, so they have to constantly send out those pulses. When bats are feeding, once they pick up on a flying insect, they send out pulses more rapidly to help them home in on that bug."

As Watrous explained it to me, "there's an evolutionary trade-off between high frequency and low frequency, because high frequency attenuates very fast in the air so you have to be very close to your target to identify it." It's the difference between a very precise but short field of view and a fuzzy but long field of view. Because Indiana bats live in forests filled with objects spaced very close together, all they need to know is what's immediately in front of them. For forest bats, the high-frequency pulses help them identify insects and trees just a few feet away while ignoring what's in the distance. Hoary bats, on the other hand, fly quickly and feed in open areas, so they use their lower-frequency pulses to detect targets a considerable distance away. "If it couldn't detect something until it was up close, it would have flown by it by the time it detected it," said Watrous.

Not only are there differences in the echolocation pulses between forest-dwelling bats and bats of open areas, there are identifiable differences even within each of these subgroups. As we continued monitoring the traps throughout the night, Darling demonstrated these differences using a laptop computer attached to another unusual device that he set beside an open field. This was another variety of a bat detector called an Anabat, which converts a bat's echolocation pulses into electronic signals that are processed, compressed, and diagrammed on the computer in real time. And since every bat species emits a slightly different pattern of pulses—called call sequences—it's possible to use the Anabat to identify the different species of bats feeding in an area.

At midnight in the Shelburne Farms forest, the darkness was complete. No moon or stars were visible, and at times it was impossible even to see the person standing beside me. Occasionally the sound of a tree frog or bird would echo in the forest, and once an opossum walked noisily through the leaf litter nearby, but the only illumination came from our headlamps—which were usually turned off—and an occasional firefly. By the edge of the forest where Darling set up the Anabat, though, the computer monitor gave off an eerie glow. Every time a bat flew by and emitted a pulse, the machine immediately detected it and converted it into an unusual graph that looked a bit like a chart of the rise and fall of the stock market.

"You need a good clear call sequence, based on the slope of the line, the duration of the call, the low and high frequencies, to identify the species," Darling said. "And each species emits a variety of different calls—

calls associated with searching for food, approaching food, or homing in on an object just as it feeds. Biologists need to begin building a call library to help distinguish between those species whose calls are very similar. And the call library needs to be regionally based because western hoary bats have a different call than eastern hoary bats, for example."

Over the course of about two hours that night, the Anabat detected and graphed eighteen bat call sequences. The hoary bat, whose call is very low, long, and nearly entirely at the same frequency, was the easiest to identify. On the computer monitor, it looked like a long horizontal line with a slight upward turn at the beginning. The smaller forest bats had short, staccato calls that looked much more vertical on the graph because they went from high frequency to lower frequency very quickly (80 kilohertz to 40). And because several forest bats, including little brown bat, long-eared bat, and Indiana bat, all have similar calls, we were unable to determine which forest bats had been flying by the detector.

"When the Anabat was developed, biologists thought that they weren't going to have to catch bats any more to study them," said Darling. "But even though you might be able to identify bats to species using the Anabat, you don't know whether it's one bat flying around and around again and again or it could be fifty different individuals. So we have to use both methods."

It was more than two hours before another bat was caught in the traps. At 12:45 A.M., we found a small bat in the double-high trap farthest from the processing station. As Darling began untangling it, I could tell from the tone of his voice that he was excited, even though he wouldn't say why. He pointed out that there wasn't much difference between the color of the fur on its face and the color on its throat, and even though the bat was still stuck in the net, Darling checked and found that the hairs on its toes weren't especially long. Both characteristics suggested that it might be an Indiana bat. Finally, the bat was disentangled and Darling took a closer look, yet still he wasn't sure. Walking back to the processing station, he stomped loudly, clearly stressed over his uncertain identification of this bat and simultaneously tense with excitement. He called vonOettingen and Watrous on the walkie-talkie and, without explaining why, told them to rush over from their trap locations to help us.

After weeks of trapping almost every night until 3 A.M. and still showing up for meetings and the other daytime responsibilities of his job, Darling was clearly weary. He hadn't found *any* Indiana bats—including at the sites where they had raised young the previous few years—so he was somewhat frustrated. And he clearly was jubilant with the possibility that he might have finally found the northernmost point in the species' breeding range in Vermont. But he also didn't want to get too excited and make a mistake, so he began trying to convince himself that it was something else.

After what seemed like an hour but was probably just ten minutes, von Oettingen and Watrous arrived from opposite directions. And ten seconds later, Darling's bubble had burst. They pointed out that this bat's feet were too small to be an Indiana, and they found one toe that had a hair long enough to convince them that it was just another little brown bat. Darling's disappointment—and mine, too—was palpable. He went through the motions of processing this bat and released it without fanfare.

The rest of the evening was a continuation of that momentary letdown, as no more bats were trapped and our exhaustion set in. The one bit of excitement was provided by a young barred owl that perched on a dead branch high above the trap nearest to the meadow and repeatedly gave an odd hooting call in hopes that its parent would bring it a meal. It didn't. The barred owl happens to be the only bird call that I can mimic accurately, so I let out a couple calls of "Whoo-hoo hoo-hoo, whoo-hoo hoo-hoo awh," and we watched as the agitated young owl flew back and forth above us expecting to soon satisfy its hunger. And then we called it a night. Or a morning.

Just a few miles south of Shelburne Farms is the center of Indiana bat breeding activity in Vermont. Discovered in 2001, the Middlebury colony is in a woodlot about 100 acres in size, adjacent to a healthy wetland, and owned by landowners who like bats. Sixty-five Indiana bats have been trapped and banded in the colony, and 270 were seen exiting from a known roost tree at dusk one day in 2004, making it one of the largest breeding colonies in the country.

"Much of the research [on Indiana bats] that has been done across the country focuses on the availability of clusters of roost trees," Darling explained. "You can look at the Middlebury site and find clusters of large, dead and dying trees. They will not necessarily be widely distributed throughout that colony's habitat and range, but just having a bunch of excellent roost trees available within proximity seems to be of significance." It also helps if some of those trees are among the tallest trees in the forest, emerging high above the canopy so the roosting female bats are exposed to a great deal of sunlight and heat in late spring, which speeds the growth of developing bat embryos.

What's perhaps most important is that the forest must have several appropriate roost trees—not just one big one—because Indiana bats like to move around. "These bats have one or two primary roost trees, and these tend to be the larger ones with large areas of bark or crevices available to many bats. And then there are alternate trees—five, six, seven of them—that are like satellite trees that they will go to periodically," said Darling. "The thinking is that these animals are dependent on a very ephemeral resource—a standing dead or dying tree which we have, in some of our earlier research, gone back to days later and found to have fallen to the ground. So these animals probably are wired to check things out, to go find another place, spend a couple nights there, go back and maybe tell everyone, just in case this tree goes down." The preferred trees tend to be shagbark hickory, white oak, and elms that have large pieces of bark that curl up or barely hang on as they get old, which the bats can get under and roost beneath. Darling said there is a clear relationship between the places where these old, decaying trees are found and where Indiana bats live. And one place these trees are found in relative abundance is the southern Champlain Valley of Vermont, especially Addison County.

Lake Champlain serves as the northern boundary between New York and Vermont. The lake runs 110 miles from north to south and is 12 miles wide. While its surface area is tiny compared to that of the Great Lakes to the west, in 1998 President Bill Clinton signed into law a bill that briefly recognized Lake Champlain as the sixth Great Lake. While the push to pass the law made the region the butt of numerous jokes on late-night television and raised the ire of many organizations working to protect the original Great Lakes, the law qualifies the region for more federal research funding, which was the purpose for seeking the designation in the first place.

The lake's strategic location between the Hudson River in New York and the St. Lawrence River in Canada has resulted in a rich maritime history, first during the Revolutionary War and the War of 1812, then as an important region for commerce and merchant fleets, and finally as a popular recreational boating site. According to Darling, the Indiana bats are closely associated with the valley's clay plain forests around the southern portion of the lake. "The elevation in Addison County is limited to somewhere in the 500-foot range, which the bats seem to prefer," he said, "and the bats are obviously linked to the forested woodlots that are a part of this landscape. The Addison County landscape below 500 feet is rather fragmented, so there are lots of woodlots and lots of fields. Fragmentation is a good thing from an Indiana bat perspective because they are found in a landscape that is between 20 and 60 percent forested. Why that is, we're not entirely sure, but it was probably a savannah species presettlement and does well with big trees at the edge of the forest."

It's obvious today that this region plays an important role as a breeding location for a significant number of Indiana bats, but in 2000 nobody knew it. "For years we've driven down the Champlain Valley and we would have laughed at the idea that the place was full of Indiana bats," Darling said. "Yet at the time we had two if not three thousand Indiana bats right here!" The revelation came as a result of a research project on the opposite shore of the lake in Mineville, New York, at a mine where Indiana bats were known to hibernate.

According to the Town of Moriah Historical Society, the Barton Hill iron mine was opened in the early 1800s on Hague Mountain on property owned by Caleb D. Barton. When he died in 1856, the mine was acquired by Bay State Iron Co. and later by the Witherbee Sherman Co., which, in the 1880s, found a pocket of ore called Lovers Hole that was considered the richest iron mine ever developed in the United States. From that one pocket, the company shipped more than 60,000 tons of Bessemer ore. Numerous new tunnels were driven into the hillside in the early 1900s in an effort to find additional rich pockets of ore. Ownership of the mine shifted again in the 1930s to Republic Steel based in Cleveland, the country's third-largest steel company behind U.S. Steel and Bethlehem Steel. But the iron-mining industry in the Adirondacks, once the major employer in the region, declined rapidly in the middle of the century, and today it barely exists. The Barton Hill mine is now owned by International Paper Co., which has logging operations nearby, and the 1,900 acres surrounding the mine is protected by The Nature Conservancy with a conservation easement to ensure that the 120,000 bats that hibernate there are undisturbed. The mine is the winter home to six species of bat, including approximately 7,000 Indiana bats, as well as little brown, big brown, northern long-eared, and small-footed bats, and the Eastern pipistrelle.

When Indiana bats return to the Barton Hill mine in August and September, they swarm around the entrance each night for weeks in a ritual that leads to mating. "The swarming behavior is the most amazing event, and all migratory bats do it," Darling said. "As it gets dark, the bats take off from their roost and begin to fly around the entrance. Bats from other caves come over, and as the night progresses, more and more bats come. We think it's a courtship display. It's the breeding season, and they're just checking out different sites, fattening up for the winter, checking out different bats, and mating." This behavior continues until October, when food is no longer available and the bats enter the mines and caves to hibernate.

In 2000, the U.S. Fish and Wildlife Service and New York Department of Environmental Conservation attached radio transmitters to twenty Indiana bats in the Barton Hill mine to see where they breed. Based on research conducted up to that time, it was believed that most Indiana bats migrate approximately 300 miles to their maternity colonies, so the expectation was that the bats in Barton Hill mine likely were raising their young in Maine or Cape Cod or Canada somewhere. But to everyone's surprise, the bats traveled less than one-tenth that distance and plopped down instead in Addison County, Vermont. Since then, state and federal biologists in both states have been working closely together to learn more about the needs of the bats and to protect their critical habitat. According to Darling, the biologists joke about whether they're protecting Vermont bats that winter in New York or New York bats that summer in Vermont.

When Darling took over responsibility for the Vermont side of the equation, he went looking for a graduate student to help him study the bats. That's how he found Watrous. Originally from Rotterdam, New York, she earned a biology degree at Hartwick College, did a couple years of work as a field technician studying Delmarva fox squirrels in Virginia, and ended up at University of Vermont looking for a research project when Darling turned up. "I'm really interested in doing work with endangered species," she said. "I had never done anything with bats before, but it sounded great. I'm most interested in mammals, but I would have done anything if it was endangered species–related. If there was money for Scott to hire me to continue this work after I graduate, I would jump at it. It's a small community of researchers, and the status of bat research is so young that every piece of data you collect is important. You feel like you're really making a dent in it."

But the initial work wasn't easy, partly because Watrous never got to sleep. "It took two field seasons to get started," she explained.

> The state needed someone to look at what the habitat is so they can manage and get a better idea of the population in the state. So we went to sites where they knew Indiana bats were—maternity sites—we captured bats, we put radio transmitters on them, and tracked them. Overnight, we would have a crew of three people following them. Every two and a half minutes, we would take a triangulation on a bat. During the daytime, we found what roost trees they were using, marked the trees, collected data on the roost trees and in a one-tenth hectare circular plot around the roost tree, and then used GIS data for landscape-level analysis. Now I'm in the analysis phase, trying to put all that data together to pop a map out that says this might be where to look next.
>
> The first shocker of the first field season that we weren't prepared for is that the bats move around so much. They'd change roost trees sometimes as often as every two days! We were under the impression that they were in these small groups of trees, and then they were gone. They were in large DBH [diameter at breast height] trees, small DBH, live shagbark hickories, dead pines that have no bark left. If it's raining, the interior of a dead tree might get wet, so maybe they'll move to a live shagbark that has more protection from the rain. If it's too hot they might move, too cold they might move,

Watrous said. "You think you know what's going on, and then they disappear again. . . . They move so fast and they zip around so often that you're constantly moving."

By the time we had closed the traps and I had driven an hour to my friend's bed-and-breakfast, it was 4:30 A.M. before I got to bed. The next afternoon, we started the process again, though this time it was just Darling, Watrous, and I. We had left most of the traps in place the night before, so set-up was a lot quicker. Darling decided to move a couple traps that hadn't caught anything the previous night and stack them three-high along the edge of a meadow. That was the site where the Anabat had detected eighteen bat call sequences the previous night, including at least one hoary bat, so we went to work setting it up. It took us nearly an hour to stack three sets of two metal poles on top of each other, attach overlapping nets from bottom to top, and secure the entire structure to trees and wooden stakes. We also set up another kind of trap called a harp trap in a tiny path that Darling thought had great potential. The 6-by-6-foot harp trap looks somewhat like the musical instrument, with two sets of vertical monofilament lines a few inches apart with a clear plastic liner below. If a bat approaches, it maneuvers to fly between the first set of lines but bumps into the second set and drops into the plastic liner.

At 9 P.M., we optimistically opened the nets once again, and at 9:30 we had our first capture, a female big brown bat. As Darling processed it, he checked for signs of pregnancy by looking at its nipples. "Whoa! Those are bigger than mine," he yelled out, then laughed in embarrassment when he saw me write down his best quote of the night. This big brown bat turned out to be the heaviest of all the bats we captured that weekend, weighing in at 20.2 grams.

For the next three hours, we didn't have a moment to rest. Every time we checked the traps, we caught at least one bat, and Darling sometimes wasn't finished processing the first captures before we had some more. At 9:50, we caught a pregnant little brown bat, and at 10:05 came a male northern long-eared bat. Then came two big browns that had faces that reminded me of fox pups, nibbling on Darling's gloved hand, closing their eyes, and turning their heads away when the offensive headlamp shone at them.

It was a warm and muggy night, much buggier than the night before, and the breeze made the triple-high net in the meadow billow and sway, which probably helped the bats see and avoid it. At 11:15, we caught our first—and only—bat in the triple, a very pregnant little brown bat that was terribly entangled and needed all three of us to remove. On our return with the bat to the truck for processing, we passed the trap that yielded the most captures during the weekend and found a bat that Darling quickly identified as a little brown. But as Watrous and I continued walking to the truck with the bat caught in the triple, we heard Darling mutter "uh-oh." When he joined us at the truck, he showed us the reason for that comment. The bat's feet were extremely small compared to the others we had caught so far, the fur on its face was dark and gave the appearance of a mask, its teeth were tiny, and it had that small lobe of cartilage on the edge of its tail that helps identify Indiana bats. But this wasn't an Indiana bat. To Darling, though, it was almost as exciting. This one was an Eastern small-footed bat (*Myotis leibii*), the smallest bat found in Vermont, a species considered threatened in the state and a candidate for the federal endangered species list. It weighed just 5 grams. Darling said that small-footed bats are probably naturally rare and are found in rock crevices with exposure to the sun, which raised a question about why it would be found in the forest at Shelburne Farms where appropriate habitat appeared lacking.

After midnight, in between catching several more little browns and a big brown, Darling excitedly returned from checking the traps and had another small-footed bat in his hands. In four years of bat trapping, he had never caught two small-footed bats in one night. Even though he didn't band the first one, he knew this one was a different individual because the previous one had numerous orange mites in its ear and this one had none.

Our excitement died down when no bats were captured in the next hour. As we began disassembling the traps, we realized that despite capturing two dozen bats of four species and seeing call sequences for a fifth species on the Anabat, we had struck out finding our target species. The absence of Indiana bats at Shelburne Farms, while disappointing, helped Darling in his continuing quest to establish the species' range in Vermont.

But it was late June, when Indiana bats should be nursing young, and Darling had yet to find even a single Indiana anywhere in the state. "We've been trapping the sites that seem to be most conducive to capturing bats," he said. "But it has been an extremely wet and extremely cold spring—the coldest May in thirty-four years in Vermont—so that seems to have really put a twist on the reproductive condition of these bats. Things are going to be very delayed this season. Even the roost trees that we've become so familiar with over the last three or four years aren't holding a bat."

He speculated that the cold weather has left the bats in poor reproductive condition. "These females mate in the fall, they store the sperm all winter, and upon emergence from hibernation, they become pregnant. The development of that embryo depends on that bat being in an active state. If the weather is cold, it's rainy, and there are no bugs available, that bat will just enter a state of torpor under a tree and not develop that embryo. At some point that embryo grows slower and slower and may not grow at all."

A month later, Darling sent me an email summarizing the season. Despite continued trapping just outside the known range of the species, he caught no Indiana bats. That negative result suggests that he has confirmed the species range in the state, although he'll probably do one more summer of surveying just in case. As for the maternity colony in Middlebury, he never found it. He captured two Indiana bats in the area one night, and counted a total of seventeen bats exiting all of the known roost trees at the site, when 270 were counted exiting from just one tree the previous year. "We can only speculate that the colony was using a roost tree that we were not previously aware of," he wrote.

Despite their absence in 2005, Darling was confident that he would find the colony again the following year. But he had less confidence about the long-term future of Indiana bats in Vermont. "I'm worried," he told me. "This is one of the fastest-growing areas of the state, and one of the areas of the state with the least amount of protected land. It's 90 percent privately owned. My goal has always been that we'll be successful when private landowners will be happy to hear that they've got Indiana bats on their property and not consider it an economic threat. How we go about doing that is going to be the challenge. The future of farmland and forestland in the Champlain Valley will determine the future of the Indiana bat. The bats are doing great right now, but I think we need to incorporate them into the plans for the future of the valley."

7

Atlantic Salmon

For several years, the National Audubon Society has made available a *Seafood Lover's Guide* aimed at educating consumers about the fish they purchase at restaurants and supermarkets. The effort is driven by concerns about the over-fishing of many species, the management of fisheries around the world, and the methods used to capture fish. For instance, the guide advises that consumers steer clear of purchasing Atlantic cod, bluefin tuna, Atlantic flounder, and Patagonian toothfish—the last a fish that the seafood marketers have renamed the more appetizing-sounding name Chilean sea bass—because these species have been depleted and their populations are not likely to rebound soon. On the other hand, Audubon says that farmed catfish, Pacific halibut, wild Alaskan salmon, sardines, and anchovies are in good shape and may be purchased without worry.

While consumers are encouraged to follow Audubon's suggestions, making the environmentally correct seafood choices is a complex challenge. That's because most of the fish consumed in America doesn't come from where we think it does. The crab used in Maryland crab cakes most likely comes from Indonesia, Thailand, or Venezuela, even when it is ordered at a restaurant on the Chesapeake Bay. Bay scallops, traditionally from New England and a popular item on menus across the country, today are raised primarily in China. And nearly 90 percent of all shrimp, the number-one seafood consumed in the United States, is now imported from farms in Thailand, India, Vietnam, Ecuador, and China rather than caught wild in traditional locations in the Gulf of Mexico.

"The globalization of the fishing industry and the decline of many fish populations in U.S. waters has meant that the fish we eat no longer comes from where it once came," said fisheries economist James Anderson of the University of Rhode Island and author of *The International Seafood Trade.* "When we shut down our fisheries here, our consumption of fish doesn't go down. We just get it elsewhere."

Further evidence of the globalization of the industry comes from the fact that fish caught or raised in the United States, such as cod and flounder, often are shipped to China to be cut into fillets and then shipped back to U.S. markets. Anderson notes that it's cheaper to do that than to have the work done here. One of the primary technological trends in the seafood industry is aquaculture—fish farming—which now accounts for more than 30 percent of the global seafood harvest, but the practice carries with it a long list of negative environmental impacts.

These issues are part of the foundation of the debate over the difficulty of restoring Maine's population of wild Atlantic salmon (*Salmo salar*), one of the rarest fish in New England and one that is included on Audubon's list of fish to avoid purchasing (though it is also generally unavailable for sale except in Greenland).

Salmon is consumed at a rate of 7.4 kilograms per capita in the United States, making it the third-most-popular seafood in the country after shrimp and tuna. More than three-quarters of that comes from salmon farms, mostly in Chile and Canada. Wild salmon consumed in the United States is caught primarily in Alaskan waters, where fishermen haul in approximately 350,000 metric tons of salmon each year, valued at about $300 million. Smaller quantities of wild salmon are also caught in the waters off the Pacific Northwest. Those who support the wild salmon fishing industry vehemently oppose expansion of salmon aquaculture farms—it's even been banned in Alaska—but that industry is growing dramatically around the world. Norway alone produces more farm-raised salmon each year than is caught by the entire commercial fishery in Alaska. Yet in the United States, the salmon aquaculture industry is "microscopic," according to Anderson, only existing in Maine and Washington. He said the industry isn't likely to grow here because it can't compete with farms in Canada and Chile, and "because regulators and landowners and rich people who own summer homes on the coast are doing everything they can do to stop it. There are all sorts of fears and phobias, only some of which are based in reality."

The commercial fishery for wild Atlantic salmon in New England is long gone. It was a major industry throughout much of the eighteenth and nineteenth centuries, with the largest run occurring on the Connecticut River. But it was decimated before 1900 by dams, over-fishing, and industrial wastes generated by the burgeoning industrial revolution, and now the species is struggling to hang on in the wild.

With the commercial fishery shut down, recreational salmon fishing all but banned, and wild Atlantic salmon reduced to a tiny fraction of its former population, biologists with several state and federal agencies are trying to figure out how to restore salmon to sustainable numbers. In May 2006, I joined National Marine Fisheries Service biologists Christine Lipsky and Graham Goulette at the Head Tide Dam on the Sheepscot River in Alna, Maine, to see how many salmon smolts—two- or three-year-old fish that are ready to move from freshwater to salt water— were migrating from the river to the ocean. Alna is just north of Wiscasset, the small tourist village where classic old New England homes line Main Street, two church steeples rise above the tree line, and a long queue of hungry visitors is always waiting to order a lobster salad roll at Red's Eats, a tiny shack in the center of town that serves up hundreds of the popular item each day.

The river is about a half mile wide at Wiscasset, but a few miles upstream in Alna, it is just 30 yards wide and an old dam holds back the flowing water, some of which spills forcefully through openings at either end and continues around and over boulders and rip-rap and under a one-lane steel bridge. The concrete dam was built in 1940 to replace a wooden dam that had been constructed a hundred years earlier to power five adjacent mills in what was once a bustling village that included a church, school, and general store, all now abandoned. It's the first dam on the river, which is tidal up to that point, and the first impediment to the salmon trying to swim upstream to spawn.

The noise of the rushing river drowned out most of the morning bird song as I awaited the biologists, but avian activity was clearly visible: a rough-winged swallow brought nesting material to a hole in the side of the dam; an osprey flew up and down the river in search of a meal to feed its nestlings; and a phoebe perched on a wire cable hanging across the river and bobbed its tail repeatedly. Below the dam were two 5-foot rotary-screw traps strategically placed so fish coming downstream and through the openings in the dam could not avoid them. Looking somewhat like a small Everglades airboat, the trap captured whatever fish swam between its pontoons yet allowed the water to continue downstream. The biologists begin trapping salmon smolts when the water temperature warms to about 10 degrees Centigrade, usually around April 15, and continue through mid-May when most of the smolts should have passed through on their way to the open ocean. The most smolts caught at the Alna dam in any one day in 2006 was fifty-five, but the day before I visited just fourteen were captured.

When Lipsky and Goulette arrived, we strapped on chest waders and lifejackets and needed just three steps in the fast-moving water to reach the first trap. We were disappointed when we opened it, as it contained just five smolts, along with six common shiners, two golden shiners, five eels, two alewives, one tiny lamprey, and one green frog. All but the smolts were tossed back into the river to continue on their way. Upon opening the second trap, however, Goulette enthusiastically called out, "We got fish!" Large numbers of fish were darting about in the holding tank, each species schooling separately. Unfortunately, most were not salmon. As Lipsky took notes, Goulette repeatedly dipped his net into the tank, pulled out several fish at a time, and called out the identification of every individual captured. In addition to fourteen salmon smolts, there were seventy-five golden shiners, twenty common shiners, sixteen creek chub, forty-three alewives, one salamander, and two pumpkinseed, the latter a warm-water pond species that was totally unexpected in the cool river.

After removing the smolts from the traps, Lipsky and Goulette set up a processing station on the nearby rocks to collect measurements and other data before releasing them back into the water. One by one, Goulette transferred each fish into a series of red buckets—the first contained an anesthetic to make them easier to handle—and measured and weighed them. Using a device like a small paper hole-punch, a tiny sample of their tail fin was collected for later genetic analysis. Finally, Goulette lightly brushed a pocketknife across the side of each smolt to collect a sample of its scales, which grow somewhat like tree rings and can be used to de-termine its age. It was a practiced and efficient process, as the biologists recorded the measurements and passed tools back and forth like a surgi-cal team so the fish could be returned to the river as soon as possible. They noted that two of the smolts had a slight red gash beneath their jaws that indicated a "hooking injury" as a result of being caught by an an-gler, and one had markings on its side from being caught in a net.

According to Lipsky, who started her career at a Pacific salmon hatch-ery in Alaska before returning east to work with Atlantic salmon in Rhode Island and Maine, the data being collected is helping to answer a wide range of questions about salmon biology and ecology. "We're tak-ing genetic samples to determine parentage and to look for commercial aquaculture influences," she said. "We take the gill samples to see how the fish are adjusting to the saltwater transition. We're comparing lengths and weights from year to year to see if there is any shift and to compare wild fish to hatchery fish. And we're looking at scale samples of smolts and adults because we're interested in seeing the proportions of fish going out to sea at age two versus at age three, and to see if that's changing. All these changes can indicate that something is going on that's different from the past.

"The perfect example is Penobscot River adult salmon. We've noticed that more fish are coming back after only one year at sea than thirty years ago, and we're wondering if that's a consequence of global warming be-cause they're growing faster. In any event, we've experienced very low water levels and high water temperatures in several rivers. This year we've had water levels that are the lowest on record for that specific day on several occasions."

Salmon are anadromous fish—they spend the first part of their life in freshwater and most of their adult life in salt water—which requires them to go through a number of life stages and complex physiological changes. Adult salmon lay their pea-sized, orange eggs in nests called redds on the gravel bottom of rivers and streams, typically in late autumn. When the eggs hatch the following spring, the tiny fish are called alevins and have a yolk sack attached to provide them with nutrition. That yolk sack soon becomes depleted and absorbed into the body, at which point the fish emerge from the gravel to feed on aquatic insects and are then called fry, a stage that lasts until they are about 2 inches long and develop camou-flaging vertical stripes and become parr. This stage lasts for one to three years until they grow to about 6 inches long and are ready to go through smoltification, a dramatic change in their body chemistry that allows them to survive in salt water.

"The timing of the smoltification process depends a lot on water tem-perature and the size of the fish," explained Lipsky. "In warmer rivers that have a salmon population, some fish may go through smoltification at age one. But for the most part in Maine, for a fish that's hatched in the wild, it's going to be two or three years old before it becomes a smolt . . . There are a lot of things that can get in the way of the smolti-fication process, which is why we study smolts. If the fish is going to have a problem, this is the one stage where it will really stand out."

After smoltification, salmon enter the Gulf of Maine and travel north to the waters off the eastern shores of Greenland, where they feed on small fish and develop into mature adults weighing 8 to 15 pounds. After one to three years at sea, they return to their natal river to spawn, typi-cally in May or June. Unlike Pacific salmon, which die after spawning, many Atlantic salmon return to the ocean or overwinter in the river after spawning—a period when they are called kelts or black salmon—and they may spawn again two or three years later.

But very few fish complete all of these stages before they die. In most of the rivers in Maine where salmon historically have bred, fewer than ten adults return to spawn in a typical year. So in 2000, Atlantic salmon from eight Maine rivers—the Dennys, East Machias, Machias, Pleasant, Narraguagus, Cove Brook, Ducktrap, and Sheepscot—were listed on the federal endangered species list. In all the other Maine rivers where salmon are found, they are listed as a species of concern. Atlantic salmon populations in eastern Canada and northern Europe are in similarly dire circumstances, while the species was wiped out entirely from southern New England rivers prior to 1865. Only in the Penobscot River of Maine, where 90 percent of Maine's returning adult salmon spawn, do Atlantic salmon still maintain relatively healthy populations, and even there Lipsky said the number of fish returning to spawn is "a drop in the bucket" compared to historic numbers.

The reasons for their decline are many, starting with two centuries of over-fishing. Ideal spawning rivers are those with clean, swift-moving water, gravel bottoms, and temperatures that never get warmer than 20 degrees Celsius. Unfortunately, every spawning river has been affected negatively by human-caused alterations. The biggest issue in the last century has been the construction of dams, which prevent salmon from reaching their spawning grounds, impede downstream smolt migrations, and increase predation on juvenile fish. But dams have also slowed down the speed of the flowing water, creating dead spots and ponds that are less-than-ideal habitat, and raising temperatures to levels that are unhealthy to salmon. Salmon are sensitive to changes in water quality and water chemistry; pollutants in their rivers—particularly pesticides from Maine's many blueberry farms, but also industrial pollutants and farming run-off—have also hurt populations. Acid rain, mostly from power plant emissions hundreds of miles away, leaches aluminum out of the soil and rocks and lowers the pH level of the river water, which makes it difficult for young salmon to complete the smoltification process. And alteration of stream-side habitat has reduced the shade on many rivers and raised water temperatures, as well as causing erosion that has led to layers of silt on what had been gravel-bottomed rivers. Other threats include predation on juvenile salmon by non-native fish, especially species such as smallmouth bass and pike that have been introduced on purpose for the fishing community; predation by cormorants when the smolts first enter salt water; climate change that may warm water temperatures too high for healthy salmon populations; commercial fishing off Greenland that may inadvertently catch large numbers of adult salmon; and salmon farming, both hatcheries used to reintroduce salmon to the rivers and commercial aquaculture.

Of all of these threats, the abundance of dams on spawning rivers is the most challenging. A report by a committee of the National Research Council in 2004 concluded that the most urgently needed action to reverse the decline of salmon populations in Maine is a program of dam removal. "Priority should be given to dams whose removal would make the greatest amount of spawning and rearing habitat available, meaning that downstream dams should be considered for removal before dams upstream of them. In some cases, habitat restoration will likely be required to reverse or mitigate some habitat changes caused by a dam, especially if the dam is many decades old," the authors wrote.

Slowly, dam removal is beginning. Removal of the Edwards Dam on the Kennebec River in Augusta in 1999 kick-started a movement to remove dams in numerous other locations throughout the state and region.

Since then, the head-of-tide dam on the East Machias River was removed in 2000, and the Smelt Hill Dam on the Presumpscot River and the Sennebec Dam on the St. George River were torn down in 2002. Plans are in place to remove two of the largest dams on the Penobscot River, the Veazie and Great Works dams, and a number of smaller dams on other rivers are also slated for removal. But to make a positive impact on salmon numbers, there are still many more to go.

"Dam removal is always on the list of things to do," said Lipsky, "but it always involves a lot of money and there are a lot of stakeholders that have strong opinions. Dams are historic sites and some people just don't want to see the area changed because it's reminiscent of the way it used to be. Dams create great swimming holes that are used by local residents." But until dam removal becomes a priority and the necessary funding is allocated, the recovery of healthy salmon populations will never be achieved.

The second most urgently needed action for salmon recovery, according to the National Research Council report, is a strategy for solving "the problem of early mortality as smolts transition from freshwater to the ocean and take up residence as post-smolts. If, as seems likely, the difficulty of the transition is due in part to water chemistry, particularly acidification, the only methods of solving the problem are changing the water chemistry and finding a way for the smolts to bypass the dangerous water. Liming has had considerable success in counteracting acidification in many streams, and the techniques are well known. Examples of its application are in nearby Nova Scotia. Liming should be tried experimentally on some Maine streams as soon as possible. Bypassing the dangerous water is best achieved by rearing smolts and acclimating them to seawater in controlled conditions. This approach is not appealing because of the degree of human intervention required and because of the adverse selection that must result from it." Strategically adding large quantities of lime to acidified sections of Maine rivers hasn't been considered seriously, but steps are being taken to gain a better understanding of the reasons behind the high mortality of smolts.

A great deal can be learned about smolt behavior and mortality by following them on their first trip into salt water. What route do they take out into the ocean and how quickly do they travel? Are there particular locations where they die in large numbers? Do they reverse course and try to return to fresh water? Do they travel in groups or individually, and do they follow currents or other features? Do wild salmon fare better or worse than farmed or hatchery fish? Many of these questions may soon be answered as a result of a complex monitoring project being undertaken by the National Marine Fisheries Service. In late May 2006, I joined biologist Graham Goulette, who I first met at Alna Head Tide dam a month before, graduate student Trent Liebich, and NOAA contractor Mike Ormsby for a day of data collection on Penobscot Bay.

We met at Belfast Harbor, a quaint village on the Passagassawakeag River at the edge of the bay, where two large tugboats, several fishing boats, and numerous recreational vessels were docked seemingly beneath the Route 1 overpass. The water was calm as we boarded the Windhorse, an almost-new, 38-foot boat chartered by numerous groups for research, fishing, and diving. Two weeks previously, seventy salmon smolts—twenty-five captured at the Weldon Dam on the Penobscot River, twenty-five from a hatchery, and twenty from the Marical Co. aquaculture facility—were implanted with tiny transmitters and released into the river near the town of Brewer. From there, the fish continued on their way into the bay and, hopefully, out to the Gulf of Maine. But as they did so, they had to pass by several electronic receivers strategically deployed in select locations across the bay. The transmitters in the fish emit an electronic ping every fifty seconds, which, when the fish swim within 500 meters of a receiver, is interpreted as data: the date, the time, and the identity of the fish. According to Goulette, the data allows researchers to track the migratory path each fish takes out of the bay. Typically, some fish go straight out, while others do a "single reversal"—beginning to swim out to sea, but reversing course and then reversing course again before reaching the gulf. Still others reverse course numerous times, suggesting that they may not be ready for their new life in the salt water.

"This data gives us an idea of where the bottlenecks are where fish predation may occur, it determines if the smolts are ready to go, their swim speed, and compares the three groups on their migration patterns," Goulette said. It was the second year of this research on the Penobscot, but it previously had been conducted for three years on the Dennys and for five years on the Narraguagus.

The first group of seven receivers were set in a line 500 meters apart in water up to 300 feet deep between the town of Castine on the mainland and Islesboro Island. A large, orange buoy indicated the location of each receiver, which were attached to ropes 30 feet below the surface of the water and anchored to the seafloor. As we approached the first buoy, Ormsby snagged it with a long gaff and pulled in the rope by hand, getting muddy and wet along the way, until he reached the receiver, a black tube about the size of a small fire extinguisher. With the receiver on board, Liebich—who, when asked for his life story, said simply, "I love tacos"—attached a small cable that downloaded the data to a laptop computer being monitored by Goulette. It took just twenty seconds before the cable was detached and the receiver and buoy were tossed back overboard. The process was repeated six more times before Goulette reported that all of the fish that passed that line of receivers did so by May 17, within eight days of being released in Brewer. That's a lot longer than I had guessed it would take them to make the 40-mile trip, but Goulette wasn't surprised. He said that those individual data points don't mean much until they are compared to the data collected at receivers further south.

It was a twenty-minute ride to the next line of three receivers across Eggemoggin Reach from Deer Island to the mainland, where the view was spectacular. Tall pine trees and scattered hardwoods lined rocky beaches, and several massive summer homes were perched in idyllic locations. The water remained calm, but skies were gray and little bird life was visible, other than an occasional gull or cormorant. Goulette pointed out a harbor porpoise in the distance, which the rest of us searched for unsuccessfully. My disappointment at missing the porpoise was erased moments later when we passed a low, treeless island covered in grasses and yellow flowers where herring and great black-backed gulls sat beside hundreds of common eiders. Black guillemots—pudgy black birds with white wings and red mouths, close relatives of puffins—swarmed around the island, and a few harbor seals were hauled out on the rocks.

The second line of receivers was in an out-of-the-way area where few salmon smolts passed the previous year. It's the most indirect route out of the bay, so it was unsurprising that just one fish was detected passing by one of the three receivers we checked. That one fish dawdled in the vicinity of the first receiver for two minutes at 7 P.M. on May 19, then continued on its way.

The next group of receivers—in a line between Stonington on Deer Island and North Haven Island—was in what should have been a main thoroughfare for the salmon smolts to travel, but out of the ten receivers we checked, just four fish were detected. And only one fish was detected by the nine receivers lined up between Stonington and Isle au Haut, the southernmost point in Penobscot Bay. The absence of salmon smolts in the southeastern portion of the bay began to raise questions among the biologists. They wondered if the smolts just hadn't made it that far yet—20 miles straight south of where many were detected by the first line of receivers—or if they died or chose a different route out of the bay. Goulette recalled that the previous year most of the smolts began their journey south through the east passage, then cut between Islesboro and North Haven islands, and completed their journey out to sea through the west passage. The next line of receivers would indicate if they followed the same path in 2006.

It took nearly an hour to reach the next group of fourteen receivers between North Haven Island and Owls Head, near Rockland, as the boat battled the wind and strong currents. The clouds looked heavy with rain, but as we finally approached our next step, the skies appeared to brighten. Hoping for positive results, the biologists pulled up the first receiver, only to find it damaged—probably by a curious lobsterman using his trap-retrieval equipment to reel in the line. The damaged receiver was replaced quickly, and the boat moved on to the next three, which recorded passage by five, eleven, and three smolts, respectively. The fifth receiver had too much data to download quickly, and so did the sixth, which sounded to me like good news. Lots of data meant lots of fish, right? Wrong. Lots of data meant dead fish. Goulette explained that when a fish dies near a receiver, its transmitter continues to ping and send data to the receiver every fifty seconds, filling up the receiver with useless data that takes up to an hour to download. When those receivers were downloaded later in the day, Goulette found that the dead smolt was an individual that was part of a University of Maine research project. It had been detected in the upper bay on May 3, traveled 28 miles in one day, which apparently is not unusual for a salmon smolt, and died near the receiver. For exactly three weeks, until we removed the receivers from the water, the transmitter in that fish sent data to the receivers every fifty seconds. "What probably happened is that the fish died and its transmitter rolled back and forth on the bottom between the two receivers for three weeks," Goulette speculated.

The rest of the receivers on that line recorded between five and twelve fish apiece, and the final line of six receivers between Islesboro Island and Little Harbor also detected good numbers of fish swimming by, suggesting that most of the smolts took the same route out of the bay as did those from the previous year. But there were still far more fish recorded in the upper bay than in the lower bay. Goulette hoped they were just in a holding pattern somewhere between the receivers and not all dead. He hoped that later analysis would shed some light on what happened and what can be done about it, if anything.

The decline of Atlantic salmon in Maine has ramifications for other wildlife as well, especially for the dwarf wedgemussel, a freshwater mollusk that is also on the federal endangered species list. Freshwater mussels are among the most threatened groups of animals in North America because they are filter feeders and especially sensitive to pollutants. "Because they're sedentary animals, they're sitting ducks for any contamination of their environment. Other animals can try to find a new environment if it becomes contaminated, but mussels can't," said Susi vonOettingen, an endangered species biologist for the U.S. Fish and Wildlife Service. "We once had over three hundred freshwater mussel species in the United States, but there have been more documented extinctions in this group than in any other group of animals." Today, 55 percent of freshwater mussel species are either extinct or endangered.

Freshwater mussels have a unique history in North America, and an even more unique life cycle. Native Americans used them for food and trade for hundreds of years, and in the late 1800s and early 1900s, they were the primary material used to make buttons. In fact, the U.S. system of issuing permits for the capture of wildlife was based on the trade in freshwater mussels.

Their link to Atlantic salmon, however, is based on one unusual stage in their life cycle. In what vonOettingen describes as a "hit or miss reproductive system," male freshwater mussels release sperm and females siphon it in to fertilize their eggs. As the eggs develop into larvae, the female lures a fish toward her using an elaborate attractant system—some mussels actually have an appendage that looks like a tiny worm to attract the fish. When a fish approaches, the adult mussel shoots its larvae toward the fish, and the larvae attach themselves to the fish's gills, mouth, fins, or tail—wherever the skin is thinnest—where they live as parasites by feeding off the nutrients in the circulatory system of the unsuspecting host. After clinging to the fish for several weeks, the larval mussel metamorphoses into a juvenile mussel and drops off the fish onto the floor of the pond or stream, where it grows a shell and lives out the rest of its life.

The challenge is that each species of mussel uses only a few different species of fish as their larval host, so not only must their water body be pollution-free, but the right host fish species also must be present. "The problem is that if the mussels don't drop off into the right substrate, they won't survive. Many are specific to a particular habitat, and that's one reason why they pick certain fish—because fish are habitat specialists, too," vonOettingen said.

The dwarf wedgemussel is found in the watersheds of seven river systems from Maine to North Carolina, although pollution has nearly wiped it out from its southernmost limits. Small populations in Maryland are also vulnerable to extirpation, in part due to a chemical spill that occurred in one stream. "Most populations have only tens or hundreds of individuals, and in some places just one or two are found," explained vonOettingen. "But here in New England there are hundreds of thousands—we've got the mother lode—but they're all in one river, the Connecticut, which is a problem. If we ever need to reintroduce them elsewhere, we could, but one chemical spill at a bridge on the Connecticut River could wipe them all out."

The primary host fish of larval dwarf wedgemussels are slimy sculpin and tessellated darters, but laboratory studies suggest that juvenile salmon also play an important role in the northern part of the mussels' range. According to vonOettingen, juvenile salmon are preferred hosts over adults because they are thinner skinned and move around less from one habitat to another. The Petitcodiac River in New Brunswick once had a healthy population of dwarf wedgemussels and salmon, but when a causeway was constructed across the river that limited the ability of salmon to swim upstream, the salmon population crashed, followed soon after by the mussel. "It may be that the salmon were maintaining the population of dwarf wedgemussels there," vonOettingen said.

Whether they were or not, the salmon in the Petitcodiac River are gone, and with them went a genetically distinct population of an endangered species. According to the National Research Council, not only is the DNA of North American populations of Atlantic salmon different from that of European populations and Maine populations are different from

Canadian populations, but "there is considerable genetic divergence among populations in the eight Maine rivers where wild salmon are found . . . It is not possible to say whether or to what degree the genetic differences reflect adaptation to local conditions as opposed to random processes associated with small population sizes or some influence of stocking."

Regardless of how the genes of wild Atlantic salmon from the Sheepscot River diverged from the genes of those from the Pleasant River, for instance, it happened. The key is to maintain the health of each population, so it's important that those genes don't become diluted. But that is happening, both intentionally and unintentionally.

The National Research Council reports that

> augmentation of wild populations of Maine salmon with hatchery releases began in the early 1870s. At first, young fish were obtained from Lake Ontario. Later, the Craig Brook Hatchery in East Orland, Maine, using eggs from Penobscot River fish, was the stocking source. By the 1920s, Canadian eggs were being used, followed in the 1940s by eggs from the Machias, Penobscot, and Dennys rivers of Maine. In the 1950s and 1960s, some eggs of Canadian origin again were used, but by the late 1960s, eggs from Maine's Machias, Narraguagus, and Penobscot rivers were used. Fish reared in hatcheries derived from Penobscot River fish were used until late 1991, when the practice of river-specific stocking was adopted. The protocol used since involves catching young, actively feeding fish (parr) in the river, rearing them to maturity in the hatchery, mating them, and releasing the resulting fry into the native rivers before they start to feed.

It's a process that essentially means that few salmon complete their entire natural life cycle in the wild, and few wild adult salmon lay eggs in the river. It means that lots of hatchery-raised smolts go down the rivers and into salt water, but almost none of them were actually born in the rivers to begin with. It's a process that suggests that wild Atlantic salmon are anything but wild.

"We use the word 'wild' kind of loosely," admitted Christine Lipsky, the National Marine Fisheries Service biologist. "'Wild' means it was hatched from an egg in the river. 'Naturally reared' refers to both wild and stocked fry. We use those two words interchangeably, because from scale analysis we can't tell the difference between the two . . . Their parents are from the river, they were just hatched in the hatchery and released. That's considered acceptable on the endangered rivers."

But a question remains as to whether the process is helping the species or hurting it. The scientists who wrote the National Research Council report aren't sure. "Even with river-specific stocking and the best available breeding protocols, hatcheries change the genetic makeup of salmon populations," they wrote.

Despite the efforts and money spent on rearing fish in hatcheries and stocking Maine's rivers [for more than 130 years], salmon populations are now at the lowest levels ever recorded. The available information is not sufficient to conclude whether hatcheries in Maine can actually help to rehabilitate salmon populations, whether they might even be harming them, or whether other factors are affecting salmon so strongly that they overwhelm any good that hatcheries might do.

Chief among those "other factors" affecting wild Atlantic salmon is commercial aquaculture, in which salmon are raised from eggs in hatcheries and then grown to market size in large pens in open water along the coast. It's an industry that got its start in Maine in the 1980s, almost exclusively in the extreme easternmost coastal communities around Eastport and Lubec, grew quickly through the 1990s, and then faced numerous difficulties that dramatically reduced the quantity of fish harvested. In 2004, it was a $40 million industry that harvested 18.7 million pounds of salmon from fifteen active farm sites and supported a thousand jobs in Maine, but it's also a key factor limiting the long-term health of wild salmon populations.

Large concentrations of net-pens holding thousands of salmon is a recipe for disease outbreaks and the accumulation of harmful parasites like sea lice, which have caused Maine aquaculture companies to go bankrupt and required net-pens to be dismantled and sterilized. In 2001, more than five million farmed salmon had to be slaughtered because of infectious salmon anemia, a lethal disease that can be transferred to wild salmon through the water. A subsequent outbreak occurred in 2003. A salmon researcher in British Columbia found that parasitic sea lice concentrate thirty thousand times higher in salmon farms than in the wild, and wild salmon migrating near the net-pens were infected by the lice at rates seventy-three times higher than in farm-free areas. Sea lice can be lethal to juvenile salmon by creating open lesions on the surface of the fish and compromising their ability to maintain their saltwater balance.

When infection rates are high enough, the parasites feed on the fish at rates greater than the fish can feed themselves, literally eating the fish alive. Since many wild salmon necessarily migrate by salmon farms on their way to and from their native rivers, and because the pens attract large numbers of predators to the vicinity, wild salmon are negatively affected by the very existence of these operations.

But the bigger concern for wild salmon comes from the large numbers of farmed salmon that escape the pens and intermingle with wild populations, competing for mates and habitat. "The Dennys River has had an influx of aquaculture escapees, and the threat comes in when the aquaculture fish go up the river and spawn with native fish," explained Lipsky. "They're going to change the genetic makeup [of the wild fish] because the aquaculture fish are being raised for certain traits—a fast-growing, larger, fatter fish. Over the years, they select for certain traits and then breed for those traits, like better flesh color, and a lot of those traits are not suitable for a wild environment." When docile, farm-raised salmon escape in large numbers, as they do every year, they dilute the genes of the offspring of the small number of wild salmon that return each year to spawn. While little research has been done in Maine to examine this impact, extensive research in other places has documented the problem.

Research in Norway, which has a small wild Atlantic salmon population and a large aquaculture industry, has found that in some rivers, 80 percent of the salmon are of farmed origin, and when those farmed fish breed with wild salmon, 30 percent fewer offspring survive long enough to leave their breeding grounds and enter the ocean. A ten-year study by researchers in Ireland found that farmed salmon grow more quickly and displace wild fish, but they have a difficult time completing their life cycle. Furthermore, the researchers found that "the inbred offspring of wild and farmed salmon are a genetic disaster, with even more effect in subsequent generations, with few surviving," according to the Atlantic Salmon Federation.

Even worse could be a proposal by Waltham, Massachusetts-based Aqua Bounty Technology to create a genetically modified salmon for aquaculture that carries a gene from another species of fish, the ocean pout, that makes the salmon grow twice as fast as normal. Salmon farmers raising this mutant may be able to double output while cutting costs up to 35 percent. "It's like improving the mileage in your car," company executive Elliot Entis told *Business Week* in 2005. But the idea is scaring a lot of people, too, from fisheries biologists to the Food and Drug Administration, which has not yet approved any transgenic animals for human consumption. If "normal" farm-raised salmon are already helping to push wild Atlantic salmon to the brink of extinction, what chance will the wild salmon have against this super-salmon if it is approved?

The known challenges to the long-term survival of wild Atlantic salmon seem nearly insurmountable, and yet there is plenty that isn't known about them as well. The biggest unknown is what happens to them once they reach the ocean on their way to Greenland and why so few return to spawn. "This year [2006] on the Sheepscot River, we've gotten 550 smolts at the Head of Tide dam, but once they leave there, we really don't know what happens to them," said Lipsky. "Once they make it to the ocean, it's a big black box. Because there's so much ocean out there, there's not really a good way to monitor them. The fish that are going out into the ocean are such a small size that we can't put in a transmitting tag because the tags are just too big. We need technology to catch up with what we want it to do."

Instead, management and monitoring in freshwater intensifies, and perhaps that's adding to the problem. There are so many monitoring agencies—the Maine Salmon Commission, the U.S. Fish and Wildlife Service, the National Marine Fisheries Service, and the Maine Department of Inland Fisheries and Wildlife among them—each working on a different aspect of the species and sometimes working from different plans, that the monitors sometimes need to be monitored. The authors of the National Research Council report worry that "the trauma associated with capturing, handling, anesthetizing, and sampling fluids and tissues from fish—especially young fish—can result in some deaths. When populations are very small, as they now are in most Maine rivers, it is essential to weigh the value of new information against the possibility of the harm to wild fish caused by handling."

It doesn't help that the monitoring agencies also have numerous constituencies and stakeholders that they feel obligated to keep happy, sometimes to the detriment of the salmon. The staff of the state Department of Inland Fisheries and Wildlife are somewhat beholden to the recreational fishing community, for instance, so the stocking of non-native fish species preferred by fishermen, such as smallmouth bass, pike, and brown trout, becomes a priority for them. Unfortunately, those species are among the chief predators and competitors of juvenile salmon, and it's not uncommon for these non-natives to find their way into salmon-spawning rivers and streams. Lipsky caught two bass in one of the salmon traps in Alna in 2006. Similarly, a number of salmon-fishing clubs in the state are still active and politically connected, despite the closure of the fishery in 1999, and various salmon-monitoring agencies are anxious to keep them happy. Many of these clubs spend considerable time, money, and energy restoring streamside habitat, planting trees to provide shade to the rivers, and removing beaver dams that may have slowed river flows. To reward them and keep their morale up, the agencies opened a fall salmon-fishing season on the Penobscot River in 2006, even though that step is considered by some fisheries biologists to be premature.

But the monitoring agencies and salmon biologists are having a hard time keeping their morale up, too. The outlook for the future of wild Atlantic salmon in New England is poor, and there seems little anyone can do about it. Christine Lipsky thinks that the species may last another fifty years if continuous active management is provided, but she also admits that the public may be unable to justify the government spending millions of dollars a year for an annual return of just a thousand fish. "On the flip side of things," she added, "dams will probably be removed over the next ten years, which may aid the return of other anadromous species, and that should help salmon indirectly by providing additional marine-derived nutrients to our river systems and by the other species running interference for the salmon's predators. In any event, the prognosis doesn't look good, and I fear that all the management in the world may not be able to prevent the extirpation of Atlantic salmon from North America."

Fisheries biologist Robert Stickney, one of the authors of the National Research Council report, isn't much more optimistic. The Texas A&M professor and director of the Texas Sea Grant Program said that most biologists believe that salmon have been extirpated from rivers in southern New England due to climate change and the warming of the ocean and rivers. "The same may be at least partially responsible for the decline in Maine's salmon," he said. "It is possible that Maine is at the very southern edge of the range in which salmon can exist in eastern North America. If so, and if predictions for continued global warming are correct, efforts at salmon recovery may be futile. If, however, we are in a thermal cycle that might reverse in the next decade or two, the environment may become more conducive to salmon survival. So, the question cannot really be answered at this time. If one takes the position that the current warming trend will continue for the next one hundred years or so, then salmon don't have a very bright future in Maine."

8

American Burying Beetle

The stench was overpowering. But that was to be expected, given that Chris Raithel was peering into a tiny jar containing a small piece of chicken that had been fermenting outdoors for a week or more. To a dozen species of beetles, though, the aroma was a tantalizing attractant, luring them to a tremendous feast. Crawling all over the bait were three or four varieties of black-and-orange carrion beetles, along with several other species that Raithel didn't identify. The largest of them all—a thumb-sized creature with dangerous-looking mandibles—was an American burying beetle (*Nicrophorus americanus*), a globally imperiled species that holds the title as the largest carrion beetle in North America.

In the hand, nature's undertaker, as it is known, is quite an attractive animal: shiny black wing coverings accented with four bright orange blotches, rust-colored head markings that differentiate the sexes, constantly moving clubbed antennae, and front legs that appear to a non-entomologist as if they have orange fur on them. I was especially intrigued to watch a hefty male groom himself as he sat in the palm of my hand. Like he was preparing for a date, he repeatedly swiped his left leg over one antennae and the left side of his face, then between his mandibles in one smooth motion. He then undertook the same process several times with his right leg. By then he appeared anxious to fly, so I placed the beetle in a container and joined the biologists at the next trap.

Raithel, a wildlife biologist with the state of Rhode Island, and Michael Amaral, senior endangered species biologist with the U.S. Fish and Wildlife Service, invited me to join them in 2000 during their annual monitoring survey of the beetles on Block Island, 12 miles off the Rhode Island coast. Best known for its appeal to summer tourists and sailors and as a fall birdwatching hotspot, the island's greatest biological claim to fame is as the home of the last naturally occurring population of American burying beetles east of the Mississippi River.

Once found throughout eastern temperate North America from New England to the Rocky Mountain front, wherever there was an expanse of meadows or prairies, the beetles are today limited to a few patches of the central plains and a couple islands in southern New England. From May to October, the winged insects cruise the night skies in search of the odor of decaying flesh. For several days each year in early summer, Raithel and Amaral are determined to make sure that the insects have no problem finding what they seek. They set out a line of pitfall traps—glass Mason jars buried in the ground to their rim and baited with rotting chicken—at Lewis-Dickens Farm and two other sites on the island to monitor the beetle population and give them a head start on breeding.

The first trap they checked on the day I visited contained a dead burying beetle. Although the trapping method is considered nonlethal, 1 or 2 percent of the beetles die in the traps if they are joined there by a mass of ants or if the beetles fight each other. According to Amaral, the beetles will sometimes even feign death in what may be a defensive measure, but blowing air softly across their antennae can make them become active again. The next trap held four live American burying beetles, and almost every other trap had at least one, along with several smaller species of carrion-eating beetles. The few traps that were empty appeared to have been disturbed by cows grazing through the meadow.

After checking all the traps at Lewis-Dickens Farm, the group moved on to a private farm, and then to Rodman's Hollow, a thickly vegetated area that appeared very different from the farm sites. "We find the beetles in shrub-dominated Rodman's Hollow, but not nearly in the numbers that we find at Lewis Farm," Amaral said. "The more open habitat is better. That's one of the reasons why we're managing for more grassland on Block Island."

Named for their habit of burying a dead animal on which to lay their eggs, the American burying beetles' preferred habitat on the islands of southern New England is sandplain grassland, a prairie-like habitat that developed on sandy glacial moraine soils that the beetles find easy to excavate. The habitat is dominated by grasses and a number of low-growing shrubs in the heath family, like blueberry, bearberry, and huckleberry. In other regions of the country, especially the few sites in Missouri and Kansas where the beetle is still hanging on, it lives in more typical prairie habitat with soft, loamy soils. In the Midwest and elsewhere in their historic range, none of which now harbor any beetles save for one site in southern Ohio where it has been reintroduced, the burying beetle lived in whatever meadow or grassland habitat it could find.

During the first two days of trapping on Block Island, the biologists clipped a tiny piece from the wing covering—which entomologists officially call the elytra—of each American burying beetle so they would know if subsequently captured beetles had been caught before. On the day of my visit, almost all of the beetles were recaptures, but a total of 182 new adult burying beetles were caught during the three days of trapping, a good total considering that strong winds on the third night likely discouraged many beetles from wandering.

The population of burying beetles on Block Island appears to be stable or increasing slightly—the only site in the country that can make that claim—but it doesn't hurt to give them some assistance finding a mate and a meal. So at the end of each trapping session, the biologists take all the beetles captured on the last day and give them a head start on breeding. They dig a hole, place a dead, farm-raised quail chick in the hole, put a male and female beetle on the chick, and cover the hole. In 2000, sixteen pairs of beetles began their breeding cycle in this manner, and dozens more have done so since.

According to the biologists, the beetles typically bury their breeding food 8 or 10 inches down by excavating soil out from under the carrion, which is why their distribution is somewhat dependent on the type of soil substrate available. They may even relocate the carcass by flipping over and using their legs like conveyer belts if the ground is too hard for digging. "They want to get it as far as possible from the surface so flies and ants can't get at the corpse," Amaral said. To monitor the success of the breeding beetles, Amaral and Raithel tied a long piece of dental floss to the foot of the quail so they could follow the trail of the floss down to wherever the beetles finished digging.

After burying the carcass, the male and female beetles then strip off its feathers or fur, work the remaining material into a ball, and coat it with a secretion from their anal gland. This secretion has antimicrobial properties and serves to retard the growth of bacteria and fungi that might destroy the carcass before the beetle eggs hatch and the larvae have a chance to feed on it. The process of excavating and preparing the prey takes about three days, after which the female beetle lays approximately thirty eggs, which hatch in just a few days. The newborn larvae start out about the size of a grain of rice, and after three metamorphoses over the course of two weeks, they turn into something that looks like a large grub or, as one biologist has described it, a tiny version of the Michelin man. The grubs then crawl off into the soil, and in forty-five days they pupate into a shiny, new, adult beetle. After feeding several times to put on fat, they burrow into the soil and overwinter.

What is particularly notable about this process is that all during the growth and metamorphosis of the larval beetles, the adults tend the larvae by regurgitating food from the buried prey and protecting them from competitors. The hatchlings even stroke their parents' mandibles with their mouths to signal that they want a meal. "Most insects don't do this," noted Amaral. "Parental behavior among solitary insects is fairly rare. That's why this group of beetles has been so well studied. Scientists have been fascinated by this high level of social behavior since at least the 1930s."

Another key element in the breeding behavior of American burying beetles is that they are quite choosy about the size of the carcass they bury. While adult beetles may feed on carrion of a wide variety of sizes, they will only bury and breed on a carcass of about 80 to 200 grams, something the size of an average human fist and more than ten times the size of the adult beetle itself. That means that dead mice and chipmunks are too small, and adult squirrels are too big. The perfect size animal is a passenger pigeon. Unfortunately, they're extinct.

The decline of the American burying beetle is directly linked to the decline and extinction of the passenger pigeon, a species so abundant at one time that it constituted 25 to 40 percent of all the birds in the United

States. When early explorers discovered America, it is believed that there were three to five billion passenger pigeons living in the country, and their migratory flights were known to blacken the skies for hours—even days—at a time. Yet by the early 1900s, they had been virtually wiped out across their entire range. The last one, a twenty-nine-year-old individual named Martha that lived at the Cincinnati Zoological Garden, died in 1914 and was donated to the Smithsonian Institution.

Although larger and more brightly colored, passenger pigeons were closely related to mourning doves, that common coo-ing bird of backyards and cornfields. It ranged from Nova Scotia, Quebec, and Ontario to the Deep South and as far west as Texas and the Dakotas. Its small head and neck contrasted sharply with its long, wedge-shaped tail and large, strong breast muscles that allowed it to fly long distances quickly and gracefully.

According to a Smithsonian fact sheet, the birds established winter roosting sites in the forests of the southern states.

> Each roost often had such tremendous numbers of birds so crowded and massed together that they frequently broke the limbs of the trees by their weight. In the morning the birds flew out in large flocks scouring the countryside for food. At night they returned to the roosting area. Their scolding and chattering as they settled down for the night could be heard for miles. . . . Nesting sites were established in [northern] forest areas that had a sufficient supply of food and water available within daily flying range. Since no accurate data were recorded on the passenger pigeon, it is only possible to give estimates on the size and population of these nesting areas. A single site might cover many thousands of acres and the birds were so congested in these areas that hundreds of nests could be counted in a single tree. A large nesting in Wisconsin was reported as covering 850 square miles, and the number of birds nesting there was estimated at 136 million.

Trouble came when the early settlers began clearing the eastern forests for farming, forcing the birds to relocate their roosting and nesting sites and decreasing their food supply. When they began feeding on the grain in farm fields and damaging crops, the farmers tried to evict them using shotguns, although it had little effect on the pigeon population. It wasn't until professional hunters began killing the birds for market in the 1800s that passenger pigeon numbers began to decline precipitously. Using nets and guns and pots of burning sulphur under roosting trees, hunters killed and sold hundreds of thousands of the birds. One of the last large nesting sites was around Petoskey, Michigan, in 1878, where fifty thousand birds were killed each day for nearly five months.

By the 1890s, the birds were nearly extinct, and it was too late to save them with legislation or changes to hunting laws. In the early 1900s, the American Ornithologists' Union offered a reward to anyone who could find an active passenger pigeon nest, but the reward went unclaimed. Breeding of the few remaining birds in captivity was unsuccessful, leaving only Martha to carry on. And soon she died, too.

"The passenger pigeon's technique of survival had been based on mass tactics," according to the Smithsonian fact sheet.

> There had been safety in its large flocks, which often numbered hundreds of thousands of birds. When a flock of this size established itself in an area, the number of local predators (such as wolves, foxes, weasels and hawks) was so small compared to the total number of birds that little damage could be inflicted on the flock as a whole. This colonial way of life became very dangerous when man became a predator on the flocks. When the birds were massed together, especially at a nesting site, it was easy for man to slaughter them in such huge numbers that there were not enough birds left to successfully reproduce the species.

So what does this have to do with the American burying beetle? The decline of the beetle across most of its range follows the decline of the passenger pigeon. That's because pigeon carcasses were the perfect size for the beetle to use as its breeding food. And given the size of the pigeon population, there were probably plenty of carcasses available to the beetles and any other carrion eaters. When pigeons were no longer a readily available food source, the beetles were forced to seek out other carrion, many of which were ample to feed upon but not the appropriate size for breeding. Slowly the beetle disappeared from the central part of its range. It survived for a while longer in pockets on the Great Plains where species like prairie chickens provided chicks of the right size to breed on, and in the east where the heath hen did the same. Then prairie chicken numbers plummeted and the heath hen became extinct, and the beetles were again forced to look elsewhere for food. Ultimately they disappeared, too.

But not everywhere.

. . .

On Block Island, American burying beetles seem pretty secure. Trapping data on the island since 1991 even suggests that the population has slowly increased. According to Howard Ginsberg, an entomologist with the U.S. Geological Survey who has analyzed the data, the presumed population increase holds up to close scrutiny. His analysis found some previously unreported behavioral characteristics, including the fact that the beetles are more active in warmer and more humid weather and less active in windy conditions. He also found that the beetles tend to fly long distances in whatever direction the wind happens to be blowing, but short-distance movements are independent of wind direction. While some of these findings may have influenced the number of beetles trapped in a given day or year, making the annual population estimates too high or too low at times, the bottom line remains that American burying beetle numbers are increasing on Block Island.

Scott Comings, director of the Block Island program of the Rhode Island office of The Nature Conservancy, noted that 2006 was the best year on record for the capture of American burying beetles on the island. In three nights of trapping, 344 different individuals were captured, about 100 more than in any other year. "The weather plays a factor [in how many are caught], and this year we had ideal weather, so take those results with a grain of salt, but it certainly means that they're doing well. It appears that the population is in the best condition since monitoring began."

Much of that success is due to efforts to protect land from development on the island and to manage as much land as possible for the beetle's preferred grassland habitat. Since 1972, about 43 percent of the island has been protected permanently through land acquisition and conservation easements, and 40 percent of that land has been outright donations of the properties to The Nature Conservancy, the Block Island Conservancy, or other conservation organizations. "There's a tremendous commitment from both year-round and summer residents to keep the land the way it was, to give it to the next generation in the way they received it," Comings said. "And many of the donors have made a tremendous personal sacrifice in doing so. A lot of people could have retired and not worked another day in their life if they sold the land to developers instead."

Due to the foresight of these Block Island landowners, the island has become an offshore refuge for many species—not just burying beetles—

that were once common on the mainland but which are now increasingly rare, including grasshopper sparrows, northern harriers, barn owls, northern blazing star, bushy rock rose, and Maryland golden aster. Like the beetle, all these species rely on grassland habitat to thrive, so as much of the protected habitat as possible is being managed so it remains grassland, especially in the southwest portion of the island. Comings said that 10 to 20 acres of additional grassland habitat is protected each year.

But not everything is rosy for the beetles on Block Island. The biologists have begun to study winter survivorship, and after the first year of research they found that just 20 to 25 percent of the beetles last through the winter. While burying beetles generally live only one year, the adults don't breed until the spring and early summer after spending the winter in the ground. If only one-quarter of them last long enough to breed, it seems remote that they will be able to sustain themselves for very long without regular human intervention.

The American burying beetle was added to the federal endangered species list in 1989. The national recovery plan that Chris Raithel and Michael Amaral prepared for the species recommends re-establishing populations of the beetles at a number of sites in its historic range. "We broke the former range into various recovery units or clusters of states," explained Raithel. "We decided we'd like to see a number of self-sustaining populations of at least one thousand individuals in each of those recovery units. 'Self-sustaining' is the key word, because we don't want them to require constant management." Since many of the recovery units didn't have existing populations of burying beetles, the most important factor in meeting the species' recovery goals was to learn how to reintroduce them to appropriate habitat within their former range. The first step was learning how to raise the beetles in captivity.

Boston University biologist Andrea Kozol spent several years in the early 1990s developing a protocol and successfully reared enough beetles for the first reintroduction effort on Penikese Island just north of Martha's Vineyard, the last known site in Massachusetts where burying beetles had been found. A 70-acre grassy island owned by the Massachusetts Division of Fisheries and Wildlife, the island is managed as a wildlife sanctuary. Between 1990 and 1993, 211 beetles were released on the island. Amaral called the releases successful because the beetles reproduced on the island, but they weren't able to sustain themselves. For eight years in a row after the reintroduction, at least one beetle was recaptured during annual visits to the island, but since 2003 none have been found.

After limited success on Penikese Island, Amaral made an aggressive decision to reintroduce the beetles to Nantucket Island, but to do so, he needed a lot more beetles. So he turned to Roger Williams Park Zoo in Rhode Island. Owned and operated by the city of Providence, the zoo has a long history of supporting wildlife conservation efforts and breeding rare and endangered species. But as zookeeper Lou Perrotti said, "Zoos are famous for the megafauna and the furry and the cute and the big animals. We've been breeding lions and tigers and bears forever, but breeding insects is a totally new thing for zoos. It's cutting edge, like reptiles were in the seventies. We're just now learning how to breed them. But because this is a local endangered species, it's a dream project for us that gives our keepers hands-on experience."

One advantage to rearing insects at the zoo, according to Perrotti, is the price. "The beauty of invertebrate conservation and using insects as conservation tools is that it's not very expensive. You can breed a whole lot of specimens in a very small area with very little cost. You can put literally thousands of endangered species back in the wild for under $1,000, whereas to reintroduce one wolf it's hundreds of thousands of dollars in logistics, raising, and rearing. . . . When we release the beetles, we don't need Land Rovers and helicopters and fancy logistical stuff, just a small Igloo cooler."

Perrotti took over an old restroom at the zoo, removed the urinal, installed floor-to-ceiling wooden shelving, and acquired some plastic containers and 5-gallon buckets. When I visited him in the winter of 2006, he took me to the zoo's Austral-Asian building where a tree kangaroo exhibit shares space with turtles, fish, and other creatures native to the Far East. Behind an entrance marked "zoo personnel only," a caged bustard yapped loudly beside the restroom-turned-beetle-rearing-room.

"Breeding is very simple," Perrotti said. "We were given larvae from the Block Island population to start with, and we kept them in these small plastic shoeboxes with a wet paper towel. Once the beetle is twenty-one days old, it's sexually active. So I take these 5-gallon buckets, pound them with soil three-quarters of the way to the top, then pair the beetles up with as much genetic variability as we can, and give them a quail resource that we buy frozen and the size that we need. We put the future mom and future dad together, put a cover on the bucket and a rock on the top, and in a perfect world, within twenty-four hours mom and dad cooperate together to excavate the quail into the soil."

The captive beetles then go through the same process they do in the wild—stripping off the feathers from the carcass, forming the remainder into a ball, secreting the antimicrobial agent from their anal glands, laying eggs, and tending the larvae. When the larvae emerge as adults, Perrotti starts the process all over again. After a few generations, there may be as many as a thousand beetles in that tiny room at one time. "The key is timing the breeding through the winter so they're not too old or too young to release," said Perrotti. "After they're eight or nine months old, they're probably too old and won't breed again."

Perrotti says he's "always been into creepy crawlies." After high school, he managed a hardware store while breeding snakes at his house, then helped start the Rhode Island Herpetological Society, led educational programs, and volunteered at the zoo. When a full-time job opened up at the zoo in 1997, he jumped at it. Now, in addition to his duties raising beetles and as zookeeper in the Tropical America section of the zoo, he's the conservation coordinator for the Terrestrial Invertebrate Taxon Advisory Group of the American Zoological Association, where he works to protect a wide range of other rare insects.

At a public lecture about the zoo's involvement in the beetle project, Perrotti's enthusiasm for insects was clearly apparent from his opening remarks. "Invertebrates are an important part of our ecosystem," he said. "Without them we basically couldn't survive on this planet for more than six months. Things would just rot. They recycle, they break things down, they produce our soil, they pollinate our plants, they have such a valuable ecological role that we couldn't live without them. They're also an important indicator of a healthy environment, and a lot of other animals rely on them as food sources."

Perrotti is also intrigued by the interrelationships among insects, particularly one involving the American burying beetle. Many of the beetles captured in the wild have a number of large, pale orange mites crawling on their bodies that play an important role in the life cycle of the beetle. When the beetle buries a carcass, there are plenty of other insects that want to feed on the same carcass, especially flies that lay their own eggs on it. So the mites help the beetle by crawling off and feeding on the fly larvae so the carcass isn't consumed before the beetle larvae have time to feed on it. Once the carcass is underground, the mite lays its eggs nearby, then climbs back on the adult beetle for a trip to the next carcass. When the young beetles are ready to emerge as adults, the young mites are also ready, and they crawl aboard for a ride.

Reintroducing American burying beetles to Nantucket—where the last sighting was in 1926—was more of a challenge than to Penikese Island, whose only residents were birds and other insects. At first glance, Nantucket doesn't appear to be a logical choice, given its large size, swelling population, and increasing development pressures, but Michael Amaral pushed for it anyway. He said Nantucket is very much like Block Island, in that nearly half of the island has been protected permanently from development, and it has a great deal of grassland habitat.

"One of my goals with the Nantucket reintroduction is to demonstrate that there can be endangered species recovery without development controversy. Though the board of selectmen was a bit upset when they first heard of our plans, there is adequate habitat available. We did not feel we needed to restrict development of private property on Nantucket because of this species."

Another factor working in favor of the beetles is the absence of mammalian scavengers on Nantucket. A likely contributing factor to the decline of American burying beetles across much of its range was the rise in the population of foxes, raccoons, opossums, skunks, and other carrion-eating mammals that out-compete beetles for carcasses. When humans hunted wolves, mountain lions, and other top predators to near extinction in the 1800s and early 1900s, the population of second-tier mammals skyrocketed, and they are now among the most common mammals in the landscape. When an animal dies, these scavengers easily beat the beetles to the meal and leave nothing behind. But Block Island and Nantucket don't have any of these mammalian competitors, leaving only insects and birds to fight over available carcasses.

The American burying beetle has several similar-looking, smaller cousins in the genus *Nicrophorus* that also feed on carrion and that are often found scavenging from the same carcass. However, none of them have the rust-colored circular patch on their pronotum, the shield-like covering over the front of their thorax, which clearly identifies *N. americanus*. The most common of its relatives is *N. orbicollis,* a medium-sized beetle with the same four orange patches on its wing-coverings but lack-ing the American burying beetle's additional rusty markings on its head and pronotum. Most abundant near forested areas, *N. orbicollis* is the most common member of the genus found in southern New England and is active from late spring through early fall, with peak activity in June. The nearly identical *N. marginatus* is slightly smaller than *orbicollis* but much less abundant in the region. The third relative in the genus, *N. tomentosus,* also has orange markings but is distinguished by golden fur-like growth on its thorax that makes it look somewhat like a bee. When disturbed, it may flop over on its back and make a buzzing noise with its wings to im-itate a bumble bee to scare off predators. It is most abundant in July and August. *N. pustulatus* and *N. sayi* are the smallest of the group, but are sel-dom found in the region.

All of the *Nicrophorus* beetles bury small carcasses and therefore may compete for carrion to some degree with American burying beetles. While *N. americanus* prefers larger carcasses, it will eat carrion as small as 35 grams when larger carcasses are not available, thereby bringing it in di-rect competition with the more abundant smaller beetles.

But it's not only *Nicrophorus* beetles that feed on carrion. Numerous other more distantly related beetles—most of them oval in shape and predominantly black—may feed side by side on the same carcasses. Early in the season, ridged carrion beetles (*Oiceoptoma inaequale*) are found in significant numbers, replaced later by the red-lined carrion beetle (*Necrodes surinamensis*), which takes over as the most abundant carrion eater in the area. In July and August, sizable numbers of the very common margined carrion beetle (*Oiceoptoma noveboracensis*) and American carrion beetle (*Necrophila americana*), a dime-sized black beetle with a black spot in the middle of its golden thorax, are found as well. Almost all of these beetles turned up when I spent a day on Nantucket in June 2006 to see how suc-cessful the reintroduction had been.

The ferry crossing from Hyannis to Nantucket was surprisingly calm, considering the stormy weather of the previous few days, but it was dis-appointingly slow in bird life—just three gulls and none of the pelagic species I was hoping to see. In fact, I saw more private planes flying to the island during the one-hour ferry crossing than birds, an indicator of the island's ritzy residents and high-profile visitors. Upon arrival, I was met by Bard College professor Bill Maple and research assistant Andrew McKenna-Foster for a walk through the bustling downtown district, which is filled with fancy art galleries, high-end shops, expensive restaurants, and throngs of tourists and traffic.

Early the next morning, we headed out to check three trap-lines for signs of American burying beetles that had survived the winter and emerged to search for a carcass and a mate. The brightening sky showed high wispy clouds and fog in the distance as we made our way to Sesachacha Heathland Wildlife Sanctuary, located on the far eastern portion of the island and about a mile inland from the coastline. Owned by the Massachusetts Audubon Society and better known as the Eastern Moors, it looked somewhat similar to the Block Island site that I had visited six years earlier, with wide open expanses of grasses and sedges interspersed with low-growing heath shrubs and scattered patches of scrub oak. Song sparrows, catbirds, yellow warblers, Eastern towhees, and robins were busy raising their first broods of young, darting back and forth with bugs and caterpillars in their beaks and occasionally bursting into song. As we approached the line of twenty pitfall traps, almost identical to those used by Raithel and Amaral on Block Island, a white-tailed deer ran across the sandy path and a northern harrier swooped low over the grasses ready to pounce on its next meal.

Maple and McKenna-Foster had opened the traps the previous day for the second of three four-day trapping sessions, so they were excited about what they would find. The first session a month earlier was partially rained out, but they still caught fifteen American burying beetles, which they judged to be a good sign. Unfortunately, things didn't start out well. The first four traps contained a total of just three of the smaller *Nicrophorus* beetles, and one trap was completely infested with ants. At each stop, McKenna-Foster removed the rotting chicken bait from the buried Mason jar and called out to Maple what beetle species he found. Maple in turn recorded the data while quickly spritzing the bait with water from a spray bottle so it wouldn't dry out.

As soon as McKenna-Foster arrived at the fifth trap, a big smile formed on his face as he yelled out enthusiastically, "Whoa, what a great trap!" Not only did this trap contain our first American burying beetle, but it also held a 4-inch-long wolf spider, the largest spider I had ever seen. In addition to the beetle project, McKenna-Foster was also spending the summer conducting a census of spiders on the island, so for him this trap was a two-fer. He carefully removed the spider with a stick and let it crawl on his rubber-glove-covered hand for a moment before sliding it into a small plastic container to include in his collection. I took a quick picture of the creature, but that was about as close as I wanted to get to it. Spiders are one of the only groups of wildlife that still give me the creeps—along with leeches and a few others—so while I was intrigued to look at it, I was also happy when it was safely away in the container. McKenna-Foster then removed the burying beetle and noted that it was a male—they have a rust-colored square patch on their heads, while females have a triangular head patch. Looking closely at the wing-coverings of the beetle, he noted that they were unmarked, indicating that it was neither a beetle that had been caught in the season's first trapping session nor an adult released by the zoo the previous year. This beetle joined the spider in the container as we continued to the next trap.

None of our target species were found in the next nine traps, although we found several *N. orbicollis* and our first *N. tomentosus*—the one that imitates bees—as well as several beetles in the genus *Geotrupidae* and something McKenna-Foster called "species C," one of a difficult-to-identify group of small black dung or scarab beetles. Trap 15 held two wild male American burying beetles, and it was my first opportunity to hold one. I was tentative at first, because their large mandibles make them look somewhat vicious, but that individual didn't seem interested in biting me at all. He just wanted to escape. As I held him firmly between my thumb and forefinger, I could tell he was a strong insect; he kept battling to push me away and escape between my fingers. After the beetle released a strong-smelling secretion in my hand, I'd had enough and placed him in the box with the others.

The remaining five traps contained two more American burying beetles, along with several other species that we had already seen and one beautiful, glossy black beetle with several perfect rows of tiny red spots that McKenna-Foster identified later as a caterpillar hunter.

Our next stop was a place referred to as the Serengeti for its grassland habitat and scattered tall scrub oaks that look like the acacia trees commonly seen on the African plains. Owned by the Nantucket Conservation Foundation, the site is mowed every other year in an effort to attract harriers to nest. The six traps there were overflowing with *N. orbicollis*, along with two American burying beetles, several *Geotrupidae*, and a few cockroaches that I decided should also be added to my list of least-favorite wildlife.

The final stop of the morning was Sanford Farm, just west of downtown Nantucket, an old farm with a mix of dry grassy areas and dense patches of scrub oak. Fewer American burying beetles had been found at this site than the others, partly because its soils are drier. Breeding of the beetles there totally failed in 2005, so the biologists weren't expecting to find new adults at the site when we visited. And we didn't. We found a fair number of *N. orbicollis,* and some crickets that McKenna-Foster saved to feed to the wolf spider, but half the traps were completely empty. The biggest surprise at the site was the discovery of an ox beetle in one trap, a radish-sized, purplish beetle with horns that doesn't feed on carrion so would not be expected to enter the trap. The biologists speculated that it may have just stumbled in and couldn't get out.

The beetle research on Nantucket is conducted in collaboration with the Maria Mitchell Association, which honors the legacy of the island's celebrated astronomer and educator who was the first person to use a telescope to discover a comet. Born on Nantucket in 1818, Mitchell earned international fame following her discovery, and later became the nation's first woman astronomy professor and the first woman elected a fellow of the American Academy of Arts and Sciences. The association was established by friends and colleagues in 1902, thirteen years after Mitchell's death, to celebrate her memory and continue her work in the fields of education, social reform, and scientific research.

Not far from the island's ferry dock is a complex of six buildings owned by the association, including Mitchell's birthplace, a natural history museum, an observatory, and temporary living quarters for scientists and students. An association-operated aquarium is located on the waterfront. The group supports a wide variety of education and outreach activities, as well as astronomical and natural history research. In addition to the American burying beetle research, other projects include ornithological, botanical, and marine studies, and the ongoing cataloging of historical collections of insects, plants, birds, and other specimens housed in the museum's basement laboratory.

After completing the trap survey and bringing the seven American burying beetles back to the Maria Mitchell lab, McKenna-Foster used a cauterizing tool to burn a tiny notch into the wing-covering of each beetle to mark them so they can be identified as to when and where they were caught if they are recaptured later. He said that marking the beetles doesn't appear to bother them as long as he doesn't harm the wings beneath the elytra. After the ten-second marking procedure, the beetles were returned to the plastic container and fed some meal worms. When the four-day trapping session was complete, all the beetles that were caught—a total of twenty-six—were paired up and given a head start in their breeding by being placed on a dead quail chick in a pre-dug hole, just like on Block Island. Between 1994 and 2005, 2,892 beetles raised at Roger Williams Park Zoo were paired up and released on Nantucket in the same way. Despite these ongoing reintroduction efforts, it's unknown how large the population of wild beetles is on the island.

"We're struggling right now to answer that question," said Maple, the Bard College biology professor who is overseeing the Nantucket beetle monitoring project. "We've been trying to reintroduce them for ten years, and for some number of those years—six or eight—we've been bringing beetles out and provisioning them with quail, and sometimes we'd dig up the nests and check on the beetles. We find beetles every summer that have emerged, that are brand new and unmarked, but whether that population is sustaining, I personally doubt. If we have a population in the two sites we've been working on that amounts to fifty beetles, I think we'd be ecstatic."

Similar reintroduction efforts, research, and monitoring are taking place in several locations in the Great Plains, and the St. Louis Zoo has learned from the Roger Williams Park Zoo how to rear the beetles in captivity, but all of these sites are facing similarly meager results. Maple says that every site is "hoping to jump-start the population, get the numbers up to a critical mass where it can be self-sustaining. Like a nuclear reaction, you just got to get to a certain number." But only Block Island has reached that unknown number.

Maple describes the burying beetle as "a very striking beetle" and "a robust, sturdy animal," particularly when compared to others in its genus. He thinks its bright coloration is a warning to potential predators that it is distasteful, so it is unlikely that the beetle is at risk from being eaten by other animals. "Field mice love to chew on a juicy beetle, but I don't think they'd touch them," he said.

But there are still plenty of other threats to the American burying beetle. While the extinction of the passenger pigeon and the heath hen, as well as increasing competition from mammalian scavengers, is probably the chief culprit in the beetle's demise, there are several other possible contributing factors. Many biologists have speculated that pesticide use may have had a considerable impact, both in killing the beetles directly and by reducing populations of common carcass species, but others wonder why pesticides wouldn't have also wiped out the other *Nicrophorus* beetles that are still so abundant today. Increasing use of artificial lighting may affect the movements and behavior of the nocturnal beetles, but again the same question arises about why related beetles weren't similarly affected. Pathogens also have been considered a possible contributing factor in their decline, but not enough research has been done to draw any conclusions.

Maple thinks that habitat loss is another key contributor to their historic decline and to the current difficulties restoring their population. Prairie habitat has been vastly diminished, both from conversion to agricultural use in the Great Plains—plowing and harrowing of fields would greatly disturb beetle brood chambers—and from the natural conversion to forests in the East. "That lack of appropriate habitat of sufficient size is really limiting them right now," Maple said. "We've had beetles that have flown a mile to a mile and a half from where we put them out. They're strong fliers, and you can imagine it's natural for them to disperse, but on an island, if you disperse you're in the ocean. In 1930, they could probably fly and find a good patch of habitat, but now if they fly off they'll land in something that's not hospitable."

A naturally upbeat and optimistic man with an Amish-style graying beard, Maple said he grew up the way most modern ecologists did—hunting, fishing, exploring the neighborhood, and turning over rocks seeking wildlife. He has studied a wide range of creatures during his career, from endangered Massasauga rattlesnakes and salamanders in the Midwest to ticks in New York and arthropods in the soils of Nantucket. "I'm an old-timey generalist biologist, in my muddy boots, and anything living has always intrigued me," he said.

His optimism is being tested the more he learns about the American burying beetle. He likens the beetle to the canary in the coal mine. "It reflects on the impact that humans have had on the environment. We have abused the habitat to such an extent that these species can't make it, can't survive, and they deserve our help to try to bring them back, even if it's ultimately going to be futile. Too many people. You spend an August on Nantucket and you'll see it."

Both Maple and Michael Amaral recognize the challenges of generating public support for spending money to protect a beetle, but they also know it's worth the effort.

"If we could outfit the American burying beetle with fur and big brown eyes, we would have it made," Maple said. "But it's not a poster child for conservation, and sometimes you need a poster child for these kinds of reintroductions. If you work hard to conserve the habitat because there may be a poster child like an ivory billed woodpecker out there . . . then a lot of species that aren't poster children benefit. And that includes fungi and lichens and worms and stuff that we don't even know about."

Added Amaral: "Although you get the occasional individual who thinks it's a total waste of taxpayers' money, almost everyone I talk to about this species is absolutely fascinated by its life history and parental behavior and thinks it's worthwhile to take care of the little things . . . It's insects that really run the natural systems on the planet, so if we don't take care of them, we're not really taking care of ourselves."

9

Golden-Winged Warbler

My trip to the northwest corner of Connecticut didn't start well. I had planned to meet my good friend and long-time birding buddy John Confer at a hotel in the area to search for golden-winged warblers (*Vermivora chrysoptera*). Several months before, Confer had learned from a state biologist where New England's last nesting golden-wings were located, but instead of directions to the site, all he was given were the site's latitude and longitude coordinates. After hours of searching until late into the night for an appropriately marked map of the region, all we could find were maps for New York and Massachusetts. That gave us a general idea of where we might find the birds, but my expectation of actually finding one was pretty low.

A biology professor at Ithaca College, Confer has been studying golden-winged warblers for close to thirty years. Shortly after I graduated from the college in the early 1980s, Confer introduced me to the world of birding, including late-night owl prowls, twenty-four-hour Big Days, and weekly birding circuits around the Finger Lakes. He and his wife Karen, a spectacular wildlife artist, got me hooked on birds and along the way taught me the ways of science and conservation, for which

I will be forever in their debt. In some ways, John's single-minded focus on his research can make him seem like an absent-minded professor, and as we raced around looking for the map that I thought he had acquired well ahead of time, it seemed to me that this trait had reappeared. He wasn't pleased when I told him so.

"Don't worry, Todd," he kept telling me, "even without a map, I can sniff out the appropriate habitat and find golden-wings just by driving around the back roads." I wasn't convinced, but with no other great ideas, that was our plan.

The next morning we awoke at 4 o'clock, had a quick breakfast, and hit the road. Even before we arrived in the target region and just as it began to get light, Confer pulled to a stop at what he assessed as the perfect golden-wing habitat. It was a mix of wet, grassy meadow, scattered viburnum and honeysuckle shrubs, and a few small maple trees. And on the last weekend of May, it was filled with birds singing, establishing territories, and performing their breeding rituals. We walked up and down the road independently for several minutes listening intently for the bee-buzz-buzz song that is indicative of a singing male golden-winged warbler. We heard most of the typical shrubland species—gray catbirds, common yellowthroats, song sparrows, warbling vireos, chestnut-sided warblers, Baltimore orioles, and alder flycatchers, among many others—but no golden-wings. What was equally surprising, we also didn't find any blue-winged warblers (*Vermivora pinus*), a common shrub-nesting species that usually are found in the same habitat as golden-wings and that are partly responsible for the golden-wing's dramatic decline in the last century.

We continued on our drive through the back roads of Sharon and South Canaan and Salisbury, Connecticut, stopping every time we saw even a small patch of appropriate habitat. Many sites seemed ideal, and at every stop we heard most of the birds that usually are found nesting alongside golden-wings, but after three hours, we still hadn't found our target bird. We even stopped at the sites that appeared only marginally appropriate— they may have been what Confer considered too wet or too small or with too many large trees—but we stopped and listened anyway. Occasionally we played a tape recording of a golden-winged warbler in hopes that the real thing would respond, but one never did.

By 7:30 A.M., we stumbled upon the site of a property owned by the Audubon Society of Connecticut, and we pulled in hoping to find someone who could direct us to the birds we sought, but no one was there. So we continued criss-crossing the region—unsuccessfully—and returned to the Audubon refuge an hour later, but still we found no one about. At 9 o'clock, we returned to the refuge once again, and thankfully found someone stirring inside the headquarters. But despite his willingness to help, it was clear he didn't know anything about golden-wings. He did offer to call someone whom he thought would likely know where to look, but that person wasn't home. So once again, we left the refuge and continued on our way, driving slowly along country roads with our heads out the windows hoping against hope to hear the soft buzzing of a golden-winged warbler.

And then we heard it. Before the car even came to a full stop, we jumped out to track down the bird. It was definitely singing bee-buzz-buzz, but we couldn't see where it was singing from. For a moment, Confer got a glimpse of the bird, but by the time he raised his binoculars it had moved away deeper into the bushes and he couldn't confirm the identification. As we scanned the area excitedly for the warbler—which had stopped singing by then—Confer commented that he thought there was something odd about the third syllable of the bird's song. I didn't care if he was a good singer or a bad singer, I told him, I just wanted to see New England's rarest songbird.

Frustrated by our inability to see it, Confer started playing recordings, first of the golden-winged warbler, then the blue-winged warbler, and then even the mobbing call of the black-capped chickadee, which often attracts birds of many species, yet still we got no response. Then, after ten minutes of searching, the bird flew up from the bushes and into a tree right in front of us and sang the same golden-winged warbler song we had heard a few minutes before. But it wasn't a golden-winged warbler. It was a blue-winged warbler. And our disappointment was overwhelming.

Other than their size, blue-winged and golden-winged warblers look almost nothing alike. Blue-wings are mostly bright yellow with a black line through the eye, blue-gray wings, and two white wing bars. Golden-wings have grayish-white underparts, a black throat and eye patch (in the male), and a yellowish crown. They, too, have gray-blue wings, but instead of white wing bars like the blue-winged warbler, golden-wings have a yellow patch on their wings.

Despite the distinctions in the two species' appearance today, it is believed that two or three million years ago they were likely a single species. And then, according to Confer, the glaciers advanced south, the population split into two populations that became isolated from each other, and as a result of random selection and accumulated genetic mutations, they diverged and became two distinct species. Yet their DNA is still very much alike.

"The ancestral separation of the birds occurred about 1.5 million years ago," explained Confer.

> The best we know is that they became isolated, with blue-wings confined to the prairie forest ecotone in the Missouri area, probably. Golden-wings may have been in beaver meadows in the Appalachians. And then man cleared the forest between them, farmed the land, abandoned the land, secondary succession occurred, and golden-wings moved in. Sometime afterwards, blue-wings moved in, too.
>
> They were separated geographically before man changed the habitat pattern, and all of a sudden this solid bulk of forest which had isolated them became an avenue of secondary succession that blue-wings followed into the heart of golden-wing range and into the Northeast. Man's changing the habitat removed the barrier.

Because the species were still genetically very similar, when they found themselves in the same place, they hybridized. The progeny of this hybridization are called Brewster's warblers, which look like a mix of the two species, with the black eye-line and white wing bars of the blue-winged warbler and the gray-white belly and yellow crown of the golden-winged warbler. When a Brewster's breeds with another Brewster's, about one out of every sixteen young will be a Lawrence's warbler, a rare hybrid that has acquired the recessive genes of both its blue-winged and golden-winged grandparents. But rather than two Brewster's breeding with each other, what is more likely to happen is that Brewster's warblers will breed with blue-wings or golden-wings.

The blue-wing that Confer and I saw singing a golden-wing song probably had pure blue-winged parents and grandparents, but two or three generations before that an ancestor likely bred with a golden-wing. While it looked almost like a pure blue-wing, it clearly had some golden-wing genes.

The bigger issue, however, is that Brewster's have a very difficult time finding a mate. "Of seventeen Brewster's that I followed over two springs, none of them got a female," Confer said. "They seem fertile, but something about their interactions leads to a failure to get mates. There's a sexual selection. There isn't an intrinsic genetic barrier, but there seems to be a sexual behavior related to plumage that, when a female comes by, she says 'I don't like you, you don't look right.'"

While that might not sound like it would have much of an impact on the golden-winged warbler population, it does. That's because golden-wings are much more likely to hybridize than blue-wings. If hybridization results in succeeding generations having difficulty acquiring mates, then the golden-wing propensity to hybridize may be a major factor in their decline. Add to that the fact that blue-wings often harass pure golden-wing pairs enough to reduce the number of eggs they produce, and the result is the total displacement of golden-wings by blue-wings. And it's happening everywhere they occur together. About fifty years after blue-wings arrive in a region where golden-wings previously had thrived, golden-wings disappear.

Golden-winged warblers historically nested throughout much of the Appalachian Ridge (they winter primarily in Nicaragua and Guatemala), but in most of those locations, with the exception of the high elevations of the Appalachians, which are inhospitable to blue-wings, they have been replaced by blue-wings. As that has happened, the golden-wing population has spread northward.

According to Confer, the range expansion began about 130 years ago as farmland was being abandoned and the early stages of secondary succession emerged. Golden-wings first turned up in coastal New England in the 1870s, and their first nesting success in Michigan was around 1900. They are now as far north as Georgian Bay in Ontario, the north shore of Lake Superior in Manitoba, and a few miles into Saskatchewan, places they had never nested before. But as they move north, they are extirpated from their southern range as blue-wings invade the territory.

"Golden-wings reached Ithaca, New York, where I live, in 1917," said Confer. "Blue-wings reached there in the 1940s, and golden-wings disappeared as a regularly occurring nesting species in about 1980. And that trend has occurred in hundreds of counties in the Northeast and the lower elevations of the Appalachian Mountains, as well as in southern Michigan, southern Wisconsin, southern Minnesota, and northern Ohio. In all these places, golden-wings arrived as early stages of succession became regionally abundant, then blue-wings arrived, and in fifty years the golden-wings were gone."

Some lineages continue to move north, but once they reach the boreal forests in Canada, there won't be anywhere left for them to go. In New England, where there isn't any appropriate habitat further north, they've just disappeared.

Except for one tiny spot in northwest Connecticut. If only we could find it.

It had been the coldest month of May in decades and we had been searching for golden-winged warblers for hours under cool, gray skies, but then the sun came out at about 10 A.M. and the temperature warmed noticeably. For birders, that's not a good sign. Birds tend to stop singing and go into hiding during the heat of the day. Since we were likely to hear the bird singing long before we saw it, our chances of seeing a golden-winged warbler were reduced further as the mercury rose. Confer and I were praying for the clouds to return.

With nothing to lose and nowhere else to turn, we stopped one more time at the Audubon Society refuge and sought out the man we had spoken to previously. Thankfully, he had received a call back from the birder he phoned earlier with vague directions to one of New England's last golden-winged warbler breeding sites.

The designated road is a narrow, dirt lane that parallels the east bank of the Housatonic River, a wide, rocky river where fly fishermen were casting their lines, kayakers paddled, and where it appeared that several rafting outfitters made a good living. The road also crosses back and forth over railroad tracks that also follow the line of the river. As we traversed the road for several miles, no appropriate habitat was within view. When we finally found a small roadside area that Confer thought could be it, we pulled up alongside another vehicle where an older gentleman was standing holding binoculars. I rolled down the window and asked the man if he was a birder, and he smiled in the affirmative. When I then asked if he knew where to find golden-winged warblers in the area, he chuckled and said, "This is the place." Introducing himself as Neil, he added that this was his fourth visit to the site and he had yet to see the bird, though he also admitted that his hearing wasn't too good.

The site was about 100 yards long and 30 yards wide with grass that appeared to have been mowed once or twice in the previous year; small patches of tall, dried stems remained from the previous year's wildflowers; dense areas of autumn olive, honeysuckle, gray dogwood, and thick poison ivy vines indicated that some areas hadn't been mowed in five or ten years; and a few scattered cedar and maple trees completed the picture of what Confer considered the perfect habitat. It was all bordered by the road and river on one side and with a forested perimeter of pines and oaks on the other. After walking around for a brief moment, Confer proceeded to set up the tape recorder to play a continuous loop of golden-winged warbler song.

The Ithaca College biologist looked like a man on a mission. He found a 4-foot-long branch with a fork at the end, called it his warbler stick, and optimistically proceeded to explore the southern portion of the site for a golden-winged warbler nest. I took off in the opposite direction, battling the thick black flies that found their way into my eyes, ears, and mouth and that were absent from every other site we visited that day. With the tape recorder still blasting away, Confer emerged from a thicket ten minutes later to say he found the nest of an indigo bunting, a beautiful finch-like bird that often nests alongside golden-wings. At most other sites we had been to that morning, we gave up after less than ten minutes had elapsed, but Confer said he was convinced our target bird was there, so we continued searching.

"It's likely that the female may be incubating eggs by now, and if that's the case, then there's no reason why the male needs to defend the territory, so he may not respond to the tape," he said. So we turned it off and Confer continued his nest search while I took some notes and glanced at the trees. Birds were abundant: yellow, chestnut-sided, magnolia, and pine warblers, eastern kingbird, chickadees, orioles, a yellow-billed cuckoo, even a yellow-bellied sapsucker. After another ten minutes, I took the tape player to the northern portion of the site and turned it on as Neil left.

Moments later, the tape recording sounded different, like there was an echo of the golden-wing's song. But it wasn't on the tape. It was 15 feet away from the recorder, a beautiful, male golden-winged warbler, who seemed to appear out of nowhere and was singing his heart out to defend his territory from the electronic invader singing from inside the tape player. I watched as the bird alternated between singing a perfect rendition of its bee-buzz-buzz song and foraging for a meal. It flitted from a dogwood to a maple, up to the top of a cedar, and then down near ground level, sometimes even hanging upside down as it searched for insects on the underside of leaves. And then it thrust its chest out, opened its beak wider than would seem possible, and let loose with another bee-buzz-buzz.

I almost couldn't control my excitement. This bird was probably one of the last golden-winged warblers to nest in New England, the end of the line of continuous breeding in the region that began in 1870 in a thicket in Litchfield, Connecticut, and I didn't want to take my eyes off it for fear that I wouldn't find it again. But Confer also was concerned that the bird on the tape recording would ultimately win the song battle with the real bird, and the real golden-wing would fly away defeated and abandon its territory. So we turned off the tape and continued to study the bird. Confer pointed out that it had a slight gold-colored wash on its chest, suggesting that it might have had a blue-wing warbler in its ancestry. Apparently feeling comfortable that he had fought back the invader, the golden-winged warbler stopped singing but continued actively foraging in the nearby trees and shrubs. I kept watching the bird intently, hoping to see it find a meal. Golden-wings usually glean insects off tree branches and leaves. They are also one of the few birds that know how to unroll a leaf that a caterpillar or spider has rolled into a protective covering to hide from predators. After a few more minutes of foraging withing sight, the bird disappeared to wherever it came from.

Which, of course, is when Neil returned.

As we drove away, Confer couldn't stop talking about the excellent habitat at the site. "Golden-winged warblers are habitat specialists," he said. "They occur in tamarack bogs, they occur in abandoned fields, they occur in managed utility rights-of-way, they occur in swamp forests with partial canopy and grass tussocks, but every place that they occur has about the same proportion of cover by grass and by shrubs and a relatively low amount of trees. Wherever they nest has to have at least 50 to 60 percent herb cover.

"So what they care about is the physiognomy of the site—the profile. If you imagined it in black and white and didn't worry about the water and the trees and just looked at the density of the grass and the density of the shrubs, there is a very specific combination of characteristics that's suitable for them," Confer said.

Ninety percent of golden-winged warblers' preferred habitat overlaps with that preferred by blue-winged warblers. On the extremes, blue-wings prefer more shrubs and trees and less grass and herbs, while golden-wings prefer more herbs and fewer trees, but generally speaking, they mostly like the same habitat. Golden-wings nest in grassy tussocks on the ground, and when they nest in areas with less grass and more trees, they tend to raise fewer young, probably because their nests are more conspicuous to predators.

The Connecticut site we visited appeared to have exactly the proportion of herbaceous growth that golden-wings prefer. It was so perfect, Confer said, that he suspected it was intentionally managed for the birds. And if that were the case, it would be one of only two places in North America where it has been done.

With that in mind, I put in a call to Jenny Dickson. She's the wildlife biologist for the state of Connecticut who is responsible for coordinating the management of nongame birds and the one who gave Confer the coordinates for the site where we found the golden-wings. She said that the state is indeed managing a number of state and private lands for shrubland birds, partly through a federal landowner incentive program, and she is specifically targeting golden-winged warblers.

"We know the species is barely hanging on in the state," she said. "How many pairs we have is uncertain because the area of the state they're found in has an extensive amount of private holdings. But you can safely say there are fewer than two dozen pairs."

Dickson acknowledged, however, the challenges of managing for golden-wings. She said she has been working to educate landowners about the importance of shrubland species and why they should manage for early successional habitat. "But it's tricky to manage for golden-wings without just encouraging blue-wings," she noted. "Blue-wings are declining, too, so it's important that we strike a balance between golden-wings and blue-wings, though it's tricky figuring out how to keep that balance. We know some of our work will benefit blue-wings and not necessarily golden-wings."

Yet the fact that she is focused on creating and maintaining the habitat at all is a huge step in the right direction.

The preferred habitat of golden-winged warblers is hard to come by, and it lasts only a short time. Before recorded history, it occurred primarily as a result of forest fires or hurricanes and tornados blowing down sections of forest. In the years following, natural succession occurred as those areas became revegetated with herbaceous plants, shrubs, and small trees. Golden-winged warblers would then move in to breed for five to ten years until the trees grew too tall and the habitat reverted to forest. The birds then moved on to find new locations where fires or blow-downs created the early stages of succession they prefer.

Beaver also played a major role in creating this habitat. According to Confer, of the total of 33 million acres within the borders of New York State, 1 million acres were historically ponds and adjacent meadows created by beavers damming streams. "At any given time, 7 to 8 percent of those beaver ponds were abandoned, the dam had gone out, the water level went down, the mud became exposed, and you would get these little clusters of successional habitat," he explained. "That's 70,000 acres of excellent golden-winged warbler habitat. That's a lot of acres. So it's conceivable that golden-wings evolved in the habitat that is formed briefly as beavers abandoned dams."

Then Europeans came along and nearly wiped out the beaver in much of the country, reducing the quantity of that ephemeral habitat dramatically. Around the same time, humans also began clear-cutting the eastern forests for agriculture. By the 1840s and 1850s, though, farmers in New England were recognizing that the poor, rocky soil wasn't conducive to raising crops, and those farm fields began to be abandoned as farmers moved west. Since farmland abandonment creates successional habitat just as beavers and fires and blow-downs do, golden-wings began to expand their range and thrive once more.

"Farmland abandonment has moved as a wave with regional synchronization across much of the eastern United States," Confer said. "It started in the Northeast, moved westward, and it's still moving northward now. The golden-winged warbler movement has followed the regional social, economic, and agricultural trends that lead to farmland abandonment over a large scale."

Unfortunately, there's not much farmland in the Northeast left to abandon. Two million acres of farmland in New York were abandoned in the first two-thirds of the twentieth century, and that land has passed through its shrubland stage and become forested again. It happened even earlier in most of New England. The great pulse of man-made shrublands created from farmland abandonment is mostly over, according to Confer, and since people are creating and managing little new acreage of this habitat, golden-wings are barely hanging on. The species' population has declined by 7 to 8 percent per year for the last forty years as its habitat in New England has declined by approximately 90 percent.

Its few bright spots are due to unexpected allies, like power companies. Electric utilities in the Northeast own and manage thousands of miles of power-line corridors that transport high-voltage electricity from power plants to electricity users throughout the region. The companies must manage those corridors so vegetation does not grow tall enough to interfere with the wires and cause black-outs, which means the companies kill off most of the trees but encourage the growth of shrubs and low-growing plants. As ugly as the towers supporting the wires may be to neighbors, these utility rights-of-way are quite attractive to golden-winged warblers. And it's not just golden-wings that like this habitat.

"There's a whole suite of birds that nest in shrublands that are declining—song sparrow, field sparrow, indigo bunting, prairie warbler, Eastern towhee, gray catbird, brown thrasher, as well as blue-winged and golden-winged warblers—and the biggest source of shrubland now is utility rights-of-way," said Confer, who spent four years studying the birdlife under power lines in New York and New England in the 1990s. "Utilities have clearly become the dominant source of shrubland, so hopefully it can be managed in a way that is most suitable for the rarest species or for the greatest abundance of species."

Another important source of shrubland habitat is forest clear-cutting. Golden-winged warblers have expanded their range into northern Minnesota and Manitoba primarily into areas where the aspen forests have been clear-cut for wood pulp. With little effort, thousands of acres of golden-winged warbler habitat could be created in New England and New York simply by allowing timber companies to clear-cut small areas in state and national forests and leaving the land to regenerate on its own. But it's an unpopular idea.

"Politically, there is tremendous opposition to clear-cutting, partially because of the belief that large contiguous forests are the best thing you can do for conservation," said Confer. "Pre-human intervention, though, there was always a patchy network of beaver ponds and burned areas within our forests where shrubland species could live . . . We should manage for that mosaic. If you say that state lands should be 100 percent forest, then where do the shrub species fit into that?"

Confer advocates that 5 to 7 percent of state forest lands—about the percentage that he says shrublands covered in pre-colonial times—should be managed on a rotating basis for shrublands, to create the mosaic of habitats that support the diversity of species that occurred before human activities changed land use over a large scale. But he knows it's not likely to happen. He supported a plan submitted by the New York Department of Environmental Conservation to do some clear-cutting in the Hudson River Valley to create shrub habitat, "but it blew up in their face and they had to retract it," he said. "Politically, you just can't clear-cut."

It seems that some of the land uses hated most by the general public are turning out to be the best land uses for golden-winged warblers, and warbler advocates like Confer are finding themselves seeking allies in unusual places. What's worse in the public's mind than joining hands with the power companies and those clear-cutting the forest? How about supporting the efforts of strip miners who don't reclaim their abandoned mine sites?

Ron Canterbury, a biology professor at the University of Cincinnati, has been studying golden-winged warblers in the mountains of southern West Virginia for nearly twenty years. He said that the sites that harbor the greatest number of golden-wings are in the Appalachian coalfields that were strip-mined in the 1960s and 1970s and then abandoned. Over the next thirty years, those sites naturally became revegetated and turned into excellent golden-wing habitat. Unfortunately for the warblers, changes in mining methods and regulations requiring mining companies to restore abandoned mines, which were designed to make the industry more ecologically friendly, have decimated the golden-wing population. Reclamation is opening up former mining sites and making them more favorable to grassland species, according to Canterbury. The birds were most abundant when there was no active management of the sites. At one time, he was monitoring eighty to one hundred sites, some for as long as nineteen years, and now he has just twenty sites left where golden-wings remain.

While mine reclamation is one major cause of the decline of golden-wings in West Virginia, suburban sprawl is the other. Unlike in much of the Northeast, where farmland abandonment has fueled golden-wing expansion over the years, what little farmland abandonment that occurs in West Virginia is quickly being developed before it has time to become good golden-wing habitat. Canterbury said that roadway projects like the Coalfield Expressway and tourism development like the Hatfield

McCoy Trail are ripping through the largest golden-wing populations in the state.

"What little refugia the birds had because of mining in West Virginia they're now losing because of reclamation," said Canterbury. "The outlook is not good. By 2020 I'm pretty sure golden-wings will be gone from West Virginia."

After a brief celebration of our successful search for golden-winged warblers in Connecticut, Confer and I drove 100 miles west to Sterling Forest in New York, one of just three sites documented in North America where blue-wings and golden-wings have co-existed for a hundred years. The 18,000-acre forest, which is contiguous with a forested state park and protected forests at the West Point military academy and adjacent areas of New Jersey, is Confer's primary research site as he tries to understand the ecology of warbler co-existence.

"If there is a hope to find something that allows blue-wings and golden-wings to co-exist, and if it's possible to manage for that, then the hope is that you can look at some place like Sterling Forest where they have co-existed, find what's special or unique or different there, and mimic that in one way or another at other sites," he explained. What Confer claims to have found in Sterling Forest is habitat segregation, a place where the preferred habitat of blue-wings is segregated from that of golden-wings so they have little interaction and therefore little likelihood of interbreeding.

When we got there the next morning at 5 o'clock with his research assistants after sleeping in a rustic bunkhouse nearby, I was totally surprised. Sterling Forest is a thick, swampy forest of red maples and uplands with a nearly closed canopy. It looked to me nothing at all like the habitat where we had spent the previous day searching for golden-wings. And the birdlife was totally different, too. Instead of shrubland species, we heard typical forest species singing, including ovenbird, wood thrush, hooded warbler, American redstart, scarlet tanager, veery, and red-bellied woodpecker.

Yet Confer reminded me of what he said the day before—ignore the trees and the water and think only about the ratio of shrubs to herbaceous groundcover. When I did that, I could see how golden-winged warblers might think the two habitats were similar, despite the obvious differences when looking at the bigger picture. Sterling Forest has a thick understory of shrubs, fallen rotting logs, scattered rocks and boulders, and plenty of forbs and grassy tussocks.

Confer and his assistants Mark and Jen spent every day from May through July searching Sterling Forest for the nests of blue-wings and golden-wings, monitoring the birds' activities, and recording reams of data about their behavior, egg-laying, social interactions, and nesting success. They also trapped individuals of both species to collect a blood sample for DNA analysis. "The hypothesis I'm testing is that golden-wings have survived here for so long because they do really well in the swamp forest and blue-wings rarely occur here," he said. Blue-wings occur nearby in a less-forested upland area where smaller numbers of golden-wings also are found, but in that habitat the two species hybridize and compete with each other. "In the uplands before blue-wings got here, that was the habitat that fueled golden-wing expansion," Confer said. "Now, blue-wings are there and golden-wings are becoming extirpated. Something changed with the arrival of blue-wings. So the model that I'm testing is that the swamp forests have really good reproductive success [for golden-wings], and they produce more young there than they need to sustain the average annual death rate of adults over an entire year. They produce excess young, and those excess young go around trying to find some place to nest besides the swamp forest because there's more than enough birds to fill the vacancies, and they end up in the uplands. The uplands are not so good [for golden-wings] because they produce hybrids and because blue-wings and golden-wings compete, so their reproductive success in the uplands isn't enough to sustain the golden-wings there." Ultimately the swamp forest is such a strong source of golden-wings that it sustains the appearance of a population of golden-wings in the uplands, but the upland golden-wings continue to succumb to the blue-wings.

The first job of the morning was to set up a net to catch a male golden-winged warbler that had been seen in the area in previous days and whose behavior suggested that a female was sitting on eggs somewhere nearby. We stretched out the 40-foot-long mist net, which looks much like a fine volleyball net but which is almost invisible to the naked eye, and attached a stuffed golden-winged warbler to a nearby shrub. The stuffed bird was killed by a car five years previous and the researchers call him Stooly because he's the "stool pigeon" that lures other golden-wings to the net for capture. Stooly looked old and battered to me, and I couldn't imagine that a real warbler would think him a threat, but the research assistants assured me that he does his job well.

We then proceeded to set up a second net 100 yards away near the territory of a different pair of golden-wings. Confer wanted to give the first birds some time to settle down after the disturbance caused by setting up the first net. When we returned twenty minutes later, we positioned ourselves about 50 feet from the net. Confer turned on the tape recording of the golden-winged warbler's bee-buzz-buzz song and then tugged on a long string attached to Stooly to make it appear that the stuffed bird was alive and singing. But instead of the target golden-wing, a male blue-wing responded, dove at Stooly, and eventually became entangled in the net. Despite the researchers' great disappointment at discovering a blue-wing in an area where they hadn't seen one before, they proceeded to remove the bird from the net and process it. While seated on a nearby log, the group went through a series of apparently well-planned steps, and they all knew their role. Confer used a tiny hypodermic needle to prick the branchial vein near the bird's elbow joint to collect blood in a tiny vial, then applied coagulant powder with a cotton swab to stop the bleeding. The bird was then banded with a series of colored bands—the right leg received a hot pink band above a purple band while the left leg received light green and aluminum bands—to identify it without having to recapture it. Then the bird was weighed and measured. Its pointy outer tail feather indicated that it was born the previous year, and a yellow bar on its wing suggested it had some golden-winged warbler genes. When the bird was released, it immediately disappeared into the trees. "We like it when the bird flies up rather than down," Confer said with a smirk.

Returning to the second net, the team found three birds entangled before even playing the tape—a previously banded male golden-wing, a female American redstart, and a male cerulean warbler. The cerulean was the big surprise, as it is almost as rare as the golden-wing; to find both rarities in one net was almost inconceivable. After releasing the captured birds, Mark went to check up on a nearby golden-wing nest he had found several days previously. The game plan was to scare the female warbler off the nest and into the net so she could be banded and so a blood sample could be collected. Confer describes female golden-winged warblers as "tight sitters" because they "sit tight [on their eggs] and hope their cryptic camouflage helps them avoid predators . . . You can walk by a female on a nest and she almost never leaves. You want to count the eggs she has and you sometimes have to poke her off the nest [with a stick]. I've had females that, when you poke them off their nests to count the eggs, the female comes right up the stick scolding me. They're really brave little creatures."

Unfortunately, that strategy didn't seem to work with this particular nest. When Mark approached, he found that the nest had been turned over and the eggs were gone, probably eaten by a medium-sized mammal such as a raccoon, since smaller predators like blue jays or chipmunks would have taken the eggs but left the nest undisturbed. Luckily, the female golden-winged warbler was heard nearby, so at least it survived and perhaps could start over again. Confer said that some golden-wings are such tight sitters that they've been consumed by predators while sitting on their eggs.

A major concern that Confer has with his research is that by monitoring nests so closely, he may be leaving human odors and creating pathways that lead predators right to nests. So he's careful to never actually touch a nest and to watch them from a distance whenever possible. That's why each member of the research team, and any visitors to the site, are required to carry what Confer calls a warbler stick: a chest-high walking stick with a fork at the end that is used in place of one's hands to move vegetation around when looking for nests. As we finished trapping for the morning and moved to a new section of the park to look for nests, the researchers went through an elaborate ritual to find me the perfect warbler stick. Once an appropriate stick was located and presented to me with great fanfare, we split up to search for nests.

The target area of the forest, designated by Confer as F2 and F3, was considerably wetter than the earlier locations we had worked in, and the songs of wetland birds became more noticeable, especially the common yellowthroat, northern waterthrush, and Louisiana waterthrush. The forest was slightly more open there, and the vegetation included three or four types of ferns, spicebush, blueberry and viburnum shrubs, and mounds of mosses, sphagnum, arrowhead, and violets. We sloshed through shin-deep water and thick mud that often nearly pulled off our boots as we used our warbler sticks to search beneath every bit of vegetation for a nest. Most of the golden-wing nests Confer has found in this area in previous years have been in the middle of sedge tussocks, so those were searched especially carefully. I was more worried about stepping on a nest

than in finding one with my stick, so my efforts proved fruitless. After an
hour of searching, Confer located a golden-wing nest with a female incubating six eggs near a spicebush in an area that I had already searched.
He memorized the location so he could find it when he returned several
days later, and he insisted that I stay away so as not to create a path to the
nest for predators.

It was the Saturday before Memorial Day, and on Saturdays the researchers only work in the field for half a day. When your day starts at 5,
a half-day of work means you're finished by 9 A.M. So we packed up the
gear and made the slow trek back to the truck, enjoying the continuing
chorus of birdsong and the beautiful scenery while remarking on what
still seemed to me to be atypical golden-wing habitat. "This is certainly
a rare habitat, an old habitat, and it takes a long time to make a habitat
like this," Confer said thoughtfully and with an apparent sense of wonder. "There's something special about it, but I'm just not sure what."

Sterling Forest isn't just special to golden-winged warblers, though. A
private landowner in the middle of the forest is threatening to build a
housing development that could affect water levels and that certainly
would result in housecats running rampant, lawn fertilizers harming the
ecosystem, and the eradication of significant swaths of natural habitat.
And that has Confer quite concerned.

"Golden-wings aren't on the state endangered list, so there's nothing
to prevent people from destroying the habitat," he said. "I've estimated
that there are twenty, thirty, forty pairs of golden-wings in the area that
is proposed for development, and there are about 250 pairs in Sterling
Forest altogether. So you're talking about jeopardizing a tenth of the
population. If you want to manage for a population, two hundred pairs
is right on the margin of . . . being too small a population to be comfortable that it could sustain itself."

The national conservation plan for the golden-winged warbler was drawn
up by a group called Partners in Flight, which ranks the conservation priority of various bird species on a state-by-state basis. Because the golden-
wing population is low and declining and there are significant threats to
its habitat, the species is a high priority for serious conservation effort.
"But the plan has no authority," explained Confer. "It's not a law. It's just
a group of state employees and ornithologists from universities who get

together and say 'wouldn't it be nice if . . .' Their idea is to create a plan that can serve as a lever to pry money out of state legislative bodies."

But it's failing miserably, at least as far as golden-wings are concerned. The plan recommends that 30,000 acres in southern New England and southern New York should be managed specifically for golden-winged warblers, yet only a small number of acres in Connecticut and New York—and none anywhere else—are being managed for the species. Confer's efforts to get funding to manage just 4 acres in Sterling Forest finally were approved in 2006 after several years of rejections. Yet he's continuing to move forward with his own research in hopes that he can find the miracle answer to stave off the species' extinction. And he's expanding his reach to see what he can learn from what's happening to the species in other parts of the country. "We need to determine in a wider geographic area if there are habitat refugia," he said.

So he's continuing his work at Sterling Forest to learn more about the population of golden-winged warblers that has co-existed with blue-wings for more than a century and strategizing with other researchers in other parts of the bird's range. But will it be enough to reverse the population trend? Confer doesn't think so.

"I've spent a good deal of my professional life trying to find the relative importance of competition and habitat and hybridization, and it looks to me like it's every one of them," he said. "It's been extirpated from so much of its range. And even in Sterling Forest where they've co-existed for a hundred years, when you sample the genes of the golden-wings, they are about 30 percent mixed with blue-wing mitochondria. If in a hundred years you get 30 percent mixing, it's a goner . . . I think in five hundred years they'll be gone. The movement north of blue-wings and golden-wings in different places and different time periods is 2 to 4 miles a year, so right now golden-wings are 200 to 300 miles north of blue-wings. That means that in sixty years blue-wings will be there. At some point, they'll be getting up to the conifer forest, and golden-wings are just not adapted to the conifer forest.

"On the other hand, three-quarters of the population now is in Wisconsin and Minnesota, and blue-wings aren't there yet. There's a chance that blue-wings aren't adapted to move that far northward, so golden-wings might be able to hang on there. I guess we'll just have to wait and see."

10

Karner Blue

Every year, Mrs. O'Brien's class of first and second graders at Beaver Meadow Elementary School in Concord, New Hampshire, study the life cycle of insects and learn about plants in the community. After a unit about butterflies and the plants they feed upon, biologists from the New Hampshire Fish and Game Department arrive laden with milk cartons, soil, and seeds to lead the children through an hour-long activity planting wild blue lupine, an uncommon perennial plant with bluish-purple flowers and light green leaves. For the next three months, the students care for the plants and watch them grow, keeping a close accounting of the health of each plant.

In May, when the weather has warmed and the lupines have matured, the students gather up their plants, hop on a bus, and take a field trip to conservation land next to the Concord Municipal Airport to transplant the lupine into the pine barrens. There they are joined by students from other schools who have also cultivated lupine, as well as mentors from Fish and Game who help them dig holes and water the plants. "The kids get very excited about the project," O'Brien said. "We do a huge study of the lupine, we create a bulletin board where eventually a butterfly arrives, and we learn lots of new vocabulary. We're even writing a book about it."

The airport site is a rare and declining habitat found only in scattered locations between 41 and 44 degrees latitude from New Hampshire to Minnesota. According to Celine Goulet, a biologist with New Hampshire Fish and Game, the pine barrens are a combination of three primary habitat types: grasslands harboring a variety of herbaceous plants; a layer of shrub that includes scrub oak, blueberry, and heath; and a pitch pine community that provides shade and protection to the plants and wildlife living below. "With all these different habitat types together, the pine barrens is in constant flux," Goulet said. "It's an environment that typically has a lot of disturbance occurring within it, so what was once a grassland could succeed into a shrubland and then into a canopy, and then there may be a fire that reverts it back to grassland. It's constantly shifting."

It's here in the pine barrens adjacent to the Concord airport that New England's last population of Karner blue butterflies (*Lycaeides melissa samuelis*) is being reintroduced after having been extirpated from the region in 2000. And its growing population is due in large part to the many schoolchildren who have grown and transplanted wild blue lupine, the only plant on which the Karner blue caterpillar will feed and on which the adult butterfly will lay its eggs. The official butterfly of the state of New Hampshire, the Karner blue is a tiny insect—just 1 inch across—and, true to its name, the males are a brilliant silvery blue outlined with a thin black line and fringed with white, while the females are a gray-brown or purplish-blue with orange crescents on the outer edges of their hind wings. The undersides of both sexes are pale silver with numerous black spots encircled in white and a row of bright orange and blue markings on the edge of their hind wings.

Although Karner blues are easy to confuse with two look-alike species—the eastern tailed blue and the spring or summer azure—their orange crescents, association with lupine, and distinctive flying behavior separates them. "They sort of look like a puppet on a string," said Goulet. "They don't look like they know where they're going, or they have no rhyme or reason to their flight pattern. They're just crazy little fluttering things. That's an easy way to find them in the wild. Just look for a butterfly that's going in a roundabout way as if it were on a little puppet string." But they're not very easy to find, even when you know where to look, partly because the adult butterflies only live for five days.

After disappearing entirely from the airport site in 2000, captive rearing and reintroduction efforts have bolstered the wild population of Karner blues in New Hampshire to 1,500 individuals. In July 2006, I joined Goulet on her daily monitoring of the Concord pine barrens to see how many butterflies were still on the wing. To get to the 350 acres of protected habitat, we drove through an industrial park behind the airport to a gate leading to a 25-acre easement owned by the U.S. Fish and Wildlife Service. A wide, sandy right-of-way through the middle of the habitat is open to the public, and since it's so close to several offices in the industrial park, numerous workers and nearby residents use it as a walking trail. As we arrived, a man in a white shirt, blue tie, dress pants, and sneakers had just completed his morning walk at the site during what must have been his coffee break, and two women strolled by deep in conversation. Although the bird nesting season was nearly over, eastern towhees and field sparrows were constantly singing, and a prairie warbler occasionally let loose with his ascending buzzy song.

We hiked in about 100 yards on a trail that was closed to the public to one of several "monitoring units" that Goulet had scheduled to visit that day. When we got there, I quickly understood her earlier description of the three habitat types that make up the pine barrens. Much of the area consisted of native grasses and forbs, such as little bluestem, spreading dogbane, and sweetfern interspersed with scattered blueberry bushes and head-high scrub oaks. Encircling the area were tall pitch pines, the only trees within sight. According to Goulet, the varied habitat meets the differing needs of the Karner blues. "The females prefer shaded areas where they can lay their eggs, while the males prefer sunny openings to roost and look for females. They mate in sunny, humid conditions, usually around eleven in the morning or four or five in the afternoon. They're often active later in the day than most other butterflies."

As she spoke, the first Karner blue of the day fluttered by, and Goulet dashed after it with her net. Her first swing missed the tiny insect, but instead of flying away, the butterfly danced around us, and Goulet ultimately slapped her net gently over it when it landed on the grass. It was only then that I noticed that the end of her net had a hole in it, which she closed by tying it into a knot. She intentionally created the hole in the net because, after she untied the knot, it allowed her to reach in easily and grasp the butterfly without having to lift the net and risk the insect's escape. Holding its folded wings carefully between her thumb and index finger, she noted that it was marked with a number six on the underside of its wing. Every Karner blue butterfly that is reared in captivity is assigned a number that is written on one wing using an ordinary fine-point marking pen, which, much to my surprise, apparently does no harm to the insect's delicate wings. But Karner number six was not reared in captivity. It was born in the wild, but it had been captured three days earlier in an adjacent monitoring unit, marked with an identifying number, and had traveled less than 200 yards since that time. Goulet made a note in her records, then set the butterfly on a leaf so I could get a good look at it, but it immediately took flight. Eventually, it landed on a nearby blueberry bush leaf. With its wings folded, I could easily read its number, and when it finally opened its wings, the gorgeous blue coloration sparkled in the sunlight.

While Goulet and I chatted about the habitat and the butterfly she had just released, another Karner blue approached us and landed on her net, followed soon after by a skipper, one of a group of small orange and brown butterflies that perch with their wings closed and are very difficult to identify. The Karner was apparently an old female—which means it was probably five days old—with slightly torn wings and some of its orange scales missing. Again Goulet noted the butterfly's number and recorded the date, time, monitoring unit, and sex before moving on.

The Karner blues share the pine barrens habitat with several other rare butterflies that feed upon wild blue lupine, including the frosted elfin and persius duskywing, as well as with the equally rare pine barrens moth, hognose snake, and grasshopper sparrow, so I kept my eyes out for those species, too. Casually strolling through the area, Goulet swung her net back and forth as she walked to flush any Karners into flying. As she did so, she picked and ate several wild blueberries, raving about how tasty they were. Soon a Karner blue took wing, and she quickly caught and removed it—another wild male—and struggled to write the number 106 on its tiny wings. When she finally released it, some of its orange coloration had rubbed off on her fingers.

The mark-and-recapture project helps the biologists learn about how far the Karners disperse, survival rates of wild and captive reared butterflies, the specific habitat they are using, and the success of habitat restoration efforts. One thing they learned early on was that the insects were not dispersing as quickly and as far as they had hoped, which may have been because the habitat at the release site was too congested. So they removed some trees and other vegetation and found that the butterflies soon scattered further away to colonize additional habitat.

At the next monitoring unit, the trail paralleled the airport fence where chimney swifts twittered and darted back and forth overhead and horseflies harassed us constantly. We had no choice but to put up with the biting insects because the use of insect repellent while monitoring the butterflies is prohibited to ensure that it doesn't harm the endangered insects. Just as Goulet mentioned that we were probably too far away from the release site for any butterflies to have moved that far, another wild male flew by and was captured and marked. Twenty minutes later as we returned on the same trail, the same butterfly was still fluttering around the exact spot where we had caught it earlier. Goulet said that most Karner blues only move about 100 yards in their entire adult lifetime, which is part of the difficulty they face at the site. They confine themselves to a tiny part of the available habitat and don't disperse to other areas that are less crowded and have equally attractive habitat.

Back at the entrance to the pine barrens, two Karner blues swirled around each other as if they were fighting. Thinking they might be preparing to mate, Goulet decided not to capture them, but they quickly separated. While Goulet kept an eye on one of them, I did my best to follow the other, which turned out to be number six, the first Karner blue we had seen earlier that morning. After fluttering up and down and around me momentarily, it settled on a thick plant stem that was leaning over on its side. The butterfly's wings were held partially open, and it appeared to adjust its position several times to find the best angle to enjoy the blazing sun. But it only stayed still for a few seconds before fluttering off to land on a root five feet away in a sandy patch of ground, where it shifted its rear wings back and forth like the swaying hips of Elvis, a behavior I noticed several more times that morning. Again it took flight, but this time it returned to perch on the same root it had just abandoned. Goulet said that Karner blues hold their wings closed when feeding and mating, but otherwise they hold them open when perching. The one I was watching also occasionally flicked its wings, like it had a twitch.

After two minutes of apparently doing nothing, it took off again, flew in small circles, then up and down, seemingly with no apparent destination in mind. "Skippers fly straight like they know where they're going," Goulet said, "but not these guys." Eventually it settled again on a root, this time about five feet behind me, where it shifted position once more to collect the sun. A red ant walked around on the same root, but the butterfly—which appeared to have a torn rear left wing—ignored it entirely. Some species of red ants have a symbiotic relationship with Karner blues. The ants protect the Karner caterpillars from predatory insects, and in turn the caterpillars secrete a honeydew solution that the ants eat. Goulet said that it's often easier to find caterpillars by first looking for red ants.

A minute later, Karner number six flew off once more, but immediately fluttered close to the ground and landed on a cinquefoil leaf that was twisted upside down. Its wing tip caught the sun at an unusual angle and appeared almost bright white, and the increasing breeze made it quiver, but the butterfly held its ground. It didn't appear to be bothered by a tiny bee that darted around it either, but as the bee tried to alight on the Karner blue's wing, the butterfly flicked its wings and the bee flew off. After getting one last close-up look at the attractive little insect, Goulet and I turned to leave.

Members of the order Lepidoptera are famous for their magical transformation from egg to caterpillar to delicate adult butterfly. In the case of the Karner blue, which produces two new generations per year, the process begins in mid-April when tiny larvae emerge from eggs that had been laid on lupine the previous August. The well-camouflaged green caterpillars immediately begin feeding on the lupine leaves, and over the course of about thirty-five days they proceed through four stages of postembryonic growth called instars during which they shed their skin and grow larger and larger, eventually becoming about half an inch long. After the fourth instar, they attach themselves to the underside of a lupine leaf and pupate, the transformation stage during which they stop feeding, become immobile, and undergo a complex series of internal changes. Seven to nine days later, they emerge as an adult butterfly.

As adults, Karner blues do not depend on wild blue lupine as much as the caterpillars do. While they feed on the nectar of the blooming lupine, they also nectar on a number of other flowering plants, preferring white or yellow flowers in particular, including New Jersey tea, broadleaf milkweed, wood lily, spreading dogbane, blueberry, and strawberry. During the five days of their adult life, they feed and mate and the females lay eggs to start the process all over again. This first group of adult Karners typically flies in late May and June. Their eggs hatch in July and another brood of adult butterflies take wing late in August. The second brood of adults know to lay their eggs at the very base of the lupine plant, which by then has fallen over and dried out, where the eggs survive through the winter and hatch in April. "A lot of people have been trying to determine what factor is most important in making them hatch," Goulet explained. "Some people think it is temperature, some think it might be light, and some think it may be some chemical reaction having to do with the lupine starting to grow. We're not sure. We try to regulate the light and temperature in the lab, and that seems to be the biggest key to cause them to hatch in captivity."

During their life cycle, Karner blues are a regular target of predators. As caterpillars, they are fed upon by wasps, ants, and ladybugs, while adults are often consumed by dragonflies, spiders, robber flies, and assassin bugs. While some species of birds eat a significant number of butterflies and moths, there has never been a documented case of a bird eating a Karner blue, though Karners have often been found with holes in their wings that may have been caused by a bird's beak. Other causes of mortality include deer accidentally eating the caterpillars while browsing on lupine plants, and extreme weather events like severe rain that prevent the butterflies from flying and feeding.

The population of Karner blues in New Hampshire is increasing, but it had dropped to zero at its last stronghold along a Concord power-line corridor in 2000, when it was officially considered extirpated. When it was listed on the state endangered list in 1987, there were about 3,000 adults in the population, but it declined steadily thereafter despite the funding that came with being added to the federal endangered list in 1992 and efforts by The Nature Conservancy to manage habitat and rear individuals in captivity. The species' decline was caused primarily by habitat loss due to development. The flat terrain and sandy, well-drained soils found in pine barrens are ideal for development, especially for airports and malls. As development increased, the habitat became more and more fragmented and isolated, leading to a decline in lupine populations. "With development comes roads, and Karners tend not to fly over pavement," noted Goulet. "The more development occurs, the more pavement is put in, the less the butterflies will disperse, and without dispersal you have problems with genetics. That will cause inbreeding and infertility, and that will be their demise." Which is probably what happened in Concord. Increasing development also requires that natural fires be suppressed as quickly as possible, which negatively affects the butterflies because fire is a key element to maintaining the pine barrens ecosystem and ensuring the health of the plants on which the Karner blue depends.

Because fire is an essential process in numerous ecosystems, if the regular fire regime is removed or altered, the ecosystem changes to something else and the species that depend on that habitat are displaced or eliminated. In fact, there are very few habitats that evolved independent of fire—only those where it is too cold, too wet, or too dry to burn. In fire-dependent ecosystems, species have evolved adaptations to respond positively to fire, and in many cases, the vegetation is prone to fire and facilitates its spread. "If you think about ecosystems being not just the vegetation but all of the organisms that live there, what you find is that there are many wildlife species that are fire-dependent, like the Karner blue, where they are dependent on an ecosystem component that needs fire to be regenerated," said Ayn Shlisky, director of the Global Fire Initiative for The Nature Conservancy. "I even heard about a salamander in California that creates a fire retardant foamy substance that allows it to walk through flames." Fire-adapted ecosystems often recover very quickly from fires, yet they can be damaged severely if fire is suppressed for long periods of time and a buildup of fuel then results in a more severe fire than usual.

In the case of pine barrens, Shlisky said that the habitat has been exposed to natural fire ignitions through time, "so it is climatically predisposed to fire because of where it is on Earth and where lightning strikes. The species there are relatively short-lived, they are fire-adapted, and the plants are prolific 'seeders' in response to getting hit by a fire. They are very dense and flammable. When fire does occur, it happens in patches, and the system rebounds through the successional process. The cycle of regeneration there is really driven by fire." During fires at pine barrens, the heat of the flames opens thick, sap-covered, pitch pine cones to release their seeds, and the scorched earth becomes a fertile place for nectar plants to take root. Government policies of fire suppression over the last seventy years, however, have resulted in many pine barrens being dramatically altered: The pitch pine trees create a closed canopy, the scrub oak creates a dense understory, and the grassy openings where lupine and other wildflowers grow get crowded out. Invasive species then move in.

Returning fire in a controlled way to fire-dependent habitats is a complex job but one that is vital to ensuring the health of native species.

"The biggest challenges are social: people's perception of fire, how they relate to it, whether they view it as a threat to their livelihood and safety, or if they understand that fire is part of the system and we need to figure out how to live with it," explained Shlisky, whose role at The Nature Conservancy has earned her the nickname the goddess of fire. "That perception puts a big constraint on what you're able to do." Environmental Protection Agency regulations governing air quality also constrain the use of fire when it gets smoky, and weather conditions, particularly shifting winds, make it difficult to plan and implement a safe and controlled burn. Yet because of the key role fire plays in so many habitats, The Nature Conservancy has developed an expertise in fire management. In 2006, they conducted 700 controlled burns totaling 100,000 acres on properties they own and manage, and they helped government land management agencies burn another 116,000 acres on federal property. The group has twenty-two full-time staff members committed to its Global Fire Initiative, which aims to assess how natural fire regimes have been altered in habitats around the world and to develop strategies for restoring fire regimes to maintain biodiversity. The Conservancy has also trained hundreds of fire managers who apply their expertise at wildlife preserves in every state in the country.

At New Hampshire's pine barrens, implementing a controlled fire plan has been a struggle. "We develop a plan each year, but unfortunately being in the heart of Concord it's difficult," Goulet said. "You try to balance managing the habitat with the fact that you're surrounded by development, and you have to be respectful of the neighbors and respectful of safety. As a result, we haven't been able to burn much. We've implemented four burns since we started habitat management in 2001. Our burns tend to be anywhere from 5 to 10 acres, and most of the time we have to stop them early due to smoke interfering with the surrounding community. So we haven't been able to do much compared to other states that are able to burn hundreds of acres each year."

Because of the suppression of natural fires in the Concord pine barrens for so many years, the habitat had begun to change considerably. The native grasslands and shrublands disappeared and were replaced by a thick forest of early successional species such as white pine, aspen, maple, and cherry trees that enclosed the canopy and blocked the sunlight from reaching the ground. Restoring that habitat to something the Karner blues would thrive in required a huge commitment of manpower to remove the undesirable species, both mechanically and by hand, to minimize the amount of competition and allow the native plants to return. When we walked through the pine barrens, Goulet pointed out a site where restoration recently had been completed. Towering trees and large scrub oaks had been removed, and an opening had been created that linked to other open areas to provide the Karners with travel corridors. In the openings and corridors, the soil had been scarified with a "brontosaurus machine" to encourage growth of native plants, and dozens of young lupines and other nectar species were planted. This work continues on an annual basis.

At the same time, the biologists are working with local landowners to encourage native landscaping in nearby neighborhoods. "If the Karners have areas with little patches of lupine here and there, that will allow dispersal to occur," Goulet said. "We need to look beyond the immediate area for other locations we can restore. If we can create connections by having landowners do this type of landscaping, it will allow the Karners to disperse and find new habitat. But it's pretty limited right now."

A native of Canada, Goulet started out pursuing an art career before switching to biology and working on snake, turtle, and peregrine falcon research projects. She took me to a section of the Karner habitat that recently had been burned to illustrate the difficulties of implementing a fire plan next to an airport. To get there, we had to drive through the airport's secure back gate and cross an inactive runway that sometimes requires wearing a reflective vest, having an airport escort, and placing a flashing light on the roof of the vehicle.

We parked at the end of the runway where a prescribed burn had been conducted the previous spring. The site is considerably grassier than the rest of the managed habitat, with an abundance of lupine and several specimens of blunt-leafed milkweed, a rare plant that Karner blues use for nectar but that doesn't look at all like the other kinds of milkweed I had seen before. Goulet said that the airport generally doesn't object to the biologists' efforts at habitat management, including fires, because they need to keep the vegetation low immediately around the runways, but that doesn't mean it has been easy. Smoky fires reduce visibility for approaching planes, so when that happens the fire must be extinguished immediately. The same is true when the wind shifts and sends smoke or ash toward nearby neighborhoods. That's what happened during the most recent planned fire, so it had to be halted before the job was complete. Walking around the site, it was difficult to notice that a fire had burned through just three months earlier. Most of the vegetation was lush and healthy. The only indication of fire was found on a few small pitch pine trees that looked dead at the bottom but upon closer inspection revealed new growth sprouting from the middle of the blackened branches.

Besides ongoing desires by the airport management to expand its operation onto Karner habitat, the other challenge that the airport location creates for the butterflies comes from the regular visits by a commercial blimp, which flew by during my visit. The structure it attaches to when it lands must be set up on grass, not pavement, and it requires 500 feet of clearance around it, so the only place available for it to land is on the habitat being managed for the butterflies. To ensure that the blimp personnel don't trample the lupine when the airship arrives, Goulet is contacted on each visit to determine the most appropriate landing location.

Less than a year after the Karner blue was declared extirpated from the state of New Hampshire, plans were under way to reestablish it in its former haunts. Beginning with fifty eggs collected from one population in New York in 2001, more than six thousand Karners have been raised and released at the Concord airport site as of 2006. The captive rearing lab is in a tiny military barracks the size of a built-in swimming pool at the New Hampshire State Military Reservation, headquarters of the 54th troop command, which is within view of both the airport and the release site. The facility was offered by the state's Army National Guard, along with ten years of project funding, in exchange for several acres of Karner blue habitat the military took over to create a new hangar for their Blackhawk helicopters. Additional funding for the captive rearing effort is provided by funds raised by a conservation license plate that state residents can purchase.

The lab where the butterflies are raised is a former Quonset hut converted to look somewhat like a greenhouse. The hut sits next to several similar barracks that are home to the National Guard's drug enforcement and awareness program offices and surrounded by knee-high grasses and mounds of dirt from the construction of modern National Guard offices nearby. Construction vehicles and a continuous movement of aircraft of all varieties made the site uncomfortably noisy, but a step inside the captive rearing lab was like entering a florist shop. It smelled wonderfully of bee balm, butterfly weed, and New Jersey tea plants that were cut from just outside the barracks and provided to the caterpillars and butterflies to feed upon. The interior of the building was lined with folding lab tables overlaid with preformed kitchen countertops and stacked from end to end with 18-inch-tall gauze-like tents, inside of which were the remains of the 2006 captive rearing operation. Some of the tents had decaying nectar plants and cotton balls that had been submerged in honey water for adult butterflies; another contained several pupa that had failed to complete their metamorphosis, each sitting on separate circular filter papers; and in still other tents were Petri dishes holding nearly invisible Karner eggs. One covered Petri dish sitting on the countertop held the bodies of dozens of dead Karner blues stacked tightly on top of each other. "Because it's a federally listed species, we can't just throw them away when they die," Goulet explained. "We've acquired a lot of butterflies through this process. We'll eventually be handing them over to the U.S. Fish and Wildlife Service, and they can determine what they want to do with their bodies."

The job of raising Karner blues in the lab falls to Heidi Holman, a wildlife technician with the New Hampshire Fish and Game Department whose captive rearing success has led to unexpected optimism for the future of the butterflies in the state. The complex process begins with eggs collected the previous August that are wrapped in hay and layers of cloth and stored outside through the winter in a secret location, the wrappings simulating a thick snow cover. In the spring, the eggs are brought into the lab and separated into Petri dishes that are monitored closely until they hatch. The tiny caterpillars remain in the Petri dishes and are fed lupine for five weeks until they begin to pupate, at which point they are placed on the floor inside a gauze tent for the eight days it takes for them to transform into adult butterflies. Their wings are damp when they emerge, so they slowly crawl up the edge of the tent and hang upside down for an hour or two until they dry. After Holman carefully selects individuals with distinct lineages to prevent inbreeding, the butterflies are paired up and transferred to mating tents containing a bouquet of lupine on which they will lay their eggs.

"At that point, the ideal temperature for them is 96 degrees," Holman said. "They like it very hot and very humid, so we do a lot of misting in the lab. We also observe them periodically through the day to confirm that they mated. They mate for twenty minutes to an hour, so it's not something that is easy to miss." All of the captive butterflies mate within a span of about ten days, and when their eggs are laid, the process begins again. In 2006, the first brood of eggs resulted in twelve hundred adult butterflies, and since only five hundred are needed to ensure a healthy genetic lineage for the captive rearing program, the other seven hundred were released immediately into the pine barrens to feed, mate, and fend for themselves.

The New Hampshire goal set forth by the federal Karner blue recovery plan is to establish a population of fifteen hundred wild butterflies in the first brood for five years in a row. The monitoring program found that nearly that many were in the total population in 2006, but the increasing success of the captive rearing efforts suggests that the target is within reach soon. Approximately two hundred butterflies were raised in captivity in 2001, with more than two thousand reared in 2005 and again in 2006, despite a cool, wet spring that made for challenging breeding conditions.

"The hardest part of the whole captive rearing process is maintaining the proper temperatures to make sure they successfully mate," Holman added. "If the sun isn't out and there's not proper light or temperature, then we spend all day with heat lamps to stimulate them to mate. Temperature at every life stage is very important."

Named for the town in New York where it was first found—though the community is now called Guilderland—the Karner blue was first identified by Russian novelist Vladimir Nabakov, the author of *Lolita,* who was also a respected lepidopterist. During the 1940s, he was a research fellow at Harvard University and was responsible for organizing the butterfly collection at its Museum of Comparative Zoology. Natural history essayist Stephen Jay Gould referred to Nabakov as a scientific "stick-in-the-mud," in part for dismissing the idea that genetics could be used to distinguish among insect species. Instead, Nabakov relied on the microscopic comparison of butterfly genitalia to identify species, which was the more traditional method at the time.

The site adjacent to the Concord airport is the only place where Karner blues are found in New Hampshire, although there are historic records for them in nearby Merrimack, Webster, and Manchester, all communities that formerly had pine barrens and healthy populations of lupine. The species was also formerly found in eleven other states and Ontario, but now only widely scattered populations are found in New York, Ohio, Indiana, Illinois, Michigan, Wisconsin, and Minnesota, with the western populations doing considerably better than those in the East. In Wisconsin and Michigan, for instance, there are tens of thousands of acres of available habitat, much of it protected from development, and relatively healthy populations of Karner blues. The state of Wisconsin, where the Necedah National Wildlife Refuge is home to the nation's largest Karner population, is even considering removing the butterfly from its list of rare species.

New York has four distinct populations in parts of the Hudson Valley sand belt that extends from Albany north to Glens Falls. Three of the populations are struggling to hold on due to limited, fragmented, and unprotected habitat. But at the Albany Pine Bush Preserve, the Karner blue is on-target to meet the goals of the federal recovery plan. Located in the heart of the city of Albany, the preserve contains 3,010 acres of protected habitat managed by a state-funded commission made up of state and municipal agencies, The Nature Conservancy, and local citizens appointed by the governor.

While firm data on the number of Karner blues found at the site are unknown, it is estimated that there are between one and three thousand there, and the butterflies are successfully recolonizing newly restored sites. An annual prescribed fire plan has been implemented since 1991, with about 70 acres burned each year to maintain the habitat. The biggest challenge at the site is black locust, a tree that grows as a clone with one root system sending up numerous stems and spreading out up to 10 feet per year. "That's our toughest plant to manage," said Neil Gifford, director of conservation for the Albany Pine Bush Preserve Commission. "It eliminates light, changes the soil chemistry, and eliminates native plants, including lupine. So we've been removing it and restoring [the site] to grassland and letting the native plants move in on their own. For us, restoration is a process rather than an event." Every year, they remove between 30 and 50 acres of black locusts, mostly young trees 6 to 8 inches in diameter, and replant the area with seeds of little bluestem, lupine, and other flowers and grasses collected in the vicinity. They still have about 500 acres of black locust removal and habitat restoration to go before the site has been restored completely.

Despite the successful prescribed burns and restoration efforts, the weather has been a major factor in suppressing the Albany population in recent years. In 1998, a tornado struck the area just as Karner blue numbers peaked, and a year later a drought dried out many of the lupine plants. Then in 2000, a cold spring reduced breeding success in the first brood, which had a domino effect on the year's second brood. The next year saw Karner blue numbers at their lowest levels on record.

Although poor weather conditions again negatively affected the population in 2006, Gifford said that the Karners are "responding well to our habitat, so if we get good climactic conditions the outlook is good." But that's not to say the species is out of the woods. Despite the extensive available habitat, the site is relatively fragmented and bisected by the New York State Thruway and numerous other roads, which has affected the butterflies' ability to disperse among the habitat as much as the biologists would like. So the commission has initiated a plan to accelerate the colonization of the new habitat with a captive rearing program similar to that in New Hampshire. The local school groups that have been growing lupine for the site will also be enlisted to help in the captive rearing effort.

"The population is still at risk in New York, but we're more optimistic than we've ever been in the last fifteen years of managing Karner blues because we've figured out the logistics of habitat management," said Gifford. "The jury is still out, however, on whether they'll reproduce fast enough to prevent their extinction . . . Here in Albany, we've protected enough acreage, but we still don't know if we've done it in time."

The biggest hurdle to ensuring the long-term health of the New Hampshire population, according to Celine Goulet, is maintaining the habitat once the funding from the National Guard ends. Most of the major habitat restoration has been completed at the site, she said, so in the future it will simply be a matter of maintaining it from year to year. "We're already starting to reach the numbers of butterflies out there we need [to meet the federal recovery goal]," she said. "We haven't reached fifteen hundred yet in the first brood, but we have reached it in the second brood. We're hoping that within a year or two we'll reach that goal, and if we can maintain that for five years then the outlook is really good. It won't be a self-sustaining population in this location because the size of the pine barrens is so small. If you look at Albany, the size [of that site] allows for natural disturbances in the system to go through their cycle, whereas

here it will always require human intervention to allow for that disturbance and the maintenance of the habitat. Once they reach that thresh-
old, though, if they can maintain enough subpopulations, I don't think
it's going to require many more years of captive breeding to keep them
going."

11

Canada Lynx

Northern Maine in winter is a place of incredible beauty, with rolling
hills, uninterrupted spruce forests, scattered potato farms, and small towns
all covered in a soft, glowing blanket of snow. It's a long way from almost
anywhere else in New England, but it's also a worthwhile trip to learn
firsthand about a culture that the more populated regions of the Northeast abandoned many decades ago, where the residents have an intimate
knowledge of the land and its resources, where the timber industry is
king and proud, where snowmobiles seem to outnumber cars and their
tracks are ubiquitous along roadsides and farm fields, where frost heaves
and massive log-hauling trucks make drivers necessarily careful, and
where melting snows and unpaved roads combine for a mud season like
no other. Northern Maine is also the only place in the Northeast where
a small population of Canada lynx (*Lynx canadensis*) ebb and flow with
the vagaries of the snowshoe hare population.

Mud season is when I made my first visit to the region. It was a nine-
hour drive from my house in Rhode Island to the town of Ashland, north
of where Interstate 95 turns east to New Brunswick, past scattered stands
of spruce trees killed decades ago by a budworm infestation, and just be-

yond a lumber mill with a pile of logs stacked 20 feet tall running a quarter mile along a bend in the road. I spent a day exploring the Ashland area—Ashland itself took just a few minutes to explore—searching for northern birds that seldom or never make it as far south as my house, like gray jays, evening grosbeaks, boreal chickadees, and a variety of finches. Stopping at every house with a bird feeder in the yard, I scanned the trees and feeders with my binoculars, trying unsuccessfully to be inconspicuous to the homeowners. Common redpolls, birds that would get the Rhode Island rare bird hotline buzzing, seemed to be everywhere, including in the middle of the street eating road salt. I checked off several other species that got my heart racing despite how common they were in this extreme northeastern corner of the country.

Back in Ashland, I met up with Sarah Boyden at the local office of the Maine Department of Inland Fisheries and Wildlife, and I climbed into her truck for the two-hour drive west on a rutted, mud-slicked, dirt road into the center of lynx country. The winding road took us through large stands of mixed species forest—balsam fir, red and black spruce, yellow and white birch, and red and sugar maple—as well as past turn-offs for hunting and fishing camps where ice fishermen and snowmobilers were enjoying the last few weeks of the season in a year of low snowfall totals but bitterly cold temperatures. Our destination was Clayton Lake, a logging camp near the Canadian border that Boyden and fellow biologist Scott McLellan called home for most of the winter. With the sun setting behind us as we arrived in camp, I was surprised to find that the camp was much larger and more modern than I anticipated. The main building housed an office, cafeteria, and bunkhouse for twenty workers; several private cabins for foremen and mechanics were scattered around the site; a garage held equipment and fuel for the massive logging trucks; and it even had an old, abandoned post office. About forty loggers were based there through the winter, although we never saw them, since they work primarily through the overnight hours during mud season when cold night-time temperatures refreeze the roads, making it easier for the massive logging trucks to maneuver.

The logging camp is the corporate headquarters of Clayton Lake Woodlands, a timber company that purchased most of the land in the area from International Paper Co. in 1999 and is owned by two sets of brothers, the Pelletiers from Fort Kent, Maine, and the Blanchettes from Quebec. Far from civilization, the company relies on satellite phones, portable electric generators, and wireless Internet to conduct their business. The workers cut whatever trees are mature, regardless of species, for use as lumber, veneer, fence posts, paper, and other products. The land regenerates new growth rather quickly, so the company doesn't bother replanting, especially since it's cheaper to buy more land than to replant.

It's the regenerating forest that makes this region excellent habitat for lynx. Or to be more precise, the regenerating forest is perfect habitat for snowshoe hare, and it's the abundant snowshoe hare that make it excellent for lynx. The hare make up 75 to 90 percent of the lynx diet (the rest consists of rodents and birds), and the lynx population somewhat tracks the hare population in an eight- to eleven-year cycle—when hare numbers are high, lynx numbers are too, and when hare numbers crash, so do lynx in most of their range. Snowshoe hare are 2- to 4-pound animals with large feet and white fur in the winter that turns brown in spring. Ranging throughout much of Canada and the northern tier of the United States, they are an important game mammal that feeds on succulent vegetation, twigs, buds, and bark. Their preferred habitat is the early stages of succession, a decade or so after a forest has been cleared and when new growth is low and thick. As a result, the timber industry plays a vital role in creating habitat to maintain a healthy hare and lynx population.

The small house at the logging camp that the lynx biologists use as an office, lab, home, and recreation center is a sparsely furnished structure with ancient fixtures and cabinetry, primitive basement bedrooms, a pantry made of plywood and two-by-fours, and a laundry line stretched across the living room. The walls were covered with lynx pictures cut from calendars and magazines; a whiteboard listed individual lynx and the number of kittens each gave birth to the previous year; and on mismatched hooks hung several old radio-tracking collars of a size that gave me my first clue that the cats we were seeking were considerably smaller than I imagined.

The windows were frosted over when we awoke at dawn the next morning, and the thermometer read zero degrees Fahrenheit as we listened to a French-Canadian swing radio station while preparing for a long day in the field. I had purchased extra cold-weather gear, so I layered it all on and worried unnecessarily about getting cold. As it turned out, the weather couldn't have been more comfortable. We left camp and drove slowly along the slushy roads for an hour to the Musquacook Lakes region and what looked like a group of six beach cabanas in the middle of a forest clearing where two snowmobiles and a bucket of chopped beaver parts awaited us. The game plan was to split up and visit each of the twenty-five cage traps scattered over 50 square miles in a research project designed to assess the lynx population in the area by studying survival rates, range, habitat, dispersal, mortality, and reproduction. I had never been on a snowmobile before, so the biologists didn't want to give me one of my own. Instead, I held on for dear life on the back of McLellan's vehicle as he traveled faster than I would have preferred down narrow paths and abandoned logging roads.

It didn't take us long to find our first lynx.

The first trap we stopped at gave me an idea of what to expect. It was a 4-foot-long and 21-inch-tall wire cage wedged between several second-growth aspen trees and covered with balsam boughs and snow at the edge of the trail. A frozen beaver head hung from the back of the trap as bait, and a metal plate half-way back triggered closure of the gate when an animal stepped on it. The whole set-up was somewhat inconspicuous, which was intended, except that with so much forested land in the vicinity it might take a long time for a lynx that may wander over 50 miles to stumble upon this inconspicuous location. So a shiny compact disk was hanging from a string on a nearby branch and danced gently in the breeze to attract attention and give any approaching cats a reason to investigate.

As I walked around the site, I learned that the snow depth was quite deceptive. The trail had been packed down hard by the frequent speeding snowmobiles, and the melting daytime temperatures and freezing nights in late March further solidified the snow in the open areas, so it was easy to walk across the surface. But as I explored around the trap, I sunk to my hips and discovered that the tiny spruce seedlings peeking out above the snowpack were actually 4- or 5-foot-tall saplings buried in the snow.

After a short ride on the snowmobile, McLellan stopped well before reaching the second trap. As we approached, he noted without further explanation that this trap was the only one set back from the trail by 20 yards or more, and that it had been the one that had captured the most lynx in recent months. One cat in particular, known as L18, was caught regularly, and it may have learned that the trap contained a free meal with only the minor inconvenience of being enclosed for a short time. Before we even left the trail, McLellan sensed that a lynx was entrapped, and as we got near, we could hear a low growl.

The approach to the trap was through a mix of mature red spruce and balsam fir with some birch and scattered scrubby undergrowth. In the shade of the trees, the waist-deep snow had not yet begun to melt, and McLellan's repeated visits to the site made it easy to push through. A frozen dead deer, placed there by the biologists to attract attention to the trap, was partially covered by snow but clearly had been chewed on occasionally by any number of predators in the area. My first glance at the trap gave me a slight smile, as the lynx's posture reminded me of the way my housecat, Socks, sits on my livingroom couch watching me watch television. Like the lion statues guarding the entrance to a big-city library, it was alert yet comfortable as it peered out the front of the trap and calmly waited for its expected release. The only indicator of its displeasure was the soft growl it occasionally emitted, which was also similar to one Socks gives when watching the neighbor's cat strut through our yard. Appearing similar to a bobcat, this lynx looked just like every lynx picture I've ever seen: grayish-buff fur mixed with blackish hairs, a large ruff of long facial hairs, tall black ear tufts that enhance hearing, and massive feet with white toes. The biggest surprise for me was how small the animal was. It was about the size of a fox rather than the size of a coyote as I expected. They average about 30 to 40 inches long from nose to tail and weigh only 15 to 30 pounds, with females being considerably smaller than males. As the animal growled more frequently with McLellan and I lingering just outside the cage, I couldn't help but be impressed with its cougar-sized feet. I knew its feet were going to be big—lynx thrive in deep snow by using their feet like snowshoes to walk across the surface of the powdery snow—but the feet of this lynx were even bigger than I imagined. They seemed far out of proportion to the rest of its body, clearly explaining why lynx have the reputation for being efficient in snow, good swimmers, and adept tree climbers.

A quick glance at the animal's radio-tracking collar and McLellan identified it as L18, the male animal that he knew well. That cat had been recaptured numerous times and had been seen just a week prior in the company of female lynx L43. His collar was equipped with a global positioning system that provided the biologists with exact coordinates of the animal's location four times a day. But to download that information, the cat must be recaptured and the collar removed. Since the battery in the collar still had several months of life left, McLellan decided to leave the collar on the cat and trust that he would be captured again.

After writing a few notes, McLellan was ready to open the trap and release the lynx. I positioned myself in front of the cage but 20 feet back behind a tree, while McLellan hid behind the trap and reached around to open the gate. The cat immediately bounded out of the enclosure, and in three large leaps disappeared from view, leaving behind an image of long legs, a short black-tipped tail, and those massive feet. But the animal didn't go far. As McLellan said was typical, it lingered in some thick brush and trees about 50 feet from the trap, just out of our view but clearly making enough noise to let us know that he wasn't gone entirely. At that moment, two red squirrels let out a loud chatter, perhaps celebrating that the animal was finally gone from their territory, and the drumming of a hairy woodpecker reverberated through the area.

The remaining ten traps that we checked that day were empty, though three of them had been tripped and closed without capturing anything. At each, McLellan adjusted the trip switch, fixed the camouflage, checked the bait, and made repairs as necessary. While we were working at one trap, a small plane circled overhead and tipped its wings at us. According to McLellan, the pilot tracks every collared lynx from the air three times a week to collect location data and make sure the animals are still alive. He reported later that the collar of one of the lynx he tracked that day was in mortality mode, sending a signal that the animal hadn't moved in several hours and was probably dead. That meant that McLellan was going to have a change of plans for the following day. He had to find the lynx, recover the collar, and determine the cause of death.

Lynx probably have been present in northern Maine at varying levels throughout much of history, according to John Organ, chief of the Division of Wildlife and Sport Fish Restoration for the Northeast region of the U.S. Fish and Wildlife Service. They may become extirpated temporarily at times, while at other times they may be abundant. "At the southern extent of their range in North America, the population can be quite volatile depending on habitat and prey base," Organ said. "The population center for Maine lynx is in the Gaspé Peninsula of Quebec. As that population grows, you're more likely to have individuals emigrating from the Gaspé and colonizing areas that are suitable, but it varies over time depending on the conditions.

"The Maine forest has varied over the years. At times it's dominated by mature forest, and at other times it contains large areas of young forest. When it's mostly mature forest, lynx may be absent from Maine, but when it's mostly young forest, they may be abundant. It's not a static population at all. It's quite dynamic."

Organ said that lynx prefer forests about fifteen to thirty years old, and to get forests of that age in the Northeast, it has to be managed intensively. In historic times, forest fires or tornados or beavers would create young forests naturally by destroying large swaths of mature forest and opening up clearings for young trees to regenerate, but that doesn't happen much any more. A spruce budworm infestation could do it, too. That's exactly what happened in the 1970s and is one reason why lynx are doing so well in Maine today. When the budworm killed so many spruce trees, loggers came through and clear-cut vast areas of dead trees. Twenty-five years later, young regenerating trees have created tremendous habitat for snowshoe hare, and lynx numbers are booming. But in ten years, as the forest ages, it will be less hospitable to hare and numbers may decline again unless other places in the forest become good habitat.

That's not likely, according to Organ. "After the clear-cuts of the 1970s and 80s there was a backlash and restrictions were imposed," Organ said, referring to the Maine Forest Practices Act that replaced clear-cutting with partial harvesting. "We're not seeing large clear-cuts any more, and that may determine the future of lynx. With a changing forest, how are they going to respond?" In the years since the legislated cutting rules have been implemented, research by a University of Maine graduate student concluded that hare are less abundant in partial harvesting sites because the new method does not create the same desirable hare habitat that is created by clear-cutting.

Organ said that biologists are just now trying to understand the relationships between lynx and hare and their preferred forest conditions so informed management decisions can be made. Now that large clear-cuts have been regulated virtually out of existence, lynx and hare are facing vastly different forest management practices. How they fare will determine the guidance biologists provide to the timber companies that control most of the land in the area. Organ and other biologists are analyzing how lynx and hare use different habitat types, and it has become quite clear that they use young, regenerating softwoods in much greater proportion to their availability in the landscape. That may mean that lynx will be in considerable trouble in another decade or two. For now, though, the Maine population seems quite healthy. One indicator of the health of the population is the average litter size, which increased substantially in the first six years of monitoring, from one to two kittens per litter in 1999 through 2002 to three to five kittens per litter in 2003 through 2005.

While biologists can't estimate accurately how many lynx live in the region, they believe it's somewhere in the hundreds and growing. Just ten years ago, it was uncertain whether even one lynx was resident in the state. Occasional surveys of animal tracks in northern Maine periodically would turn up a set or two of lynx tracks, and in 1998 five sets of tracks were found, but three of them were seen together on the Canadian border, leaving considerable uncertainty about where the animals resided. The first effort by biologists to trap and track lynx in Maine occurred in 1999, with the first cat captured in March of that year. When the animal gave birth that spring, it confirmed for the first time in recent memory that the state had a resident lynx population. Since then, 127 different individual lynx have been identified and marked. The center of the population appears to be in the northwestern part of the state in an area of unorganized townships having no local government and little or no human population. Owned mostly by timber companies, the townships are divided into 36-square-mile blocks and identified simply by combinations of letters and numbers.

Maine isn't the only state just learning about its lynx population. In 1997, a federal court case was brought by environmental groups asking that the lynx be added to the federal endangered species list. (It was eventually listed in 2000 as threatened in fourteen states.) The case raised enough questions that biologists in several areas met to talk about the animals. What they learned in those meetings was that they knew very little about the natural history of lynx. Alaska has a large, healthy population of lynx, and Washington once had a sizable population as well. Maine's research program was launched soon after Montana confirmed a resident population of the animals. In 2002, Minnesota biologists were surprised to learn that they, too, had a small population of lynx. And in Colorado, lynx have been reintroduced successfully to the mountainous regions of the state, after a rocky start when four of the first five animals released into the San Juan Mountains in 1999 starved to death. Nearly two hundred lynx from Canada have been released in the state since then, and in 2003 they began reproducing. Some of them have even been found wandering into Wyoming, Utah, and New Mexico.

One thing the various state biologists have learned is that the ecology of the eastern populations is quite different from those in the West. "In the West where they have more arid forests, lynx are probably using thicker forest more than in the East," Organ said. "Home ranges in the West are much larger, which means that they have to range farther to meet their food requirements." Lynx densities in Minnesota, where the forest ecology is somewhat similar to that in Maine, appear to be more like those in the East than in the West.

After checking each of the lynx traps, McLellan took me on a designated route to the north through a township he seldom spent much time in, to conduct a survey of lynx tracks. Riding slowly along the snow-covered trails and abandoned logging roads, we found abundant animal tracks, and my learning curve to distinguish among them was short. Moose tracks were easy to identify, since they are the only large mammal that sinks deeply into the snow. Hare were also distinctive, with their long hind feet. McLellan even pointed out the markings of a river otter sliding on its belly down a shallow hill. The more difficult distinction was between lynx and the abundant coyote—on close inspection, lynx tracks are wider and with rounder toes while coyote tracks usually show toenail marks— but I quickly learned to distinguish between them even blazing by at 40 miles per hour on the snowmobile.

The first road we traveled had an abundance of tracks of several different species; we often found lynx and coyote tracks traveling in the road for upwards of 100 yards at a time. Every time we found lynx tracks, we took a GPS reading to identify their location and noted where the tracks entered and left the trail and in which direction the animal had traveled. Along the next road, we found miles and miles of nothing but coyote tracks. When McLellan pointed out the habitat the second road traversed— mostly thick, mature forest with few of the balsam firs in which hare like to hide—it was clear why lynx and hare were absent. After taking a wrong turn and losing the path in dense shrubbery, we followed a third road that also had mostly coyote tracks. The only lynx tracks we saw there intersected with the only hare tracks we found.

I was exhausted by the time the day was done, mostly from the challenge of hanging onto the back of the snowmobile, and my face was chapped and sore from wind burn. Relaxed and jovial, McLellan took his work seriously and seemed to enjoy every minute of it. He grew up in

Maine, spending his teenage years in the northern part of the state when his father, a state forest ranger, was transferred to the town of Smyrna. He graduated from the University of Maine in Orono and had extensive research experience with predators before joining the lynx research team. He studied American marten in Maine, swift foxes and coyotes in Colorado, and for six years worked in North Carolina in numerous capacities aiding in the recovery of red wolves. Due in part to burn-out and a desire to study a different species, he returned to Maine just four months before my visit and was already an expert on the life history and behavior of lynx.

"I'm fascinated by northern mammals and how well-equipped they are for dealing with the weather conditions," said McLellan, an avid hunter and fisherman who enjoys searching the backcountry for antlers that have been shed by deer and moose. "And I like the isolation of the fieldwork out here." Unshaven and wearing a t-shirt emblazoned with an image of his old college dormitory, the thirty-year-old looked five years younger, yet his confidence and comfort with his place in the world suggested someone older.

While we were chatting back at the logging camp, I glanced at a map of the region and noted a number of handwritten name changes to area logging roads. Isolated far from civilization and with little to occupy their free time, McLellan and Boyden obviously had to create their own entertainment. The main road that Boyden spent the day traversing alone is officially designated as Long Lake Road, and most regulars in the region referred to spurs off that road simply as LL1, LL2, and so on. McLellan and Boyden, however, know those same roads as LL Bean and LL Cool J, among others. Anything to keep things interesting, they said.

During her day checking traps, Boyden caught a single lynx, L26, which had first been caught a month earlier and was then caught every three or four days thereafter. She said the animal appeared quite calm in the trap, but it bluffed charging her when she approached the trap, an unexpected behavior she hadn't encountered before.

Despite the long day in the field, the biologists were anxiously looking forward to dinner in the cafeteria in the main building of the logging camp. The camp's cook, a thickly accented French-Canadian named Royden (not to be confused with biologist Sarah Boyden), had been a cook at logging camps for fifty years, and every Saturday throughout the winter months—the one night the loggers have off and have returned to town—he cooks dinner for whatever researchers, fishermen, and hunters happen to be in the vicinity. Royden is a very likable character who speaks in a colorful mix of French and English and dresses like a typical grandfather. Seeming somewhat simple, he happily puts up with everyone's requests and gruff personalities, and in return is treated protectively like a little brother. The day I visited, however, was the last dinner of the season, and probably the last one ever for Royden, who had plans to finally retire (though he had reportedly said that in past years as well). As is usually the case, Royden made a huge quantity of food—steak, pork, seafood casserole, chicken wings, French fries, carrots, fiddleheads he picked and canned himself the previous spring, and whoopie pies, a chocolate and whipped cream dessert for which he was famous. Among those who arrived to partake were three potato farmers from Frenchville who were ice fishing nearby, three snowmobilers boasting of their exploits crossing open water on their vehicles without sinking, and the husband-and-wife owners of a hunting camp and back-country guide service who lived even further from civilization than the logging camp. They were a loud, raucous bunch who drank heavily and flirted with Boyden all night long. Long after Royden went to bed—an hour past his usual 7:30 bedtime—Boyden and I returned to the research camp and left the rest to continue their drinking and boasting.

Boyden grew up on a dairy farm near Waterville, Maine, and was an avid skier in high school. She spent two years in the AmeriCorps after graduation, cutting trails, thinning forests, and repairing camps in Maine and California, all while camping in small tents in remote locations for long periods of time. She then took seven years to complete her undergraduate studies at three different colleges in Maine and Vermont, mostly taking classes in the fall semester and skiing or traveling widely during the spring. Three years of often-unpaid wildlife jobs followed—first studying an endangered desert fish in Utah, then more fish studies in Colorado, a volunteer position on the Maine lynx project, a salmon restoration job in Vermont, and finally a paid position on the lynx project. A soft-spoken woman who enjoys working in primitive conditions, Boyden considers the lynx project a dream job, but the weekend I visited was the end of the field season, and the following day she was packing up to move on to another temporary biology position near Portland, this time involving migrating birds.

After ten years of jumping from job to job and college to college, what Boyden wanted more than anything was a secure job as a biologist with health benefits somewhat close to her boyfriend in Vermont. Acknowledging that it would be difficult to go from working intimately with a rare, charismatic mammal like lynx to smaller, "lesser" animals, she knows she could be happy working with a shrew, fish, or insect if she had a guaranteed paycheck coming in every week. At the end of the lynx field season, she was clearly weary and ready to move on. But not before one more day of checking the traps.

Winter trapping of lynx to learn about home ranges and kitten dispersal is only one small part of the year-round research project. In addition, prey abundance surveys are conducted during the winter months to count hare, red squirrel, and grouse tracks; hare pellet counts are conducted twice a year along 672 transects to determine the density of hare; lynx dens— usually in hollow logs or other sheltered places—are visited in June to count and tag kittens; and intensive habitat analyses are conducted in the fall by counting tree species, identifying vegetation, and assessing canopy density in areas where lynx dens are found. In addition, volunteers conduct backtrack studies. These studies require that the trackers find the track of an adult female lynx and follow it back to determine the number of kittens traveling with her, assess behavior, find kill sites, analyze habitat, and find where her tracks intersect with those of other lynx. By combining several years of this kind of data, the biologists hope that a clearer picture emerges of the Maine lynx population, prey, and habitat needs.

One thing that has surprised McLellan and Boyden during their field studies is how difficult it is to catch female lynx. Are they inherently more cautious than males, perhaps because of their need to protect their kittens? Are males more willing to accept being captured in order to get an easy meal? McLellan said that the lynx clearly are making a choice to go into the trap, and for some as-yet-unknown reason, the males are much more willing to make that choice.

The other unexpected result has been the increasing number of lynx sightings. The biologists expected to see lynx only in the traps, particularly since the animals are supposed to be primarily nocturnal, but more and more they have seen them wandering around in the daylight. Perhaps that means that lynx numbers are increasing. More likely, McLellan thinks the lynx are becoming somewhat tolerant of people, even those lynx that have been trapped and therefore should be frightened of people. The cats appear quite relaxed in and out of the traps, he said, and they seem to take their time to observe calmly those who are observing them.

One potential reason for this calm behavior is because they have little to fear from people. According to John Organ, hunting and trapping of lynx in Maine isn't an issue—a bounty on lynx in the state was revoked in 1967—and human-caused mortality of any kind isn't a factor in the species' survival locally. The primary threat to lynx is the declining abundance and distribution of snowshoe hare, which is driven by habitat availability. But while lynx are considered to be at the top of the food chain, that doesn't mean they don't face pressures from other predators. While most mortality in the Maine lynx population is linked to natural causes like starvation, fishers have killed a number of cats as well. Once nearly wiped out of much of New England due to the clearing of forests for agriculture, fisher populations have rebounded in recent decades. Strong, aggressive members of the weasel family, fishers wander over large home ranges and are one of the only animals known to prey successfully and regularly upon porcupines. Based on what has been learned in Maine, it's not just porcupines that need to be wary of fishers. Lynx do, too.

While humans aren't responsible for directly killing many lynx in Maine, the animals are being trapped legally in Canada, including hundreds a year in the Gaspé Peninsula region that is the source of Maine's lynx population. John Organ noted that transborder issues are going to be crucial to conserving the species in the state. "Lynx in Maine are going to depend upon lynx from the Gaspé, so we need to recognize that and ensure that this metapopulation has no barriers to prevent the free interchange of animals. That's something we're going to need to address down the road."

Organ is more concerned, however, with the impact of global warming on lynx. "Climate change is certainly an issue," he said, "if it results in deep snow areas receding farther north, and if the snow patterns continue as they have over the last thirty or forty years, with a reduction in the average snow depth and that reduction moving farther and farther to the north. Lynx are adapted to deep snow, [and if the deep snow recedes] you may have an expansion of bobcat and fisher, which could have an impact on lynx."

A receding snowpack isn't the only concern lynx face with warming global temperatures. A biologist at the University of Alberta has discovered that the consistency of the snow is also an issue. Stan Boutin says that lynx populations are divided into three genetically distinct populations, with those in the West isolated from eastern populations by the Rocky Mountains and two eastern groupings separated by a climate factor. The Atlantic Canada population is adapted to hunting on slightly crustier snow, while the central and northern Canada population is adapted to hunting on fluffier snow. These differences in snow conditions are based on a weather pattern known as the North Atlantic Oscillation, which causes chilling and warming periods that result in crustier snow in eastern Canada and fluffier snow in central Canada. Boutin's concern is that as global temperatures rise, central Canada will have crustier snow and lynx in the region that are adapted to fluffier snow will find it more difficult to hunt, especially when hare populations are low and lynx survival skills are put to the test. He also worries that increasingly crusty snow in eastern Canada will make it even easier for the crusty-snow-adapted lynx to capture hare and throw off the balance between the species. And that could cause a domino effect throughout the northern forest and affect many other species.

As he told *National Wildlife* magazine in 2004, "this lynx-hare cycle is an amazing phenomenon. It has proved to be a very robust relationship that has sustained both species for thousands of years. If we start to get climate warming and a crusting of snow without long, deep cold spells, it could change the interaction and disrupt this robust system. It's one more way in which global warming is giving us an ecological warning."

With temperatures barely reaching above zero the next morning, global warming was far from my mind as I began the second day of monitoring the traps. McLellan and I revisited the same traps we had checked the day before, but in reverse order. It was Easter Sunday, and hare tracks seemed appropriately abundant. The sixth trap was closed as we approached, and inside, much to McLellan's surprise, was a snowshoe hare, just the third hare caught all season. The animal probably sought refuge in the trap because it looked like a good hiding place, certainly not because it sought a meal of frozen beaver parts. As we glanced into the trap, the hare clearly was agitated, remaining at the far end of the trap and periodically standing on its hind legs in an effort to get out. When we stood back from the trap, the animal relaxed a bit.

I had seen a snowshoe hare the previous summer on a vacation trip to Alaska, but that was in the summer and that animal was mostly gray-brown. This one was pure white—though it was obvious that many hairs were gray at the base—with dirty yellowish feet, and black eyes and whiskers. Its nose twitched constantly, and its ears seemed to shiver nervously. When McLellan opened the trap and stepped aside, the hare took a few tentative steps toward the open gate, then darted out in several large, bounding leaps and dashed toward the protection of the nearby trees. All he left behind was a large pile of pellets in the trap and a few clumps of soft fur.

After resetting the trap, we continued on our way. It had been a busy night for traveling coyotes, as we found numerous tracks on top of the snowmobile tracks we left the day before. We also saw our first grouse tracks crossing the path. What we weren't finding were captured lynx. Our expectations were high as we approached the second-to-last trap of the day, the same one in which we had captured L18 the day before. McLellan was certain the cat would be entrapped again, and when we got near it was quickly apparent that the trap was closed. But it was just a blue jay that was captured, the third one of the day. They'll eat almost anything they can find, so it's not unusual to see them feeding on carrion, but that individual seemed pretty unhappy about being in the cage. It fluttered around noisily, and its plumage was worn and wet. When McLellan opened the trap and the bird flew away, the jay appeared relieved as it disappeared into the forest. For McLellan and I, on the other hand, it was a major let-down. We were both counting on catching one more lynx, and that particular trap was the one for which we had the highest hopes.

As Sarah Boyden and I left town that afternoon, McLellan still had one more important job to do. He needed to find the lynx that the pilot had reported had a radio collar emitting a mortality signal. Just once before had the biologist had to track down a dead lynx, and it took many hours of walking through deep snow to find and recover it. McLellan wasn't pleased with the prospect of doing it again, especially not that day. It was the last day of the field season, and he had planned to head home and relax for a day before moving his new wife up to Maine from their previous home in North Carolina. Instead, he headed into the forest.

McLellan emailed me a few days later to report on what he found. "The collar had been cut with a knife, separated from the animal, and tossed away from the body," he wrote. "We tried finding the body using both personnel and dogs, but did not succeed. I picked up the collar miles from where the normal home range of this animal was. This means that the animal was most likely (99.99%) taken illegally. Law enforcement has issued a reward for insight into the illegal nature of this event."

U.S. Fish and Wildlife Service

12

Shortnose Sturgeon

The extreme weather was the biggest news story in 2005. Globally, it was the second-warmest year on record, and not one state in the United States was cooler than average. Hurricane Katrina nearly erased the city of New Orleans from the map, and twenty-five other named storms made the year the most active hurricane season on record. Wildfires burned more acreage in the country since records have been kept, most of it in Alaska, and drought hit the Pacific Northwest and the Great Plains. Boston endured the snowiest January in its history.

And then there was the flooding. Record October rains in New England washed away the foliage season, threatened to collapse numerous dams, and killed more than a dozen people. Providence, Hartford, Concord, Worcester, and Bangor all experienced their wettest month on record. It was also the wettest month ever on Mount Washington, as well as its snowiest October in history, with 79 inches of accumulation. As a result, the ski season in northern New England got off to an excellent start.

But the wet weather also made rivers overflow their banks and turned their flows a murky brown. Worse yet, the flooding was the likely reason for the complete failure of the breeding season of the endangered shortnose sturgeon (*Acipenser brevrostrum*) on the Connecticut River. An ancient fish that lived during the era of the dinosaurs but was nearly wiped out by overfishing in the 1800s and 1900s, shortnose sturgeon stop feeding in November and don't start again until April. But the high, murky water conditions in 2005 made it very difficult for the fish to feed from late September until they began their fast in November. "That's two of the seven months that these guys feed that the high flows made them feed very inefficiently, when they couldn't get access to their feeding areas, and when if they could get access they had to expend much more energy than they normally would to get any particular food item. So energetically they didn't do themselves very well," said Boyd Kynard, a fisheries biologist at the Conte Anadramous Fish Laboratory in Turners Falls, Massachusetts. "And then the water stayed up even after they got into their wintering period when the water temperature gets down below 7 degrees Celsius. Even then they had to exert more energy, take in no food, and so we think what that created in these fish is an energy deficit. Basically, during the winter their bodies made the decision to either spawn or survive. It's just that simple."

Only four sturgeon—three males and one female—arrived at the Connecticut River spawning grounds near the town of Montague, Massachusetts, in the spring of 2006, while about seventy-five fish spawn there in an average year. But it wasn't totally unexpected. High water in the fall was implicated in the spawning failure of shortnose sturgeon once before in the sixteen years that Kynard has been monitoring the species in the river, and springtime flooding has a lesser impact on a more regular basis. As daylight gets longer in the spring, female sturgeon experience hormonal changes during a three-week period leading up to spawning. "They have this three-week window when they either have to spawn or abort, and that's it," Kynard explained. "During that three-week window, the river—the biggest unpredictable environment they have—has to give them the kind of discharge that will give them the water velocity over rocks that they require. If it's too fast, they won't spawn. If it's too slow, they won't spawn. There's a range of acceptable velocities, and if the river comes up, as it has done about every four years, nobody spawns."

Shortnose sturgeon are one of the smallest of the twenty-five sturgeon species found around the world, rarely exceeding 3 feet in length, with four rows of bony plates called scutes along their bodies and armor-like scales on their heads. The olive-colored fish has a whitish belly and a rounded, shovel-like snout with an unusual mouth on the underside that can protrude a considerable distance from its body. This odd mouth is an adaptation for foraging on the bottom of the river and enables the short-nose sturgeon to pick up particular food items easily and to avoid others. As an adult, the fish feed primarily on small mussels, though they also will eat a wide variety of other aquatic invertebrates. "They use an electrical sensory organ on the bottom of their snout to detect the slight muscle twitch of a worm or crustacean or mussel," Kynard said. "They can just put their nose right over the bottom and detect where exactly that electrical impulse is coming from and discretely pick it up." It is uncertain how they manage to open the mussel shell and get to the flesh, however. They don't crush the shells—Kynard has studied the stomach contents of shortnose sturgeon and found empty hinged shells intact—so they may use digestive juices or their huge gizzard to open the shells.

The rare fish live mainly in large, slow-moving river systems along the eastern seaboard of the United States, from the St. Johns River in Florida to the St. John River in New Brunswick, each river population genetically distinct from the others. The southern populations grow faster and become sexually mature earlier than those in the northern regions, where females first spawn at about age ten and males do so at age six or seven. Shortnose sturgeon are diadramous, meaning they spend some of their life in freshwater and some of their life in salt water, but unlike salmon, they never enter the open ocean, preferring to stay in estuaries at the mouth of their spawning rivers. "They go down to the estuary to forage and never stay longer than sixty days—most stay just thirty days—and then they come right back up to freshwater," Kynard said. "After they get through spawning, they move downstream and into the estuary sometime during the following summer, which suggests that they're going to be foraging on organisms that they would not have access to in the freshwater reach of the river. We think they are foraging on invertebrates down there where they get some essential mineral elements that simply don't exist in the abundance that they need."

Shortnose sturgeon require a river that is at least 200 kilometers long because that's how far upstream they tend to breed. Rivers of this length typically have rocky areas at their uppermost reaches that provide the increased flows that sturgeons prefer for spawning habitat. This length also ensures that there is plenty of downstream freshwater habitat in which young fish can feed. Beyond the river's length, however, shortnose sturgeon are quite tolerant of other habitat variations. Water temperature, depth, shading, and shoreline vegetation don't seem to matter, and they have been successful even in somewhat polluted rivers and those with a wide variety of substrates. "It's that spawning area that's the unique environment in their whole life history," Kynard said, "and it's a place that they only visit when they're spawning. Rocks and sturgeon don't get along at all, except during spawning. The hard surfaces of rocks and their hard scutes don't go together. We've documented all kinds of injuries when they make these migrations past rapids and move into spawning areas with rocks. You'll find scutes that are worn and bleeding. But the fact that they will go through that to put their eggs in that kind of habitat tells you how important it is."

Mature shortnose sturgeon winter together about 15 kilometers downstream from the spawning area, and in April they migrate upstream to spawn. The females emit a pheromone to attract males, then emit another pheromone to indicate to the males that they are ovulating. They produce up to 300 very sticky eggs—each about 4 millimeters in diameter—every fifteen minutes for two or three days continuously, and the males immediately fertilize them. Small females may spawn approximately 30,000 eggs while especially large ones may spawn as many as 250,000 to 300,000 eggs. The eggs are heavier than water, so they settle toward the bottom and stick to whatever they come in contact with. Ideally that's going to be the rocks in the spawning habitat, but some may drift downstream a bit and end up in a wide range of habitats. Under typical water temperatures of about 12 to 15 degrees Celsius, the eggs will hatch in nine days, long after all of the adults have completed spawning and moved back downstream to feed. After the eggs hatch, the free embryos have large yolk sacks attached to them, making it very difficult to swim. They prefer darker areas at this life stage, so they hide amidst the rocks where they were born, feeding off the yolk sack and slowly developing fins, sensory organs, and swimming abilities. Ten days after hatching, they start to feed on their own, swim out from underneath the rocks, and drift downstream for three to five days, ending up about 8 to 10 kilometers from where they were born. That's where they spend the next year of their life. In the Connecticut River, the young fish spend that year in the vicinity of the town of Deerfield, Massachusetts.

As yearlings, sturgeons undertake a dualistic migration pattern, with half the population migrating further downstream and the other half remaining in the Deerfield area. "It puts progeny of each generation throughout all of the areas that the species uses in the river," Kynard explained. "There are advantages and disadvantages to moving downstream or staying upstream, but it balances out. If you stay upstream, it gives you poor foraging but great opportunity to spawn, since you don't have to go anywhere and you don't have to pass any barriers. If you go downstream, you get foraging advantages because you have access to the estuary, but you have horrible access to spawning because you have to pass two major rapids systems to get back up here."

Kynard is one of the leading experts on the sturgeon of the world, especially shortnose. A native of Mississippi, he has studied a wide variety of other rare fish during his career, including spine sticklebacks, mosquito fish, and desert pupfish, as well as shad, salmon, and sea lamprey. With the general decline of so many sturgeon species around the world, almost all of his time is now spent on that group, including visits in 2006 to China and Italy to work with fisheries biologists on native sturgeons in those countries. In the United States, there are nine species of sturgeon, and all but two are rare or endangered. The shovelnose sturgeon in the Mississippi-Missouri River drainage is secure enough to allow for commercial harvesting, while the lake sturgeon in the Great Lakes can only be captured by spearfishing. There is a sport fishing season for the white sturgeon in the Columbia River of the Pacific Northwest, although its status is variable and uncertain, and it may be added to state endangered lists in the near future. The green sturgeon in Oregon is another species that probably should be added to the endangered list, according to Kynard, and the Alabama sturgeon is in worse shape than the closely related shortnose, with none in captivity and only two captured in the last fifteen years. The pallid sturgeon, another species found in the Mississippi-Missouri River drainage, is on the federal endangered list, and the Atlantic sturgeon is headed in that direction, too, though it is doing well in the St. John River of New Brunswick. Atlantic sturgeon, including the Gulf sturgeon subspecies found in many rivers emptying into the Gulf of Mexico, can grow to 15 feet long and live for sixty years, but little is known about their population other than that a small number of them are living in the Hudson River of New York.

When Kynard moved to Massachusetts to study anadramous and diadramous fish about thirty years ago, he sought out a lab with the facilities to conduct scientific studies and test the hypotheses generated by fieldwork on these species. When he found no appropriate labs in the region, he proposed that the federal government build one. "We had a restoration program that had been going on for twenty years, but no commitment to gathering information about these fish," he said. "This laboratory would do that." The U.S. Fish and Wildlife Service director suggested he talk to Massachusetts Congressman Silvio Conte about funding the lab, and within days Conte proposed the project on the floor of the House of Representatives. Opened in 1990, the Conte Anadramous Fish Laboratory contains a remarkable array of research facilities, including an indoor artificial stream, complex fish passage systems, and dispersal tanks designed to study a wide range of physiological, behavioral, and ecological issues. As a result of research conducted at the Conte lab, more is known about shortnose sturgeon in the Connecticut River than about any other sturgeon population.

Kynard invited me for a tour of the facility in May 2006 at what should have been the peak of spawning season, but the double whammy of major fall floods and heavy rains in April and May eliminated any chance I had of seeing a wild sturgeon. The lab is on the northern tip of an island in the Connecticut River separated from the western banks by a canal that directs water to a hydropower station and the lab's research facilities. The island has a small village of old homes, one stop sign, and a red brick schoolhouse, and the approach to the lab goes through Cabot Woods, a tiny forest and fishing access owned by the power company Northeast Utilities. The Cabot Station powerhouse includes a fish lift that aids migratory fish in getting past the Turners Falls Dam a quarter-mile upstream. As I drove along the canal with a light rain falling, hundreds of tree, barn, bank, and rough-winged swallows soared and swooped close to the water surface in search of insects, while chimney swifts darted about high overhead. I paused for a few minutes to look for cliff swallows, the most difficult swallow to find among the five species native to the East, but none were apparent.

When I finally met Kynard, he looked to me like the assistant principal at the high school near my old office, a short, stocky, square-faced man with an easy smile. He quickly pointed out several physiology and ecology labs on our way to the behavioral labs where he works. He said that sturgeon are the fastest-growing fish in the world, so the only time they are vulnerable to predation is in their first fifty days, when catfish and other benthic fish might feed upon them. They are also highly adaptable. By the time they get to be about ten months old, they can live in either freshwater or salt water without having to proceed through a period of smoltification like salmon do. "That's the advantage of having been around for sixty-five million years," Kynard said. "They've adapted to be able to go anywhere."

Kynard first took me into what he called the wet lab, an area of sixty large holding tanks on two levels, each tank about 10 feet in diameter and 4 feet high. The tanks held a wide variety of sturgeons from distinct locations and of particular ages. With a large net, he reached into one tank and pulled out a shortnose sturgeon born three months earlier in the Savannah River in Georgia, and then from another tank came an older shortnose from the Connecticut River. The local fish was about 2 feet long, and its scutes and armor-plated head made it feel like it had an external skeleton. Like sharks and all species of sturgeon, it had a heterocercal tail in which the upper lobe is much longer than the lower lobe. The shortnose sturgeon in the tanks exhibited a wide range of coloration: Some looked almost black above, while others were gray-brown or olive green, and the juveniles showed some spotting beneath. While Kynard held the fish above the tank, he stuck his finger in its mouth and demonstrated how its mouth protrudes several inches below its body when feeding. To me it looked unnatural, like grotesquely oversized lips or an extra appendage that could be extended on command. After he showed me green and Atlantic sturgeon in other tanks, I asked why the water in the tanks was so brown. He noted that all of the tanks have a continuous flow of water coming in from the Connecticut River, and the flooding in previous days had made the river turbid and murky. Most of the year, the river is clear and the fish are visible in the tanks. Kynard said that using actual river water in the lab ensures that the fish grow under natural temperature and water-quality conditions.

The cramped facilities that Kynard uses in his research were on the second level, separated from numerous additional sturgeon holding tanks. He studies the very early life stages of the fish when potential problems are most likely to occur, so his equipment was much smaller than I expected. A 6-inch-diameter tube standing vertically about 5 feet tall is used to study how high in the water column the young fish prefer to swim, while a small tank containing dark- and light-colored rocks is used to assess their light preferences. The tank that I found most interesting looked like an 8-foot-long racetrack oval that Kynard called a dispersal tank. When filled with water to a depth of 18 inches and continually pumped so the water flows in one direction, the tank becomes a "microcosm of the river," he said. "The day they hatch, the fish are put into the tank, and we [use video to] count the number of times they swim around the track, twenty-four hours a day for forty-five or fifty days. It's a measure of their innate migration, how far they swim downstream after hatching. It's a key question to understanding the impact of dams and reservoirs. If they only disperse short distances and don't reach dams, then the dams might not be a problem for the young fish."

Next to the wet lab is a Quonset hut with larger holding tanks for bigger sturgeon. As we passed through, Kynard knocked on the side of one tank and several 4-foot-long lake sturgeon immediately surfaced and swam toward us expecting a meal. Their size, aggressiveness, and lack of fear was somewhat disconcerting, but when they saw we were empty-handed, they disappeared back beneath the murky water. The last building in the complex is called the flume building, and it contains a massive, concrete, oval track about 20 feet deep and 80 feet long where fish passage studies are conducted. Although it was dry when I visited, rocks of all sizes and configurations were set up to evaluate the kind of substrate in which various species prefer to forage, spawn, and migrate. Just outside the flume building are the facility's spawning tanks, which looked like another concrete track—this time with continuous switchbacks—with fast-moving water piped in from the adjacent river. The four wild shortnose sturgeon that migrated upstream to spawn in 2006—along with two additional females captured the previous fall—had been placed in the tanks three days before my visit. The fish had already spawned and been returned to the river by the time I arrived, but several tiny eggs were visible in the tanks, a clear indication that despite the small number of spawning adults, another generation of shortnose sturgeon was in development.

The decline of shortnose sturgeon, as well as most of the other sturgeon species in the United States, can be traced to an organized effort by European fish processors to capture them between about 1880 and 1920. The fishermen started along the East Coast and later moved to the West Coast and the Mississippi River. Commercial fishermen caught the sturgeon on their spawning grounds and delivered them to fish-processing ships staged at the mouth of the Delaware River, while other ships made regular trips back and forth to Europe to deliver the processed sturgeon. It was the first example of factory fishing in North America. But the fishermen did not capture the sturgeon for their flesh. Instead, they were after their eggs, which were as valuable as gold.

Unfertilized sturgeon eggs are known around the world as caviar, which has been considered a delicacy since at least 1100 B.C. Lavish banquets in ancient Greece were concluded with heaping platters of salted sturgeon eggs, and early Persians considered it a medicine that was consumed in stick form for energy and stamina. The first written record of caviar—a Turkish word then spelled khavyar—was from the writings of the grandson of Ghengis Khan in 1240, while it first appeared in print in English in 1591. King Edward II claimed sturgeon were royal fish and declared that all specimens caught in England belonged to the imperial treasury. The oldest sturgeon fishery is in the Caspian Sea, where seven sturgeon species are found, including the most famous of them all, beluga sturgeon, which can live for 150 years and grow to nearly 20 feet long and 2,500 pounds. While beluga caviar has always been considered the most prized variety, the United States produced 90 percent of the world's caviar in the late nineteenth century, although much of it was exported to Europe, where it was labeled "Russian caviar" and imported right back to the United States. As many as 3,500 tons of caviar—mostly from shortnose and Atlantic sturgeon—came from the Delaware and Hudson rivers before fish stocks were depleted.

Today, most caviar comes from just four species, all in the Caspian Sea and adjacent waters. Fishing rights are shared by Russia, Azerbaijan, Kazakhstan, Turkmenistan, and Iran, and most of the caviar produced from those countries is exported to the United States and Europe. Based on data from the National Marine Fisheries Service, the United States imported more than 80 tons of caviar per year in 2000 and 2001, down from 114 tons in 1999, most of which came from Russia and Kazakhstan. At approximately $50 per ounce, U.S. caviar imports are worth about $100 million annually. Unfortunately, there have been few regulations governing sturgeon fishing in the Caspian Sea, so it has been fished at unsustainable rates for many years. In 2005, the United States announced a ban on the import of beluga caviar, a year after it placed the beluga sturgeon on the federal endangered species list.

The end of the unregulated commercial harvest of shortnose sturgeon for caviar came in the 1920s, and yet the species has struggled to rebound. Populations of shortnose sturgeon in southern rivers are in the worst shape, while the Delaware River—which has no dams to hinder upstream migration—may be home to as many as 15,000 of them. The species is doing the best in the Hudson River, with a population of about 50,000, in part because the lowermost dam on that river is far upstream, allowing the fish to complete their entire life cycle without encountering any physical barriers. Many fisheries biologists believe this segment of the population is strong enough to be removed from the endangered species list, but not enough is known about its spawning and early life history for government agencies to risk de-listing it yet. The Connecticut River has just 1,500 shortnose sturgeon in two divided populations, and less than 100 are left in the Merrimack River of Massachusetts and New Hampshire. "We believe the natal population of shortnose [in the Merrimack] was extirpated along with Atlantic sturgeon during the fishing fanaticism in the latter part of the nineteenth century," Kynard said. "But we think there are large populations in Maine in the Androscoggin River (10,000 to 12,000) and the Kennebec River (12,000 to 15,000). What's typical is that when populations get up to that 10,000 level, all of a sudden you get a lot of coastal migrants. It's advantageous for females to look for a better place to put their eggs where their young won't have to compete with all these other fish. Our hypothesis is that it is very likely that it's coastal immigrants that have come down from those large Maine rivers and established the Merrimack population."

So what has kept the Connecticut River population so low? It doesn't appear to be water quality, according to Kynard. While water quality in southern rivers may be a concern, the fact that the species survived the massive dumping of chemicals and dyes and wastes into waterways during the Industrial Revolution in the Northeast suggests that pollution isn't a major factor, especially now that most rivers are much cleaner today. The most significant threat to the shortnose sturgeon is dams, which segment populations and prevent fish from reaching their historical spawning sites. On the Connecticut River, the chief culprit is the Holyoke Dam.

Beginning in 1848, the first Holyoke Dam across the 1,000-foot-wide river was constructed of wood by the Hadley Falls Company as part of a canal system designed to provide power to its cotton mills and textile machinery. When the company went bankrupt in 1859, its assets were sold for $325,000 to Alfred Smith, who used it to establish the Holyoke Water Power Company, which grew considerably during its first thirty years by using waterwheels to provide mechanical power to local mills through a series of gears, belts, pulleys, and shafts. In 1884, the company connected its waterwheels to a generator and began furnishing electricity to streetlights in the city of Holyoke. The dam was rebuilt out of concrete and granite in 1900, and ownership of the dam and the company was transferred to the city two years later for a price of $702,000. During 1905 and 1906, two 600-kilowatt hydroelectric units and a 1,000-kilowatt steam unit were constructed between the dam and the canal to boost electricity output. These power stations were later replaced by two 15,400-kilowatt hydroelectric units, the first built in 1952 and the second in 1983.

In 1949, the company received a fifty-year operating license for its dam and hydroelectric facilities from the Federal Power Commission, but it was required to install fish-passage facilities at the dam to allow salmon, shad, herring, and other fish access to upstream waters. Fish ladders had been built at the dam in 1873 and 1940 as required by the Massachusetts legislature, but both efforts had failed. After experimenting for several years, company engineers designed a totally new fish-passage concept—an elevator-like fish lift—for which it received a Conservation Service Award from the U.S. Department of the Interior. By 1990, more than 750,000 anadramous fish had used the lift to bypass the dam. Unfortunately, it hasn't been much help to shortnose sturgeon. Just 100 of the endangered species have been lifted past the dam to give them access to their spawning grounds.

The federal recovery plan for shortnose sturgeon addresses each river population individually. The strategies for recovering the Connecticut River population focus almost entirely on ensuring upstream and downstream passage by the Holyoke Dam. "It just so happens that they built this dam right in the middle of the population that goes from Montague to Long Island Sound," said Kynard. "The fish have this innate drive to move downstream, and when they go through the turbines they get killed. We've done studies on it, and it kills 100 percent of the adults." That's not to say that it is impossible for sturgeon to successfully pass the dam going downstream. It's a matter of size and timing. Small juvenile fish pass through the turbines with just a 2 or 3 percent mortality rate, according to Kynard. Adult sturgeon that pass over the spillway at the top of the dam during high-water events typically survive as well, but the fish don't know enough to wait for high water to migrate downstream.

"The other thing the dam is doing is preventing upstream passage. The fish-passage facilities there were not designed for sturgeon," Kynard said of the award-winning fish lift.

Nothing about them—not their operation, not their location, not their access to them, not any aspect—was designed with sturgeon in mind. In years when there have been as many as a hundred fish right at the dam that I've been tracking, not one has passed. The only way this population can ever hope to get back up to ten thousand, which would be a reasonable population for the Northeast, is to reconnect the upper group with the lower group and allow the lower group to get back up. I think you can re-connect them with the fish elevator they've got in place. I know they work for passing sturgeon. But no attention has been directed toward helping them get there or operating it in a way that the sturgeons are going to be moved. For instance, the fish lift only operates in the daytime, and every species of sturgeon that we've tested wants to go up at night. If they op-erate it appropriately, put enough water down there, and make access to it, it can be done. It can be done.

The Holyoke Dam was issued a license for another fifty years in 2000, but only on the condition that it install downstream protections and up-stream passage for shortnose sturgeon. Since then, the Holyoke Water Power Company has been funding studies to see how best to meet these conditions. Before the studies began, no one really knew how deeply the fish swim when migrating. "When they're feeding, grazing, and resting, they're on the bottom, but when they're swimming they appear to be in the water column, and we didn't know that three years ago. That makes a huge difference when designing a bypass for them," said Chris Tomichek, senior fisheries biologist at Kleinschmidt Associates, an engineering and environmental consulting firm hired by the company. "We did a study along the louvers in the canal system that showed that one-year-old stur-geon moved in the water column, not on the bottom. So maybe we don't need to build a bottom bypass. Maybe we need a surface bypass instead."

A wide range of downstream fish-passage technologies are available, though there is no agreement on what works best for sturgeon. Conventional measures start with a physical barrier like a screen or net to keep the fish from entering the turbine intake, and they may include a louver or other structural guidance system to direct the fish to an engineered by-pass around the dam. Alternatively, behavior-based guidance systems use sensory stimuli to elicit actions to avoid the turbines and move elsewhere. Lights, noises, electric fields, and bubble curtains have all been tested and are effective in diverting some species of fish away from turbines. There are even fish-friendly turbines that kill far fewer fish that could be installed. Regardless of the system selected, it likely will be expensive and will have to be effective not only for sturgeon but also for shad, eels, salmon, herring, and other anadramous and migratory species that live in the Connecticut River as well.

To learn more about the behavior of shortnose sturgeon as they approach the dam, Kleinschmidt Associates is conducting a five-year study that involves capturing one hundred adult sturgeon upstream, fitting them with electronic tags, and tracking them as they migrate to the dam. In September 2006, I joined Kleinschmidt biologists Jen Burton-Reeve and Kevin Nebiolo as they set gill nets to trap adult sturgeon to implant them with the tracking devices. It was a cool fall day as I arrived at Brunelle's Marina in South Hadley, Massachusetts, to meet the biologists, but thick fog had settled over the Pioneer Valley so it was impossible to see even to the end of the dock. At 9:15, as the fog was burning off, we loaded up the 20-foot John boat with nets, anchors, floats, and boxes of unseen equipment and headed north. We were joined by Brian Hanson, a fisheries biologist with another consulting firm who is responsible for tracking the sturgeon once they arrive at the dam. The foliage on the trees that lined the river was just beginning to change colors, so it was easy to get lost in the beauty of the landscape. Little wisps of fog lingered at the water surface as we headed northward, and a double-crested cormorant was perched on a buoy at the water intake pipe of the Mount Tom Power Station on the west bank, a 136,000-kilowatt, coal-fired electricity generating plant.

Just north of the power plant is a 70-foot-deep hole in the river bottom where an underwater camera the previous week had revealed at least one sturgeon swimming. With Nebiolo and Hanson manning the net in the bow and Burton-Reeve maneuvering the boat, they tried anchoring a 6-foot-tall and 100-foot-long gill net to the bottom of the river across the hole. But after dropping the anchor at one end and trying to ease out the rest of the net carefully, they found that the mesh was "like a nasty hair net, all tangled and hideous," according to Burton-Reeve, making it impossible to release. They tried again with a second net, which went out with ease, but the anchors didn't catch on the bottom so the net quickly drifted out of position. It took thirty minutes of adjustments, but finally the net was set, although still not in an ideal location. A third net went out even faster, but the strong current and light-weight anchors nearly entangled it in the first net, so both were pulled back in and we moved to another location. "Isn't gill netting fun?" Nebiolo joked sarcastically, clearly frustrated at the slow progress of the morning. Burton-Reeve added that "gill netting is frustrating, even in good conditions." But they kept at it, and at the second location—adjacent to a rocky ledge directly opposite the Mount Tom Power Station—they quickly set three nets in a row with no troubles.

The protocol was to leave the nets in the water for an hour before checking them for fish, so the biologists sat in the boat and shared stories about the thousands of pumpkins from nearby farms that floated down the river the previous fall following the massive flooding. After an hour, we approached the nets to retrieve our catch. The biologists had concluded two days of gill netting the previous week without capturing any sturgeon, so they weren't feeling optimistic, but I was excited about the prospects. With the boat in position, Nebiolo and Hanson tugged on the first net and immediately knew something was wrong. The net was unnaturally heavy, and when the first few feet of it broke the surface, it was clear why. The net was completely covered with filamentous algae—probably the result of excess nutrients being dumped into the river upstream—so much so that the netting material was invisible and the space between the mesh was totally clogged. With the water-logged algae weighing perhaps 1,000 pounds, it took more than ten minutes of back-breaking effort to pull the net aboard. "Never in my life have I seen anything close to this," Nebiolo said. "If the others are like this, our fishing is done for the day." And they were. The biologists tried to use the power of the boat's engine to pull the second net in, but it did little good. Nebiolo and Hanson were completely exhausted by the time they had retrieved it, so Burton-Reeve and I pulled in the third one after first releasing the anchor from one end and hoping the current would wash away some of the algae. It didn't. What began as a beautiful morning on the river turned into a depressing day of wasted effort, brightened only briefly by a smiling Hanson who noted that "if we were out here trying to catch algae, these nets would probably be filled with sturgeon."

Ensuring that sturgeon can survive downstream passage by the Holyoke Dam is only one step in meeting the conditions of the dam's license. Getting the fish back above the dam would at first appear to be the bigger challenge. While the existing lift system, with a few modifications and evening operating hours, could do the trick, it's not the only technology available. Boyd Kynard has been studying how sturgeon use a variety of fish-passage systems, and while he knows sturgeon will use fish lifts, he also knows that most traditional fish ladders do little to help sturgeon. He said that sturgeon are poor at what he calls "burst swimming," whereby a fish puts on a quick burst of speed to pass an obstacle and then rests before bursting past the next obstacle. With names like Denil, Alaska steep-pass, and pool and weir, fish ladders designed for salmon and most other fish have structures built across them like steps that allow the fish to proceed up the ladder in stages by using their leaping or burst-swimming skills. As sturgeon swim up fishways, however, they prefer to swim at one continuous speed without stopping until they reach the top. Cross-channel structures and resting places interfere with their ability to maintain a continuous swimming speed, so typical fish ladders are ineffective for sturgeon.

At the Conte Anadramous Fish Laboratory, Kynard has been testing how sturgeons navigate a unique, new fishway designed with the particular needs of sturgeon in mind. The structure is a large spiral device that takes two loops totaling 90 feet at a 6 percent incline to raise the fish above an 8.5-foot dam. It is fitted with valves to control water quantity and water speed through the spiral, as well as video cameras and other monitoring equipment to count the number of tail beats—a measure of energy expended—required for the fish to reach the top. While the structure was designed with lake sturgeon in mind, shortnose and other species have also been tested. Most take between fifty seconds and five minutes to complete the journey, though one uncooperative fish took six hours because it didn't appear interested in making the effort.

Whether the owners of the Holyoke Dam decide to use the fish lift, the spiral, or some other fish-passage system to get shortnose sturgeon above the dam—even trapping them below the dam and trucking them above it is an option some dam owners have selected, although it is controversial—the key is to do it sooner rather than later. Kynard believes the long-term outlook for the species is "very definitely positive," adding that if there were a litany of other threats to the species, "I would waiver on that. But the major impact on this population just happens to be this one physical structure. Just like we can build higher walls in New Orleans [to keep floodwaters out], we can fix this dam."

Photography by New England Wild Flower Society/Lisa Mattei.
For more information on New England Wild Flower Society's plant
conservation programs visit www.newfs.org

13

Jesup's Milk-Vetch

Returning home from a two-week birding vacation to South Texas back
in 1992, my wife and I opened the door and knew immediately we weren't
alone. The house was filled with ladybugs, thousands of them, swarming
around the windows and light fixtures. Once considered a harbinger of
good luck, especially to farmers and gardeners who love them because they
eat unwanted pest insects that might otherwise devastate plants, those in
my house made me feel anything but lucky. While not harmful, the challenge of ridding them from my house resulted in dull orange stains on
my walls and numerous dead bodies scattered on the floors, regardless of
how delicately we tried to remove them. And as much as I wanted to rescue them and return them outside so they could continue sucking the life
out of unsuspecting pests, the ladybugs weren't even native to the area.
Instead of the common two-spotted or nine-spotted varieties found in
my childhood garden and across North America, these were imports
from Asia with anywhere from two to twenty spots.

Officially called the multicolored Asian lady beetle, the critter was intentionally released in several locations in the United States in the 1970s
and 1980s, most notably in Georgia and Washington, to control aphids

and scale insects. Others arrived accidentally on ships in the port of New Orleans and elsewhere. They quickly spread across the country, and as their population skyrocketed, they found their way to the Northeast. With no known natural predators, there was no stopping them. The Asian lady beetle now thrives in much of the country and is displacing native ladybugs.

Unfortunately, this is a common occurrence. Invasive species like the multicolored Asian lady beetle are the second-biggest conservation problem in the world—behind only habitat loss—and they are leading to a great loss of biodiversity and changes to ecosystem functioning. Forty-two percent of the species on the federal endangered species list are there in large part due to invasive species, and these unwanted invaders have a $138 billion a year impact on agriculture, horticulture, fisheries, recreation, and water supplies.

"Most people think of it as an issue of exotic plants spreading and taking over everything, keeping other species out," said Lisa Lofland Gould, founder of the Rhode Island Wild Plant Society and the Rhode Island Natural History Survey, and a regional expert on invasives. "But it's much more than that. Invasives change the soil chemistry, they bring in diseases, and they clog up water systems."

Gould offered lots of examples. Autumn olive, an attractive shrub that produces berries that birds love to eat, enriches the soil and makes it more fertile, which forces out the numerous native species that prefer infertile soils. Other exotic plants create toxic compounds that inhibit the growth of competing plants. Introduced earthworms from fishing bait gobble up the duff layer of the forest floor, wiping out spring wildflowers and opening up the forest to additional invasives. The invasion of exotic garlic mustard and Japanese stilt grass is almost always preceded by Asian earthworms, Gould said. Gypsy moths, winter moths, and Asian longhorn beetles also have devastating effects on American forests, as have introduced pathogens such as Dutch elm disease and chestnut blight, the latter of which was responsible for wiping out up to 90 percent of the black bear population and half the squirrel population in some parts of Virginia in the 1940s due to a lack of food. Abundant deer add to the problem by feeding exclusively on native plants and avoiding introduced species like multiflora rose and Japanese barberry, in effect selecting for invasives in an evolutionary sense. Monarch butterflies are now found to lay their eggs on the introduced black swallow-wort, a plant that looks much like the milkweed that monarchs prefer, but when the eggs hatch and the caterpillars feed on the swallow-wort, they all die.

According to Les Mehrhoff, director of the Invasive Plant Atlas of New England, the problem of invasive species in the region is growing by leaps and bounds. Shrubs and vines tend to be the worst offenders, because birds feed on their fruits and disperse the seeds widely. Unfortunately, other than scattered efforts by land managers on private nature preserves and other lands, little is being done in a coordinated way to control most of these species because state and federal funding is limited.

"The impacts on wildlife from invasives are two-fold—directly from the species themselves, but also indirectly from management efforts," Mehrhoff said. He points to multiflora rose as a prime example. Introduced from Japan in 1886, it was advocated by the U.S. Soil Conservation Service from 1930 to 1960 for use in erosion control and as natural fences, but it outcompetes native plants and spreads in dense thickets across the landscape, taking over pastures and lowering crop yields. "In this case, as in many others, one conservation activity negated another. These control efforts have ramifications," said Mehrhoff.

One ramification of the spread of multiflora rose has been an expansion northward of the range of mockingbirds and an increase in the number of robins that stay in New England through the winter months. These birds, along with cedar waxwings, thrive on the hips from multiflora rose, and they have helped spread the invasive shrub north to Maine in recent years. While the birdwatching community might argue that the increase in mockingbirds and wintering robins in the area is a good thing, most conservationists would agree that the spread of multiflora rose certainly is not.

"Part of the problem with many of these exotic species is that they arrive in the United States without the pests, diseases, and competitors that keep them in check in their native lands," Gould said. "They're here in a vacuum in the absence of those things that would otherwise keep them under control."

Sadly, despite what is known about the devastating impact of some of these species, they continue to be released intentionally. Sixty percent of invasive plants come from the horticulture industry, and they continue to be sold while the industry fights all regulation.

Invasive species are one of the prime reasons that Jesup's milk-vetch (*Astragalus robinsii jesupii*) is clinging to life in New England. A perennial

member of the pea family and one of just three plants in New England
on the federal endangered species list, Jesup's is found at only three sites
along a 15-mile stretch of the Connecticut River in central New Hampshire and Vermont. Preferring steep, rocky areas close to the river's edge
with sediment-filled crevices where the plant can take hold, the plant requires periodic scouring by the breakup of river ice floating down the
river, which removes competing vegetation from the riverbanks.

New Hampshire Natural Heritage Bureau biologist Sara Cairns describes Jesup's milk-vetch as "an inconspicuous, pea-like plant with small,
compound green leaves and pale purple flowers" that bloom in late May
and early June. One of six variants of a more common vetch found primarily in western states, Jesup's grows up to fifteen tall stalks (called inflorescences) per plant, with eight or ten flowers per stalk. By mid-June,
the flowers have dropped off and been replaced by seed pods, which then
dry up and twist open, depositing their four to eight seeds within a few
feet of the original plant. Pollinators include several varieties of bee and
small flies, although under experimental conditions they also have been
known to fertilize their own seeds when pollinators are absent, in effect
cloning themselves. When plants are submerged during high-water years,
some seeds have even germinated while still clinging to the parent plant.

Cairns invited me to join her for a canoe trip to one of the sites in June
2006—it's only accessible by boat—for the annual census of Jesup's milk-
vetch. It was a hot and sticky morning with threatening skies when we
met at a public boat launch near Claremont, New Hampshire, at a sharp
bend in the river. The launch site was lined by tall aspens and oaks with
abundant bird life. Song sparrows, catbirds, and common yellowthroats
lurked in the understory while American redstarts and warbling vireos
sang from above. A tufted titmouse and yellow-throated vireo could be
heard singing in the trees 200 yards away on the Vermont side of the
river, which was very quiet, with only a few riffles and no visible current. I realized that the census was a bigger job than I had guessed when
four cars carrying two canoes, two kayaks, and five more census-takers
pulled into the lot behind me. After unloading the vehicles and getting a
brief orientation to the project from Cairns—focusing mostly on the importance of not stepping on the plants—a lengthy debate ensued about
what qualified as a plant to count. The debate sounded somewhat hu-
morous to the uninitiated, but it became obvious why it was important
once we arrived at the site.

In the plant's first growing season, it rises only an inch or two from the ground and doesn't flower, so it looks more like the clover in my lawn than the 10- to 20-inch-tall plant it would become the following year. Only a small percentage of these seedlings survive long enough to reproduce the next summer, so Cairns directed the group of volunteers not to bother counting them during the census. Instead, she said to count each adult plant with at least one inflorescence and also to count the number of inflorescences per plant.

With our orientation and debate over, we loaded into the canoes and kayaks and steadily paddled up river. There was little wildlife to note on the trip: a few spotted sandpipers characteristically bobbed up and down on the banks or flew across the river with their distinctive shallow wing beats; two groups of barn and tree swallows darted about in circles feeding on insects just above the water's surface; and an eastern kingbird flitted to and from its riverside perch in search of a meal. I kept expecting to hear the loud rattle of a belted kingfisher calling out from a snag on the banks or flying upstream ahead of us, but one never appeared.

Approaching an area where the riverbank became steep and rocky, Bill Brumback turned his kayak in to shore to look for Jesup's and to verify that we had arrived at the right place. He said we had, but to my untrained eye, there weren't any pale purple flowers visible. The previous year the site had twenty-five thousand inflorescences—far more than had ever been counted before—and yet it appeared at first that the plant had disappeared totally. Brumback, director of conservation for the New England Wild Flower Society, said that there were a few scattered plants around, but most had already dropped their flowers and had started growing seed pods.

The site, the most southerly of the three Jesup's locations, is about 400 meters long but is split in half by a small break in the rocks that made it impossible to cross from the upstream section to the downstream section on foot. So we broke into two groups to complete the job. I joined Brumback and Heather Herrmann, a New Hampshire state biologist, in tackling the downstream section, but we got off to a slow start as we debated the best way to proceed. Tiny metal pins had been driven into the rocks at 20-meter increments along the bank, and each section was divided into three levels from the top of the slope to the water's edge. By stretching a rope between each metal marker, we could easily see the three levels and determine in which cell each plant was found. But finding the metal pins was the biggest challenge, and sometimes we just had to fudge it and guess. I served as data recorder, so every time Brumback and Herrmann found a Jesup's milk-vetch, they called out to me how many inflorescences it had. After counting all the Jesup's in each section, they started over again and counted the competing invasive species: black swallow-wort, Japanese honeysuckle, purple loosestrife, cypress spurge, and poison ivy.

While poison ivy is a native plant and not technically an invasive species, it is abundant at all three sites and is included with the invasives because, like the exotic species, it grows aggressively and takes over the growing area, effectively out-competing the endangered Jesup's milk-vetch for limited soil, water, and nutrients. It's also likely to become even more aggressive due to global warming. Research in 2006 at Duke University concluded that increasing carbon dioxide levels in the atmosphere—the prime culprit in the warming of the planet—will make poison ivy grow faster and larger. The scientists experimented by increasing carbon dioxide levels in a forest to those expected in 2050 and found that the poison ivy plants grew three times larger and produced more of the rash-causing chemical urushiol.

There were few Jesup's or invasives in the first section we checked, but in the second they were both abundant. Brumback and Herrmann constantly called out numbers for me to record in different cells, often overlapping their words and making it a challenge to record the information accurately. But we soon got into a rhythm and quickened the pace. We continued to be challenged, however, by the steep, slippery slope we were working on and by our determination not to step on any endangered plants. All three of us fell more than once trying to maneuver along the muddy rock face, and Brumback even fell backwards into the river once, muttering abbreviations for profanity to himself as he climbed back out. The other challenge was avoiding the poison ivy. Since we often found ourselves on all fours as we traversed the site, and because poison ivy was the most abundant plant there, it was impossible not to come in contact with it. Besides, we had to count each poison ivy stem we found, so Brumback and Herrmann had no choice but to touch it. Brumback wore rubber gloves to protect himself from the plant's oil, but within twenty minutes of starting they were torn and useless. Hermann didn't bother with gloves, but before our lunch break she washed her hands in the river and worried that poison ivy oil on her hands would get on her sandwich and then in her mouth. But it didn't stop her from eating. By the end of the day, we had counted 3,730 stems of poison ivy.

Brumback and Herrmann provided much-needed entertainment during the heat of the day, reciting obscure lines of dialogue from the movie *Princess Bride* in between calling out the numbers of invasives and inflorescences they found. Brumback started his botany career propagating bulbs and perennials for commercial flower growers in Holland, then returned to the United States and eventually took a job cultivating endangered plants for the New England Wild Flower Society, where he has worked for twenty-six years. Herrmann grew up in a sporting camp in northern Maine where her family led canoe trips for adventuresome tourists and fishing parties. She intended to become a veterinarian, but one of the camp employees that she had a crush on convinced her to study wildlife biology instead. While she's embarrassed that she chose a career path based on the advice of a youthful crush, she's happy about the decision. After earning degrees at Houghton College and the University of New Hampshire, she worked a series of temporary field biology jobs in New York, Maine, and New Hampshire before landing her current position with the New Hampshire Natural Heritage Bureau. She works mostly with small mammals, but the Jesup's milk-vetch project helped her develop an appreciation for the conservation challenges of protecting plants as well.

Twice during our six hours of counting plants, Herrmann pointed out a red-spotted newt sitting on a rock, and once we found several small eels wriggling in the wet sand where they were trapped by the receding water. But mostly we were focused on the tall Jesup's inflorescences and the invasive species, most of which were found to have more than doubled in abundance since the previous year. Purple loosestrife, a tall spike of beautiful flowers when in bloom but an aggressive invader from Europe that takes over wetlands, was only found growing in the area just at the water's edge where few Jesup's milk-vetch grew, and cypress spurge—which increased by six times over the year before—was mostly found in the southernmost sections of the site. Native to Europe, it was introduced to North America in the 1860s and now grows abundantly along roadsides, fencerows, and meadows, where it makes fields unfit for cattle or growing hay. Another European import, black swallow-wort is a perennial vine in the milkweed family that twists itself around other plants and can quickly take over several acres of land. Like the cypress spurge, it was only found in the downstream sections of the site. The one exotic species found scattered equally throughout the site was Japanese honeysuckle, an ornamental shrub native to Asia that crowds out other species.

Despite the seemingly high number of invasive species at the site, Cairns said the upstream sites are worse. "That site [where you were counting] is blessedly free of lots of the invasives, especially the down-stream side," she said. "The other sites have lots of black swallow-wort and Japanese honeysuckle, even though we've tried removing seedpods and cutting it back. It's still there in spite of all of our manual controls." The concern, she explained, is that with so little soil accumulated in the cracks of the rocks, there is a great deal of competition among the plants' roots to maintain a hold, and the aggressive exotics are winning out.

What we hardly noticed during our census was the huge number of tiny Jesup's milk-vetch seedlings scattered in bunches around the site. While the total number of reproducing plants was relatively low in 2006, the apparently large number of seedlings suggested that the following year would be a good one. And that reinforced a worrisome trend that Cairns was tracking. Since 1997, a pattern has emerged showing a boom-and-bust cycle of Jesup's numbers at all three sites, which could be ex-plained if most of the plants are the same age. During a boom year, there are large numbers of mature plants and inflorescences but very few seed-lings because plant numbers were low the previous year and few seeds were dropped. During a bust year the opposite happens—there are few reproducing plants but an abundance of seedlings as a result of the large number of plants that dropped seeds the year before.

The cyclical nature of wildlife populations isn't uncommon, so why is it a problem for Jesup's milk-vetch? "My concern is that having one age cohort makes them much more vulnerable," Cairns said. "If they have bad environmental conditions in the year that they're supposed to put out a lot of seed, it would make it hard for them to recover, particularly if we had a couple bad years in a row."

During the boom-and-bust population cycle of Jesup's milk-vetch, 2006 was a bust year. Just 514 plants with a total of 1,090 inflorescences were counted at all three sites, while total invasive numbers were twenty-one times that many. That compares with 29,000 inflorescences the pre-vious year and over 4,600 inflorescences in 2004. The last bust year was 2003, when just 404 plants and 814 inflorescences, the lowest numbers in a decade, were counted. The good news is that huge numbers of inflo-rescences in 2005 bodes well for a big rebound year in 2007.

. . .

The specimen used to describe what became known as Jesup's milk-vetch was collected on the Vermont side of the Connecticut River by S. N. Eggleston in May 1896, although it was first mentioned in print two years earlier in the journal *Minnesota Botanical Studies*. The species was named for Henry Griswold Jesup, the first botany instructor at Smith College and the first professor of botany at Dartmouth College. While Jesup made pioneering contributions to the botany of the Connecticut River Valley during his lifetime, he didn't become interested in plants until after aborting an earlier career. A graduate of Yale and the Union Theological Seminary, he was ordained a minister in the Congregational Church in 1853 and preached in Stanwich, Connecticut, until he resigned due to poor health nine years later. He took to studying botany as a diversion from his ailments and moved to Amherst, Massachusetts, where he soon began collecting plant specimens, many of which are now housed in the herbarium at the University of Massachusetts. Among them are a spikemoss from the summit of Mount Holyoke, orchids from a wetland in Belchertown, sedges from a Deerfield swamp, and willows from an island in the Connecticut River. Jesup helped found the Connecticut Valley Botanical Society in 1873, the first such group open to both men and women, and he served as its first president.

In 1876, Jesup joined the faculty at Dartmouth and expanded the college's herbarium by giving prizes to the students who brought in the most specimens. Now called the Jesup Herbarium, the archive contains approximately one hundred thousand pressed and dried plant specimens, including two collected by Henry David Thoreau. Despite his continued ill-health, Jesup explored much of the area around Dartmouth and in 1882 published *A Catalogue of the Flora and Fauna within Thirty Miles of Hanover, N.H.* and followed it up in 1891 with *A Catalogue of the Flowering Plants and Higher Cryptogams Found within Thirty Miles of Hanover, N.H.* He also continued collecting plant specimens for the Dartmouth herbarium, as well as for his personal collection, which was rescued from a fire in his living quarters in 1881. Jesup retired from teaching in 1899 at the age of seventy-three, and died four years later. A collection of letters to Jesup from botanists around the region is maintained in the archives of the Gray Herbarium Library at Harvard.

The site where the first Jesup's milk-vetch was found still has a small population of the plant, but it's also the site that is most threatened by invasive species. That's because above the rocky bank where the vetch grows is a railroad bed, and according to Cairns, "invasives love transportation corridors. Up by the railroad bed the black swallow-wort is very abundant, and it rains down onto the ledges where the Jesup's plants are. Despite efforts to get rid of it, the swallow-wort is there to stay."

The third site, and the one farthest upriver, faces a different challenge. It is located at a natural constriction of the river where there is swift-moving whitewater, which makes it a very popular place for kayakers and other boaters. Like the other sites, it has a steep slope leading to the river, but below the slope is a relatively flat section of grass-covered ledges. The Jesup's grows in small numbers on the flat ledge in between two sites where the boaters play, picnic, and launch their watercraft. The fear is that the delicate plants will get trampled and not survive long enough for their seedpods to mature and drop seeds for the following year.

What makes these three sites unique is their geology. According to Scott Bailey, a research geoecologist with the U.S. Forest Service who has studied the sites, the rocks in all three locations have high calcium concentrations and high weathering rates, which means that the calcium is easily released from the rocks. He said that the rocks include a metamorphosed volcanic rock called amphibolite, which is often found in association with rare plants requiring calcium-rich soils, and a metamorphosed sedimentary rock called phyllite that contains marble layers. "In contrast, we visited a number of sites that seemed suitable [for Jesup's milk-vetch] based on physical conditions and generally similar geology," he wrote in an email. "However, amphibolite and marble interbeds were not present at uncolonized sites in the vicinity. In general, calcium-rich outcrops are pretty rare in this region. These lithochemical conditions coupled with the particular physical conditions (ice-scoured ledges along rivers) makes the habitat requirements of this plant pretty exacting and unusual. . . . We don't know if the *Astragalus* requires higher calcium availability or if the geologic conditions are changing the availability of some other nutrient that might be important."

The geology of the sites has also attracted the attention of the New Hampshire and Vermont chapters of The Nature Conservancy. Calcareous riverside seeps are a rare habitat type where a number of other imperiled plants are sometimes found, and the adjacent floodplain forest habitat also hosts rare species, among them the hackberry tree and the green dragon, an odd plant similar to jack-in-the-pulpit that only grows in enriched forested wetlands along rivers. Doug Bechtel, director of conservation science for the Conservancy's New Hampshire chapter, said that the organization is studying the entire length of the Connecticut River as a "macro-site" because it has a high diversity and density of unusual species, especially along the stretch where Jesup's milk-vetch is found. The cobblestone tiger beetle, for instance, lives on several river islands nearby, and the dwarf wedgemussel lives in the river sediments adjacent to the upstream Jesup's site.

Like Cairns, Bechtel is especially worried about the impact of invasive species on native plants along the river. But while invasives are the most obvious threat to the long-term survival of Jesup's milk-vetch, they're not the only one. In fact, the invasives may not even be the biggest threat. Cairns said that the most worrisome issue may be the limited habitat available. The plant has never been seen anywhere but the three sites that are currently being monitored, despite extensive searches up and down the Connecticut and White rivers and elsewhere. With all of the plants confined to just three small sites, the risk is high that environmental conditions or vandalism or something else could wipe out the plants at one site or another. Cairns even imagines the possibility of a railroad car becoming derailed at the site on the Vermont side of the river and falling on the plants. The ensuing removal of the car would certainly have devastating effects on the plant.

The recovery plan prepared for Jesup's as part of its inclusion on the federal endangered species list requires that the plant be introduced at two new sites, and that at least two of the combined five sites be on permanently protected conservation land. That's the other concern Cairns has—all three sites where the plant is currently found are on privately owned land. While the owners of all three properties have allowed biologists to monitor the plants, none has agreed to sell the property or enter into a conservation management agreement, making long-term management of the species uncertain. Thankfully, none of the landowners appears interested in selling the properties to developers any time soon, but that is always a lingering concern.

The other major threat to Jesup's milk-vetch is the dams on the river and the management of the water flowing over and through those dams. The Connecticut River is the largest river in New England, flowing 255 miles from Fourth Connecticut Lake in Pittsburg, New Hampshire, to Long Island Sound while dropping nearly 2,500 feet in elevation along the way. It drains a watershed totaling 11,250 square miles, which includes forested mountains and valleys, rolling hills, residential areas, and major urban centers like Springfield, Massachusetts, and Hartford, Connecticut. The river was formed at the end of the last ice age, about eleven thousand years ago, as the Laurentide ice sheet receded northward. During the retreat, a glacial lake was formed near Middletown, Connecticut, when a mass of sand and gravel sediment acted as a dam and backed up meltwater between the sediment and the retreating glacier. The lake, known as Glacial Lake Hitchcock, grew slowly and at its peak extended 200 miles from Rocky Hill, Connecticut, to St. Johnsbury, Vermont.

As the glacier disappeared, Native Americans moved into the area to hunt caribou and wooly mammoths, and as the climate warmed, native populations flourished. The first Europeans to explore the Connecticut River were led by Dutch fur trader Adraien Block, who was looking to establish trading posts in the Hudson River area. On his return trip to Holland in 1613, Block's ship caught fire and was destroyed near the mouth of the Hudson. Block and his crew overwintered on Manhattan Island and built a new boat, and on a trial voyage in 1614 sailed 60 miles up the Connecticut River. According to Henry Howe's book *Prologue to New England,* Block wrote, "In some places it is very shallow, so that at about fifteen leagues up the river there is not much more than five feet of water. There are few inhabitants near the mouth of the river, but at the distance of fifteen leagues above they become more numerous . . . The depth of water varies from eight to twelve feet, is sometimes four and five fathoms, but mostly eight and nine feet. The natives there [South Windsor] plant maize, and in the year 1614 they had a village resembling a fort for protection against the attacks of their enemies . . . The river is not navigable with yachts for more than two leagues farther, as it is very shallow and has a rocky bottom . . . This river has always a downward current so that no assistance is derived from it in going up, but a favorable wind is necessary." In 1624, the Dutch established a trading post on the river, and later acquired land from the Indians near present-day Hartford, Connecticut, where they built a fort. English colonists from Plymouth followed suit soon after.

As Block noted, while the first 60 miles of the river were navigable, natural barriers—especially a 50-foot falls near South Hadley, Massachusetts—prevented further navigation upstream, negatively affecting the growing economy of the region. In 1792, local merchants and political leaders initiated construction of a two-and-a-half-mile-long canal around the falls that led to rapid population growth in upstream communities when completed three years later. The tolls collected from canal users also stoked the local economy for more than fifty years, until competition from the expanding railroads made it no longer useful.

During this same time period, the river supported a thriving Atlantic salmon fishery, but overfishing and a series of man-made dams prohibiting upstream migration to traditional spawning grounds extirpated the species from the river, despite the fact that 150,000 salmon fry are still stocked in tributaries each year. The dams have also kept river flow levels relatively constant year-round, reducing the highs and lows that create a diversity of wildlife habitat. In New Hampshire, the North Hartland Dam near West Lebanon has the biggest impact on Jesup's milk-vetch.

"*Astragalus* grows in rocky ledges above the summer high-water level but below flood levels along the Connecticut River," explained Cairns. "The ledges are rocky because they get scoured in winter by ice. The exposed rocks collect a little soil in between the cracks, and that's where the vegetation grows. About 20 feet from the water is where the woody vegetation like shrubs and trees begin to grow, which produces shade to the area. Grasses, sedges, and wildflowers thrive everywhere that soil settles, and it gets densely populated. The ideal habitat is one where enough scour takes place to take out the woody vegetation, but there's still soil for [Jesup's] to grow."

Unfortunately, the dams don't allow flood stages to get as high as they would naturally, so the scouring of the river banks by ice and rock doesn't reach high enough to keep the woody vegetation from taking over the areas where Jesup's grows, reducing available habitat for a species that is already confined to a tiny space. The Nature Conservancy's Doug Bechtel said that the dams are affecting numerous species all up and down the river. "Flow in the river is a major issue," he said. "It influences ice scour, sediment build-up, where the floodplain forest and riverside habitats are, and in some cases it influences invasive species. Lots of species are affected by this one factor."

Sara Cairns is somewhat surprised that she is helping to lead the charge on behalf of Jesup's milk-vetch. She's not even a botanist. She started out interested in animal behavior and earned a doctorate from Cornell

University in evolutionary biology by studying the behavior of lions in Africa for sixteen months. The quantitative analysis she did for her lion research made her an expert in statistics and data analysis, which first led to a job as an environmental consultant in Baltimore, then to a teaching position at Middlebury College and a volunteer position with the Maine Natural Areas Program. Her primary responsibilities with the New Hampshire Natural Heritage Bureau involve data analysis—designing data tools, using mapping software, and maintaining records of rare species in the state—all to help the state make informed conservation decisions. The Jesup's project has allowed her to get back to the fieldwork she enjoys.

But it hasn't been easy. The efforts to combat the many threats to Jesup's milk-vetch have met with only limited success. Manual control of the invasive species has been ongoing at the two upstream sites where the infestation is greatest, but while it has kept the invasive numbers down it hasn't eradicated them entirely. Even herbicides haven't been as successful as had been hoped at controlling the black swallow-wort. Starting with a small, controlled effort at one site in 2002, herbicide was sponged on by hand, leaf by leaf, to ensure that only the invasive plant came in contact with the chemicals. "The results weren't as dramatic as we would have liked," Cairns said. "We knock it back, but the seeds keep raining down from [the railroad tracks] up above and it keeps coming back. We held it back relative to where it would be if we weren't doing anything, but the swallow-wort is still doing reasonably well."

From 1998 to 2001, biologists also tried augmenting the population of Jesup's at the smallest site with seeds and plants cultivated by the New England Wild Flower Society. During those years, alternating floods and drought complicated the process considerably—in a dry period, the plants remained healthy when watered regularly, but when just one week of watering was missed, they all died. "We tried using seeds, and the first time we did it the river rose up in an incredible flood and washed everything away," explained Brumback, who has cultivated numerous endangered plants, including Jesup's milk-vetch, at the Wild Flower Society's headquarters in Framingham, Massachusetts. "The second time we had an incredible drought, and the third time it worked a little bit but we didn't make a permanent dent in the population. Since then we've experimented with putting in larger plants rather than seed, which typically puts you in a better position than starting from seed." Despite the limited success, Brumback said that techniques were developed that will aid in future reintroductions.

The ongoing monitoring of Jesup's has generated a considerable data set that might provide additional insight about what other strategies to employ to protect the species, but no one has yet thoroughly analyzed the data. A close examination of that data might identify weather patterns, flooding frequency, or other elements that affect the population cycle of the plants. State biologists have discussed conducting DNA studies of Jesup's from the three sites, but experts at the labs that might do that work said it probably wouldn't yield anything useful.

So Cairns just keeps on doing what she knows is useful—annual monitoring to keep an eye out for when active intervention is necessary, and manual control of invasives at the most significantly impacted sites. She hopes that the constant ice scouring and the challenging habitat might just be inhospitable enough to keep the invasives from totally crowding out the Jesup's milk-vetch. "I'm mostly optimistic about its future because we're focusing attention on it, because the government is providing funding, and because lots of people are interested in it. I know it's at risk due simply to the sheer size and location of the sites, and I'm constantly amazed that it hasn't been trampled out yet. While I wouldn't be surprised if it winked out, I'm still hopeful because even in the case of a catastrophe, we could re-establish it. We've saved their genes [in a seed bank], so we've got a good chance to save the species."

Brumback is also somewhat optimistic, though he also worries about some random event that might prove to be the death knell of the species. "I've gained a lot of respect for this plant and its toughness for hanging on out there. That river is a double-edged sword. It has allowed it to survive there, and it's also what has kept it from gaining bigger population numbers. If that river weren't there, [Jesup's] would have been overrun by invasives by now. But the river wipes the slate clean every year."

14

Roseate Tern

Bird Island in Buzzards Bay, Massachusetts, is well named. As one approaches the treeless mound of rock and sand by boat in summer, it teems with nesting birds like bees at a hive. But these aren't sweet songbirds that shy away from approaching humans. They're aggressive terns, close cousins of gulls but with a more delicate physique, which attack anyone and anything that encroaches on their territory. And since virtually every square yard of the acre-and-a-half island has a tern nest on it, it's impossible *not* to visit the island without appearing to be an unwanted trespasser.

On my first visit to the island on Memorial Day 2005, I was unprepared for the birds' attacks. When I climbed out of the small motorboat after the short trip from the marina in the town of Marion, I was immediately given a stick found on the shoreline and instructed to hold it vertically above my head. Apparently the marauding terns usually attack the highest point on any intruder, so the stick was supposed to get the birds to avoid my head. It didn't help much. Carefully watching every single step to avoid crushing a bird's nest and with eyes averted from the nesting birds so as not to cause them unnecessary stress, I hoped for the best as I maneuvered my way to the lighthouse at the island's midpoint. But with every few steps, a half-dozen birds flew from their nests to defend their unhatched young with their piercing beaks and perfect aim. After just three minutes on the island, I had been stabbed on the top of my head several times and defecated on more times than in my previous forty-three years combined. And I still had six hours left to spend on the island. (It wasn't until I got home that I realized that several of the birds' fifty-plus jabs to the head that day had drawn blood.)

I visited Bird Island to learn about its nesting roseate terns (*Sterna dougallii*), a federally endangered species whose North American population totals just thirty-four hundred pairs, almost all of which nest on a few scattered islands off the New England coast. They look somewhat like a small gull—light gray back and whitish undersides—but with a black cap and a long, sharp-pointed black beak. Bird Island and nearby Ram Island are the summer home of more than a third of North America's roseate tern population, and a team of biologists, interns, and volunteers, led by Carolyn Mostello of the Massachusetts Division of Fish and Wildlife, spend nearly every day from May through July monitoring the birds to ensure their continued nesting success.

On the day of my visit, Mostello and several assistants started the day the way they start every day—with a nest survey. Walking carefully through several sections of the island, they counted the eggs in known nests and hunted for new nests. Eggs are buff-colored with large chocolate splotches and smaller brown speckles, and the researchers often grasped the eggs in their hands to check to see if they were warm. Cold eggs indicate that the adults may have abandoned the nest, so those eggs were turned on end. If the nest wasn't abandoned, the adult birds would turn the egg back on its side when they returned to incubate. Over the course of three days, the birds lay two eggs, and each is labeled by the biologists with the letter A or B in magic marker to indicate in which order they are laid. Generally just one chick per nest survives to adulthood, and it's usually the first egg laid.

Roseate terns prefer to nest in somewhat protected locations, and on a treeless island like Bird, that usually means beside boulders or large plants. Their preferred vegetation on Bird Island is seaside goldenrod and bind weed—a variety of mourning glory—and early in the nesting season these plants are small and provide little protection. To keep the birds from abandoning the island, the biologists have created a variety of nest-protection devices—tiny plywood teepees and large sheets of plywood laid across cinder blocks—under which the birds build their nests. Checking the status of those nests is more challenging, but by the end of the survey we had found several new nests and a dozen freshly laid eggs.

Mostello's team of biologists aren't the only ones protecting the endangered roseate terns on Bird Island. More than four thousand pairs of the similar-looking common terns also nest there, and their aggressiveness helps to protect the roseate tern nests. "Roseates look for sites where common terns already nest. The two species have an acrimonious relationship in that the common terns are much more aggressive and will drive roseates away," said Mostello. "But at the same time, the common terns are more aggressive toward predators and intruders as well. So the roseates benefit from the common terns' aggressiveness."

That aggressiveness was the greatest challenge during my visit. I kept my head down with every step, partly to ensure that I didn't crush any nests, but mostly to protect my face from the attacks. I was constantly feeling tense, knowing that at any moment I would receive another stab from a tern beak. Occasionally when I glanced upwards I'd see a marauding tern preparing its next aerial attack, mouth wide open, hovering just above my head, and then folding its wings inward and diving straight at me. Rather than try to avoid the inevitable, I found it easier to just stiffen up and accept the beating. Eventually, though, I got used to recognizing tern nests, so I was able to move more quickly through the colony and learned which parts of the island I could stand on more safely and relax.

Several boaters also visited the island on the day of my visit. One couple, who was collecting sea glass, knew that if they entered the nesting colony they'd get pooped on. Another stopped for a picnic and to take pictures of the birds. With every visitor, Mostello dropped what she was doing and walked over to chat with them. She even escorted one curious kayaker into the colony to climb to the top of the lighthouse so he could take some pictures. Educating local boaters about the peril of the tern colony was clearly a priority for the Mass Wildlife biologist.

Mostello grew up in New Jersey and went to graduate school at the University of Hawaii. After graduation, she took a job studying gray-backed terns on some of the remote Hawaiian atolls, and that's where she caught what she calls the seabird bug. "I really enjoy working with seabirds, because they're very charismatic," she said. "They're also a little bit more tame than a lot of other bird species, so you can get close to them and observe and interact with them a little easier than you can with some other species. I admire their feistiness. They're little birds but they can pack a punch, and you have to admire them for that.

"I also enjoy working on islands. I like small places you can get to know well. There are a lot of people who would love to do what I do during the summer—to work outside, to work with birds in the field, to work on the coast, and to work on islands that not many people can get to. That's a real privilege," she added.

From as early as the American Revolution, Buzzards Bay saw a great deal of marine traffic. Long before the Cape Cod Canal was built, all sorts of cargo vital to early colonists was shipped into Cape Cod Bay from the north, brought over the narrow arm of land by wagon, and loaded onto ships again at ports in Buzzards Bay to continue the journey southward. In addition, nails made in nearby Wareham and wood cut from the Rochester area were hauled south on ships through the bay.

In 1819, the first lighthouse in the bay was built on Bird Island as an aid to navigation, and the first lighthouse keeper, William Moore, took up residence. According to Charlie Bradley, the former harbormaster for the town of Marion and the island's unofficial historian, Moore didn't take the job voluntarily. "He was known as a sometime pirate, and he was assigned lighthouse duties as an alternative to a prison term and as a way to keep him away from the public," Bradley explained. "He went out there with his wife, a Boston socialite who had a drinking problem. Rumor was that he murdered her out there, but it's never been proven.

"Life on the island in the early 1800s was as desolate as could be," he continued. "It was an awful place to live. It's not very high above sea level, so numerous times during the winter, storms would over-wash the island. The cistern would fill with salt water, so they'd have to go for months without fresh water. The original building was made of stone, and construction was rather poor, so they faced drafts and cold winter winds. They'd be cut off from the mainland through the winter months." Moore remained on the island for ten years.

The island and lighthouse were originally owned by the Federal Board of Lighthouses, which eventually turned it over to the Coast Guard. By the early 1930s, after most of the shipping in the bay had shifted further to the east and the large Cleveland's Ledge lighthouse was constructed, the Coast Guard decided it no longer needed the Bird Island light. The island was purchased by the Fisk family in 1935, but by the early 1950s they no longer wanted it either, at which time the town of Marion took ownership.

Massachusetts Audubon Society biologists began monitoring the terns on the island in the 1970s, but they had no interest in the lighthouse, which fell into a state of disrepair. Bradley said that several feeble attempts had been made to restore the lighthouse over the years, most notably during America's bicentennial celebration in 1976, but it wasn't until Bradley began working for the town in 1994 that a major fundraising campaign was launched. On July 4, 1997, at 9 P.M., just before the town's annual fireworks display, the lighthouse was relit and it has remained so ever since.

While roseate terns have a longer record of nesting on Bird Island than on any other known nesting site, the island doesn't have any characteristics that make it more amenable to tern nesting than many others. "Because terns are long-lived birds—they've been known to live up to twenty-five years—this tradition of nesting is hard to break," said Mostello. "In some ways, Bird and Ram islands aren't the best sites for tern nesting because they're pretty close to the mainland and thus accessible to predators, but they do have this history of nesting there and so they're reluctant to leave. And that's fine, because we don't have too many other sites in Buzzard's Bay that are suitable for nesting any more."

During my visit to Bird Island, several other biologists were monitoring the common tern population, counting nests, trapping and banding adults. The banding effort helps identify individual birds and is designed to track the birds that return to the site in future years and help determine their age. It was a surprisingly easy process. The traps are 18-inch cubes of wire mesh with a small trap-door opening that are placed over a nest. The birds fly away when the biologists approach to set the trap, but their nesting instinct overcomes their fear and they immediately return to the nest. When they find the mesh trap over the nest, they walk around until they find the entrance and calmly return to incubating their eggs. The first bird took less than one minute to enter the trap.

Once the bird was collected from the trap, it was placed head-first, upside down into a conical device that restrains the bird from fluttering and allows the biologists to weigh it. Then measurements were made of the bird's beak length, the distance from the tip of the beak to the back of the head—which helps determine gender (that distance is smaller in females)—and then the birds are banded with aluminium rings on their legs.

While the trapping and banding continued, I climbed to the top of the lighthouse to look out over the island and the bay. The lower level of the lighthouse is mostly used for storage by the biologists, who apparently seldom venture to the top. The narrow, circular stone staircase is criss-crossed with cobwebs and active spider webs, and the door out to the ob-servation platform is rusted and creaked loudly when I pushed it open. The view was impressive, with swarming terns continually squawking beneath me and making regular forays over the water in search of food. They are agile fliers, soaring into the wind, darting about, preening their feathers in mid-air, hovering, and accurately diving into the water to catch small fish beneath the surface. I even saw one drop its fish and swoop down and catch it again before it hit the calm, blue water. There were few recreational boats around, but the nearby coastline was clearly busy and highly developed. While I was at eye level with the island's flag-pole, I noticed it was at half staff in honor of Memorial Day.

From above, it was easy to see that erosion on the island had caused a relocation of nesting sites from what Mostello said had been the case in earlier years. The common terns prefer nesting in more open areas in the lower portions of the island closer to the water, allowing the roseates to nest on higher ground near the vegetation that they prefer. But as the is-land erodes, the lowest common tern nesting sites become washed out by encroaching sea water, so the commons have moved into what tradi-tionally had been the exclusive domain of the roseates. In my earlier walk around the island, I saw numerous washed-out nests, not only of com-mon terns but also of common eider, mallards, and American oyster-catchers. A sea wall had been built around the island in 1850, but it does little to protect the island today. A plan is in place to rebuild the sea wall and fill in the area that had eroded away to provide additional common tern nesting sites, but Mostello said that several years of quibbling over refining design details of the sea wall have left the $2.3 million project long delayed.

As I retreated from the observation platform on the lighthouse, Mostello was assigning one of her assistants to try to identify the species of fish that the terns were catching and feeding their young. That sounded to me like a tremendously challenging job, but she said it was easier than it at first appears. Terns catch small fish in their beaks by flying over the water and diving head-first beneath the surface. During my observations at the island, it appeared they were successful more often than not. "Roseates primarily feed on sand lance," Mostello said, "a long, skinny, silvery fish. It's not a hugely diverse diet, but it seems to be a resource that's predictable here. The roseates' nest productivity seems to be much more constant than the common tern productivity, at least in Buzzards Bay, which says something about the availability of food." Sand lance swim deeper beneath the surface of the water than other bait fish, but because roseates fly higher than common terns when they are feeding, they can dive deeper and reach the abundant food source. Common terns are less picky and feed on a more varied diet. Using a cheat sheet with pictures of the most common bait fish found in the bay, I was able to identify that one common tern returned to its nest near the lighthouse with a large mummichog, a yellowish fish with vertical stripes on its sides. Another ate something I couldn't identify but that looked like a small seahorse.

Before leaving the island, Mostello and I crammed together into a tiny wooden blind set up near a large group of roseate tern nests to try to read the numbers on the birds' leg bands. One of the bands put on the left legs of the roseates is called a "field readable" band with larger numbers that supposedly can be read without having to capture the bird. It's less stressful on the birds, but it seemed like another impossible task. And even using binoculars and a telescope, we were only able to identify a few. But it got us close to the birds without disturbing them and allowed us to observe interesting behaviors. Many of the birds were exhibiting courtship behaviors that looked like an impressive dance. They pointed their long, white tails skyward, dropped their wings almost to the ground, puffed out their chests, and pointed their beaks in the air. And then they appeared to stomp their feet and dance around each other. Sometimes the dance occurred spontaneously for no apparent reason, and other times it was initiated when the male arrived back at the nest to feed his mate. Mostello also pointed out the wide variety of vocalizations the roseate terns make, from a honking sound to an odd squeak to what she called "gakkering" but which to me sounded like the evil laugh made by the main characters in the old Beavis and Butthead television program.

After a day on the island, perhaps the one thing I was most pleased with was my newfound ability to distinguish between common and roseate terns as they flew by me. With so many species of similar-looking terns in the Northeast, I have always found it difficult to tell them apart unless they are sitting still. But after seeing so many of them flying by on Bird Island, the long white tails of the roseates looked almost like streamers compared to the shorter, grayer common tern tails. And the common terns looked darker and dirtier overall, especially on the neck and chest. I was also finally able to see clearly the feature that many birders use to distinguish between the species: the roseates' much paler wings. But despite all the incredible close-up views I had, I still didn't see what the birds are named for: the rosy coloration on their bellies.

The species names of birds have always been a curiosity to me. Some, like California quail and canyon wren, are named for the geographic region in which they live or for their preferred habitat. Many are named for the color of their plumage, like the indigo bunting or vermillion flycatcher. Still others are named after a typical behavior, like the turnstones and roadrunner. My favorite bird names, though, are those that are named for how people have described the sound they make. Chickadees are named such because that word seems to describe—at least to some listeners— the common call they make. The same is true for whippoorwills, bobo-links, dickcissels, and killdeer, though I struggle to hear any of those words when listening to their calls.

As often as not, however, birds are named for attributes that are entirely untrue or for minor characteristics when major ones would seem more appropriate. Many of the forty-plus species of warblers in the United States are misnamed, by my reckoning. Prairie warblers are almost never found on the prairies, Connecticut warblers seldom turn up in Connecticut, and palm warblers nest on spruce bogs in Canada, more than 1,000 miles from the nearest palm tree. Likewise, red-bellied woodpeckers have a beautiful zebra-striped back and red head, but instead of being named for those distinctive characteristics, they are named for a well-hidden pinkish smear on their lower belly that I've seldom seen despite years of watching them daily at my bird feeders.

It was with that in mind that I saw my first roseate terns in 1986 at the tip of Napatree Point in Westerly, Rhode Island. Seven species of terns can be seen in a given summer in New England. All terns have short legs and long, pointed beaks and wings, and all but the black tern have a pale grayish back and light undersides. Distinguishing among them can be a

challenge. Given its name, one would guess that the roseate tern would
be the easiest one to identify. Just look for the one with the pink feathers, right? Wrong. When I finally saw my first roseate tern, it seemed to
be another case of the bird with the poorly chosen name. There was
nothing rosy about it.

Sightings of this bird for me were few and far between over the years
as it migrated through my favorite birding spots along the coast of southeastern New England. During those infrequent sightings, never once did
I see even a hint of rose on a roseate tern. Until, that is, I found myself
caught in a downpour while walking out the mile-long peninsula to Napatree in 2003. When I got there after an hour's drive from my house, the
rain had begun to pummel the parking lot. Never one to let a little water
interrupt a birding trip, I started walking to the point anyway. As expected during migration, shorebirds of a dozen species were immediately
in evidence—black-bellied and semipalmated plovers, ruddy turnstones,
sanderlings, willets, dunlin, semipalmated sandpipers, and even a rare
Baird's sandpiper. When I neared the end of the peninsula, where it curls
back like the tip of Cape Cod, large numbers of terns were congregated
on the beach. Before I could even raise my binoculars, it was clear there
were two different species mixed together. Through the heavy raindrops,
I could see that one had a darker overall look and a seemingly grayish
belly compared to the other, which had a light belly that appeared to
glow despite the poor lighting. Through my binoculars, that glow turned
to a gorgeous pink like the last moments of a setting sun. Despite my
cynicism and years of telling myself otherwise, roseate terns really are
rosy. At least in the rain.

They're also highly endangered. But unlike the majority of endangered wildlife, most of the troubles the terns face aren't caused by humans. Since the birds nest on remote, uninhabited islands and feed in
adjacent waters, people seldom have a direct impact on them. Their primary limiting factor during the breeding season is predation by gulls,
owls, and an occasional mammal that finds its way to the nesting islands.
In 2004, a mink killed twenty-seven roseates on Bird Island, the first time
a mink was known to have made its way to the island. Its appearance
forced many terns to relocate to Ram Island instead. Raccoons have also
occasionally been found preying upon the birds. But because of the difficulty that mammalian predators have of reaching the islands, they're not
the biggest cause for alarm. Other birds are. At Falkner Island in Con-

necticut, for instance, the primary predators have been black-crowned night herons, which eat eggs and chicks and caused the nesting population there to plummet. At Bird and Ram islands, Mostello and her team are constantly battling to prevent gulls from taking up residence on the islands. Any nesting attempts by gulls are thwarted by the constant vigilance and daily visits by the biologists.

"Gulls have been a big problem in the past as competitors for nesting sites," explained Mostello. "That's one of the reasons why terns declined so much this past century. Because the gulls return to the nesting sites early, they're able to displace terns. They prefer the same offshore sites that the terns do. But gull populations have declined a bit recently, and we've controlled gulls on the island early in the season through nest break-ups, so it's no longer as big an issue." But even if gulls don't nest there, the predatory birds still visit the island regularly and are a prime threat to the eggs and young chicks. On my visit to Bird Island, a few herring and great black-backed gulls lingered menacingly on the periphery of the island.

"The more serious predators are great horned owls that kill adults," said Mostello. "They also force the adults to abandon the colony at night, and that chills the eggs and it takes the eggs longer to hatch. Once the eggs are starting to hatch, visits by owls cause quite a bit of mortality because the chicks are left unprotected, they get chilled, they get wet, and that obviously has some serious effects on productivity."

That's exactly what happened at Ram Island in 2005. I visited Ram in July of that year after most of the eggs had hatched but before the young had fledged. The island is slightly smaller than Bird Island, but with a small lagoon in the middle where an abundance of early-migrating shorebirds were resting, including short-billed dowitchers, willets, and greater yellowlegs. Tern numbers on Ram were similar to those at Bird, but the adults were surprisingly less aggressive despite the hundreds of chicks huddled throughout the island. Happily, not once did I get dive-bombed or pecked in the head on my visit.

But it wasn't an entirely happy visit. There were about as many dead tern chicks scattered about the island as live ones, and probably as many unhatched, cold eggs as well. As for the eggs, Mostello said that "the adults will sit on them for a while, but eventually if they don't hatch they'll just give up on them." Despite the smell of death lingering everywhere, she said that it was a typical year.

What wasn't typical were the nightly visits by a great horned owl. More than thirty adult roseate terns were killed by the owl by mid-July 2005, along with another twenty common terns, and that concerned Mostello even more than predation on chicks. "When you're dealing with seabirds, it's the adults that are important because they're really long-lived. Predation on adults is a lot more problematic than predation on eggs or chicks. With a couple dozen adult roseates gone, that's pretty significant in a small population."

The night before I arrived, one of Mostello's assistants, Adam Doucette—who moved to Mississippi the following week with his girlfriend—stayed on the island overnight to try to capture the owl using a trap attached to the top of a pole they believe the bird perched on. The biologists had spent a month trying to trap it without success, so Adam wanted to try to observe the owl and monitor the trap in person. He said that most of the adult terns left the island at about 9:30 P.M.—no one knows where they go—and they returned just before dawn the next morning. Fear of crushing some of the hundreds of chicks and eggs scattered everywhere kept him from leaving his tent after dark. Despite his all-night vigil, he didn't see or hear the owl. Unfortunately, when we walked around the island that day we found the decapitated head and wings of an adult roseate tern, clear evidence of owl predation. Since all dead adult terns are buried by the biologists the day they are found, it's likely that this one was killed despite Adam's vigil. Its remains were quietly and solemnly buried at the spot it was found.

While predators appear to be the primary factor limiting the growth of the roseate tern population, they aren't the only factor. According to Mostello, it is believed that most roseate tern mortality occurs during migration or on their wintering grounds. And since no one is certain exactly where most of the birds spend the winter, it's especially difficult to protect them once they leave their breeding islands.

"A number of years ago there was a guy in South America who was netting them and eating them, but that has apparently stopped," Mostello says. "But we haven't seen an increase in adult survival since he stopped, so nobody is really sure what the major source of mortality is."

Helen Hayes, a biologist with the American Museum of Natural History, has done extensive searches up and down the Atlantic coast of

South America seeking out the roseate's wintering grounds. Despite checking from south of Punta Rasa, Argentina, to the north coast of South America, she only found them in the Brazilian state of Bahia. The largest concentrations were around the historic city of Salvadore, the country's first capital. "I think in all probability there are places in addition to Bahia where roseate terns concentrate, [but] these still remain to be discovered," she wrote in an email in 2005. Jeff Spendelow, a research wildlife biologist with the U.S. Geological Survey's Patuxent Wildlife Research Center who has studied roseates for nearly thirty years, thinks the birds may spend a considerable portion of the winter season far out to sea. But that has yet to be proven conclusively.

Compounding concerns about the survival of the New England roseate tern population are questions about the impact of oil spills and other hazardous wastes. In late April 2003, a barge operated by the Bouchard Transportation Co. struck an unknown obstacle in Buzzards Bay and spilled approximately 98,000 gallons of #6 heating oil out of a 12-foot gash in its hull. Oil washed up on 90 miles of shorelines, including portions of Ram Island, and hundreds of birds were killed, from loons, ducks, and cormorants to oystercatchers, piping plovers, and terns. Shellfishing in much of the area was closed, and many recreational uses of the bay were curtailed for months.

The spill came at a bad time for the rarest of the affected birds. The endangered plovers are early migrants, and they had already begun nesting when the spill occurred. Nearly all of the beaches where they nest and feed in the bay were oiled, and Barney's Joy Beach, which hosts the region's largest concentration of nesting plovers, was particularly hard hit. Even a small amount of oil on feathers can be fatal. An unknown number of roseate and common terns were also killed after diving into the oily waters to feed.

Funding for the annual monitoring of the roseate terns has come about due to another human-caused environmental impact. An 18,000-acre section of the nearby Acushnet River and New Bedford Harbor has been declared a Superfund site as a result of the industrial discharge of PCBs into the waterway for three decades. As the cleanup of the site continues, the New Bedford Harbor Trustee Council allocates funds to restore natural resources that were harmed by the PCBs. The Council has provided most of the funding for the tern monitoring since 1999.

In an effort to reduce the impact of the 2003 oil spill on the terns,

Costello and her team spent the month following the spill using propane cannons and other noisemaking devices, along with bright lights at night, to keep the terns away. About 250 pairs eventually nested on nearby Penikese Island and many others moved to Bird Island, yet the following year they returned to Ram in their usual numbers.

"One of the goals of the federal recovery plan is to increase the number of nesting sites and get them to spread out so large numbers aren't concentrated on only a few islands. We had hoped that the hazing on Ram in 2003 would encourage them to nest elsewhere permanently, but they're going to nest where they want to nest," Mostello said. According to the recovery plan, roseate terns will be considered for removal from the federal endangered species list when there are at least five sites where two hundred or more pairs of roseates are breeding. Penikese Island is one site the biologists have targeted to establish a breeding colony, and common terns have already begun nesting there in considerable numbers. But Mostello says that attracting roseates to the island is a waiting game. The same is true at two newly formed islands off the Monomoy National Wildlife Refuge near Chatham. They have attracted about ten thousand pairs of nesting common terns, but roseates have yet to arrive in any significant numbers.

Beyond the ongoing tern monitoring work required by the recovery plan, a great deal of research is also underway to learn more about tern biology, movements, and population dynamics to better understand how to protect the species, much of it conducted by biologists Jeff Spendelow and Ian Nisbet. Spendelow began studying roseates at Falkner Island, Connecticut, in the late 1970s, trying to get a handle on survival rates and factors limiting population growth. "Based on Falkner data, on average about 75 percent of adults were surviving and coming back to breed each year, but for seabirds that's not a good survival rate," he said. "So the question is, were the missing 25 percent dying or going somewhere else?" By comparing data from Bird, Ram, Falkner, and two breeding sites on Long Island—Great Gull Island and Cedar Beach—he found that 5 to 10 percent of the breeding population relocates to a different colony the following year. "The movement rates are very dependent on where they're nesting. Some colony sites aren't as good as others, so there's a lot of movement in and out of those sites. As the birds become successful at one place, their likelihood of moving is less and less. Fidelity to an area builds up based on the success they have." The colony at Cedar Beach was wiped out by predators in 1995, and the Falkner Island population dropped from 150 pairs in 1995 to 40 in 2003 after predatory black-crowned night herons discovered the colony.

With just Ram, Bird, and Great Gull hosting nearly 90 percent of the remaining breeding terns in New England—smaller numbers are widely scattered on about a dozen islands in the Gulf of Maine—Spendelow relocated his research to Bird Island. In 2005, he trapped and color-banded the adult birds so he could determine where they nest in succeeding years. This project was an effort to determine what makes a new colony successful. The hazing of the birds at Ram during the oil spill was very instructive to Spendelow. He said that a quarter of the Ram Island roseates relocated that year to Bird Island, and another quarter nested on Penikese Island, a larger nearby island that historically was used by the roseates but which has fallen into disfavor in recent decades. "Productivity wasn't as good as it could have been, but we expected that forty to fifty pairs would come back and nest at Penikese in 2004, but that didn't happen," he said. "We had fewer than ten pairs there. Most of them went back to Ram Island." Spendelow was surprised, however, that seventy to eighty pairs of roseate terns nested on Penikese in 2005, perhaps because bad weather early in the breeding season delayed nesting and the abundance of sand lance at traditional locations was down. "Many more nested on Penikese that year than we expected, but they were mostly older birds. And it wasn't just the ones that had been to Penikese the previous year. So Penikese is obviously attracting birds on its own, even without the hazing on Ram, but it wasn't attracting young birds. I'm suspecting that most of the 2005 Penikese birds will go back to Bird and Ram. For the future of Penikese to become a growing roseate colony we need to attract three- and four-year-old birds in their first years of breeding, but we only had one three-year-old bird in 2005. The older birds are aware of it and use it when they have to, but it's still not attracting the younger birds it needs to grow into a sizable colony."

Next on Spendelow's list of research projects is to learn what the birds do after they leave the nest but before they migrate south. He knows that nearly the entire population of adult and juvenile birds from throughout New England congregate on Monomoy Island off Chatham, Massachusetts, as they prepare to migrate. It's a time when they are especially vulnerable. In 1991, the eye of Hurricane Bob crossed the island and wiped out nearly all of the birds that had hatched that year, along with many adults. The population is still recovering from the devastation. Spende-

low wants to learn more about how much moving around the birds do
before they get to Monomoy, and that's an important question given the
175 offshore wind turbines that have been proposed for installation between Monomoy and Nantucket. "I'd like to know to what extent the
birds are going back and forth in the area where the wind turbines are
proposed. At the very least, all the birds that breed in the area have to go
through there twice on their way to and from their wintering grounds,
but it could be that the fledglings and their parents move back and forth
more than that during staging. And I wonder if they do it when it's hard
to see, like in the early morning or in bad weather." Mostello notes another concern posed by the proposed wind farm: "The terns might use
the wind turbine bases as courtship areas. During courtship the birds spiral up to really high altitudes—300 feet or so—which could bring them
in touch with the rotors. So we're greatly concerned about wind farms,
but there's not much information to say how much of a risk they're actually going to be."

My visit to Ram Island in July 2005 was timed to help the biologists band
the downy chicks, but the day started out much like my previous visit,
with a nest survey. This late in the season, Mostello wasn't expecting to
find any new nests or eggs—which we didn't. What we did find were
hundreds of chicks huddled in every corner of the island, squeaking loudly
while waiting for their parents to feed them. It was a hot, sunny day, with
the thermometer topping out above 90 degrees and little breeze, but it
was hard to decide what to wear, given the potential attacks from the
terns. One of Mostello's assistants, Jenny Cunningham, folded a hand-
kerchief inside her floppy hat to protect her head from tern beaks, and
intern Adam Doucette wore a hooded sweatshirt all day despite the heat
to keep the poop bombs from reaching his skin. I chose to keep my
hooded windbreaker on, though I felt somewhat wimpy when Mostello
stripped down to her t-shirt.

Before banding the chicks, we first had to trap the last few adult birds
that hadn't been captured yet that season. Unlike the common terns on
my previous visit, the first few roseates we tried to trap were uncooperative. They seemed to take much longer to decide to enter the traps. Instead, they perched on top of the trap, even when they had a fish in their
beak and a calling chick inside. Eventually, though, they got used to the

traps and were almost eager to enter. At one point we had four birds in our hands awaiting processing.

Holding a roseate tern in each hand was a magical experience for me. I had handled plenty of small, delicate songbirds before, but the terns were strong and sturdy animals, constantly struggling and jabbing their beaks at me or painlessly biting my fingers. Their black eyes were virtually hidden within their black cap, and they were beginning to show a bit of red coloration at the base of the beak that wasn't visible earlier in the season. Mostly, though, I simply felt honored to be surrounded by these beautiful creatures. They had traveled thousands of miles to return to their island to pass on their genes, mostly just following some unknown innate need to do exactly that. They had overcome severe obstacles, both natural and man-made, and despite being trapped and indelicately handled, they were driven to return to their nests to complete the job and then start the whole process over again. When Mostello finished processing the birds, she opened her hand to release them one by one. The first bird anxiously flapped its wings, dropped briefly to the ground, and flew away towards its crying chick. The other bird, however, simply stood on Mostello's hand for about ten seconds, preening and realigning its feathers, appearing to be more concerned with how it looked than with its own safety. And then it, too, flew away.

We focused our "mass banding" effort in a corner of the island where thick mats of beach pea and seaside goldenrod had grown up knee high around the nests, making it difficult to see the chicks. By carefully pushing aside every plant, we soon uncovered dozens of chicks hiding in the vegetation and awaiting delivery of their next meal by their parents. But finding them was only part of the job. Most of the chicks were at an awkward age, no longer cute downy babies but not yet attractive adults, more like awkward pubescent teenagers with acne. A few wing feathers had grown in, but they were mostly still downy with oversized beaks and feet. And they weren't happy at all about being handled. Many of the young I picked up almost immediately jettisoned what seemed like every liquid in their body, regurgitating partially digested fish from one end and defecating fully digested fish from the other. It was warm, slimy, and disgusting, and it was impossible to avoid. With three biologists wielding banding pliers and me responsible for record-keeping, we captured and banded sixty roseate and ten common tern chicks in ninety minutes within a 30-by-100-foot section of the island.

Despite a moderately successful year of breeding in 2005, the outlook for the birds remains bleak. "Oddly enough, I'd feel more confident about their future if I thought some of the reasons for their decline these days were human-caused," Mostello said. "But at least on the nesting grounds, we don't think they are. I'm not optimistic because we haven't even identified what the main problems are yet, why we're not seeing better adult survival over the winter. That's really the key to recovering the population."

Spendelow is only a little more optimistic. "I don't trust predictions into the future, because there are just too many things that can happen to change things," he said. "But as we lose nesting sites here and there, the birds are crowded more and more into fewer places, and that makes them vulnerable to a single event like an oil spill. Given the fact that we've lost most of the birds on the south shore of Long Island, and we're losing them in Connecticut, that's not a good sign. The overall trend in terms of their distribution is not good."

Even if the birds have a string of good years, both biologists expect a constant need for active management on the nesting islands. "Everyone is working so hard now to keep the sites suitable for roseates and to control predators on the islands," Mostello said. "We seem to be doing a pretty good job at that. But they're not self-sustaining, and neither are the common terns, without continual management in terms of keeping the sites gull-free and controlling predators throughout the season," she says. "Without that intervention, they'd be in rapid decline very shortly."

Acknowledgments

When I first decided to write *Golden Wings and Hairy Toes,* I thought the biggest challenge was going to be convincing the leading biologists who study my chosen species to allow me to join them in the field to learn about—and help them with—their research. I needn't have worried. Every biologist I contacted enthusiastically welcomed my visits, and many of them have encouraged me to visit again when the pressures of note-taking aren't so great. To these skilled and knowledgeable scientists, who toil under challenging conditions to protect creatures that most people have never heard of but which are critical components of our natural heritage, I offer my heartfelt thanks. While the fieldwork was often dirty, wet, and sweaty, it was also some of the most exciting times I've ever had. Thanks are also due to the dozens of graduate students and research assistants who put up with my missteps in the field, for it is they who do much of the hard work and get little of the recognition. Dozens of other biologists and others also played key roles in the completion of this book by agreeing to be interviewed and providing additional insights on everything from biology, geology, and turf science to mining history, captive rearing, and seed banking.

The idea for this book came to me fully formed in the summer of 2004 while I was reading Elizabeth Royte's *The Tapir's Morning Bath,* a captivating account of a year she spent at a biological research station in Panama. Although we've never met, I owe her a debt of gratitude for inspiring me to write my first book. Deciding which species to include in the book was easier than I expected, until it came to the birds. Thanks to ornithologists Peter Paton, Scott McWilliams, John Confer, and Ken Rosenberg for joining in the debate over which birds are New England's rarest.

Long after the fun of the first year's fieldwork ended and I was struggling to stick to my writing schedule, literary agent Charlotte Raymond's enthusiastic response to the first few chapters injected the motivation that I needed to keep going. Later, similar enthusiasm from editor Phyllis

Deutsch at the University Press of New England kept that motivation flowing to the end. Their response was exactly the boost I needed.

Finally, my greatest appreciation is owed to my wife Renay, who put up with my frequent last-minute trips to join researchers out of town despite our previous plans, who wasn't bothered that I was often motivated to write at 2 A.M., and who understood that household chores took a back seat to writing during the life of this project. Thank you. I'll cut the grass tomorrow.

Bibliography

The numerous biologists I spoke with—all of whom are referenced in the text—were the primary sources for this book, and their in-depth knowledge about the species they study is extensive. In addition, every plant and animal included on the federal endangered species list has a formal recovery plan; those documents were extremely useful in understanding the threats the species face, the monitoring research currently being conducted, and the goals and objectives that will lead to recovery of the species' population. Those plans are available on the Internet at www.fws.gov/endangered/recovery.

I referred regularly to fact sheets and reports on rare animals and plants that are provided by state wildlife agencies, the U.S. Fish and Wildlife Service, the National Marine Fisheries Service, and several nongovernmental organizations, especially The Nature Conservancy. Online databases maintained by NatureServe and the Center for Plant Conservation were also helpful for multiple chapters. And I referred often to field guides to birds, mammals, reptiles, insects, marine mammals, and plants, especially to those guides in the Peterson and National Audubon Society series.

Beyond these general reference materials, several specific publications were particularly useful. The member magazines of The Nature Conservancy, the National Wildlife Federation, the Wildlife Conservation Society, and the National Audubon Society each had several helpful articles, as did *Northeast Naturalist, Northern Sky News, Birding, Birder's World, Habitat, Northern Woodlands,* and *Sanctuary* magazines. The Canadian government maintains an excellent website on the Bicknell's thrush (www.atl.ec.gc.ca/wildlife/bicknells_thrush) that I referred to often while writing that chapter. And because rare wildlife are often in the news, I regularly found myself updating various chapters during the two-year process of researching and writing this book based on news reports from the Associated Press, *Boston Globe,* and elsewhere.